670
S   Seymour, John, 1914-
        The forgotten crafts / John Seymour. --
New York : Knopf, 1984.
        192 p. : ill.

        ISBN 0-394-53956-7 : 18.45

                                32229

        1. Handicraft. 2. Do-it-yourself work.

                        dc19   Mr85
                                        84-47646

4

19

THE
FORGOTTEN
CRAFTS

THE
FORGOTTEN
CRAFTS

JOHN SEYMOUR

Alfred A. Knopf
New York 1984

For Angela

THE FORGOTTEN CRAFTS was conceived, edited and designed by
Dorling Kindersley Limited, 9 Henrietta Street, London WC2E 8PS

Project Editor David Lamb   **Art Editor** Flo Henfield
Editor Simon Adams   **Designer** Julia Goodman

Managing Editor Jackie Douglas   **Art Director** Roger Bristow

Major illustrations by Eric Thomas
Wood engravings by Robert Kettell and Peter Reddick

THIS IS A BORZOI BOOK
PUBLISHED BY ALFRED A. KNOPF, INC.

Library of Congress Cataloging in Publication Data

Seymour, John, 1914–
  The forgotten crafts.

  Includes index.
  1. Handicraft   2. Do-it-yourself work.   I. Title.
TT145.S49 1984   670   84-47646
ISBN 0-394-53956-7

Printed and bound in Italy by A. Mondadori Editore – Verona

First American Edition

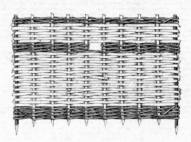

CONTENTS

CRAFTS OF THE FIELD 52

WORKSHOP CRAFTS 64

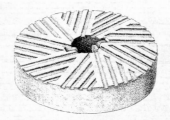

TEXTILES & HOMECRAFTS 166

INTRODUCTION

ractically every artifact that a person uses nowadays can be made from oil-derived plastic, in a large factory, by machine-minders whose chief quality is their ability to survive lives of intense boredom. Even the machine-minders are being replaced rapidly by robots who, we are told, don't get bored at all.

Artifacts so produced often do their jobs perfectly well. They are ugly and short-lived but, by and large, they work. That, unfortunately, is the best that can be said for them. Their manufacture tends to obliterate the livelihood of artisans, while their wreckage clutters and pollutes the world.

Are we justified in using articles, no matter how convenient it may be for us to use them, that we know were produced in conditions which bored and even stultified the human beings who had to make them? It was in an attempt to be able to feel a little less culpable in this respect that I began to look around and do the research that led to the writing of this book.

I found, thanks be to God, that the Forgotten Crafts are not completely forgotten at all. In spite of the machines, there is not a human skill that was ever developed that is not still practiced somewhere on this planet. And, further, there are, almost everywhere in the so-called developed world at least, the beginnings of a revival of the ancient arts and crafts. More and more people are becoming fed up and disillusioned with mass-produced rubbish and are seeking for and demanding good craftsmanship.

THE CHATTI OR THE DEBBIE

The great Bengali poet and mystic Rabindranath Tagore once compared a *debbie*, a four-gallon gasoline can, with a *chatti*, an earthenware pot created by a village craftsman. The *debbie*, he wrote, carried water just as well as the *chatti*, but while doing so the *debbie* looked ugly. *The chatti* not only did the job of carrying water just as well as the *debbie* but it did still

more – it delighted and pleased both the user and the on-looker. He could have added that even a pretty woman looks ugly carrying a *debbie* on her head – even quite a plain one looks graceful and beautiful carrying a *chatti*. He could also have added that the use of the *chatti* helps to give a living to a friend and neighbor in the village: the use of the *debbie* merely compounds the pollution and degradation of our planet.

THE DISCIPLINE OF NATURAL MATERIALS

The use of artifacts made from natural materials gives a pleasure far in excess of the pleasure that we may derive from simply doing the job. The form, the texture, the subtle feel of such artifacts, together with an awareness of their origins – in trees, a crop growing in a field, part of the hide of an ox, part of the living rock – add greatly to the pleasure of seeing and using them. Wood, iron and steel (including that excellent material stainless steel), other metals both precious and base, beautiful gems and stones, stone, leather, natural fibers such as wool, hemp, flax, cotton, silk, jute and manila, clay: these materials, shaped and put together by the hands of skilled human beings, provide all the artifacts that we should legitimately need. If something cannot be made with these natural materials I don't want it.

The very intractability of a natural material imposes a discipline that forces the craftsman to produce something beautiful as well as useful. It is the grain of wood with its liability to split along one plane and not the others, that forces the carpenter, the wheelwright, the cooper, the turner or the shipwright to fashion it in certain ways, to use the qualities of wood and overcome its disadvantages, that

imposes a pattern of beauty on wooden objects. It also forces the craftsman in wood to learn the mystery of his craft and this elevates him high above the mere factory worker.

It has been the limitations of stone as a building material which have forced the builder, over the centuries, to develop the great beauty of arch and vault, of column and arcade and flying buttress. Concrete, which, when reinforced, can be made to any shape, is rarely made into anything beautiful at all. Look at a modern skyscraper, you might say. Yes, but compare it to the fan-vaulted ceiling of Sherborne Abbey, in Dorset, a photograph of which is stuck to the side of my filing cabinet and which overcomes me with awe every time I look at it.

Hand-crafted goods often cost more – but do they when you really consider the matter? Surely it is more economical to pay money to a friend and neighbor – a local craftsman – to make something good for you than to pay a little less money for some rubbishy item mass-produced far away. By helping to keep your neighbor in business you are enriching your own neighborhood. Furthermore, you are increasing the sum of real enjoyment in the world, for your craftsman almost certainly enjoys making the article for you and you will certainly enjoy owning and using it. The worker in the factory

that produced the mass-produced object may enjoy the wages he or she gets but the work, well, no.

Slowly and steadily, I am ridding my home, as far as I can, of mass-produced rubbish, and either learning to do without certain things or else replacing them by articles made out of honest materials by people who enjoyed making them and who, by long diligence and training, have qualified themselves to make them superbly. This has brought me into contact with many craftspeople in Ireland where I live, in Wales where I used to live, in England where I was born, in France, Germany, Austria and Italy, in Crete and mainland Greece, and even in the Middle East and in Africa. Some of these people were poor, some were struggling for a living, but poor or not they had one thing in common – they enjoyed their work. They took a great pride in it and, if you showed an intelligent interest, they loved to show what they were doing and how they did it.

History

To learn something about crafts and craftsmen is to learn about the history of the race. Each craft is the rich repository of many years of practical experimentation and knowledge by men and women whose very lives were shaped and enhanced by the work of their hands. More than wars, more even than literature or the chronicles of kings and great men, the crafts reflect our universal past. They also demonstrate, with beauty and precision, how generations of creativity went into developing and refining hundreds of regional

variations that are only now blending, losing their identities.

Many of the crafts in this book appear to be distinctively British – Irish, Welsh, English, Scottish – because they are the ones I am in the best position to describe. But it should be recognized that most of these same crafts were carried with emigrants from the Old World into the New, from Ireland to Australia, from Germany to Pennsylvania, from Africa to Brazil. And while they may have survived longer in one place than another – thatching, for example, may still go on in Devon but be extinct in Massachusetts – it is fair to say that the crafts shown here were once common very widely indeed, in places where machinery has long since driven them out. In the hollows of Appalachia, for example, where the old ways linger, crafts dating back to Elizabethan times or earlier survive to this day, identical with the practice of a crofter in the Highlands or a peasant craftsman in the Var.

Of course many variations developed depending on local conditions: many an English countryman made a profession of coppicing because he could easily sell the forest products within the local community, but a settler in Ohio, with no such market, produced entirely for himself and his family.

Similarly, the art of hedge laying especially suitable to the softer, wetter, English climate, never took hold in New England or Australia. But wheelwrighting was universally practiced, along with different kinds of basket making, workshop and building crafts, and dozens of others.

REWARDS

The older craftsman still has that ancient attitude to the reward for work that used to be universal but is, alas, now

seldom found. And that is the attitude that there should be a fair reward for good work. Nowadays the predominating attitude is "I charge what the market will bear." I will never forget the time I finally persuaded that great craftsman Mr. Harry King, the boatbuilder of Pin Mill in Suffolk, to build me a 14-foot dinghy. This was just after the Second World War when it was hard to find craftsmen to make such an item. For a long time he refused and I looked elsewhere. Finally he relented.

"How much will you charge for her?" I asked. Later I learned that you do not ask such people how much they will charge, at least not in Suffolk.

"Three pun' a foot," he snapped.

"But, Mr. King, everyone I have been to charges *four* pounds a foot! You must have made a mistake?"

"Three pun' a foot's my price. If you don't like it you can go somewhere else!" he replied. "I don't hev to build ye a dinghy!"

The real craftsman does not need more than enough. In our times of social mobility, everyone is after more than enough. We no longer ask "What is our product worth?" or "How much do I need?" but "how much can I get?" I have known many young people who have tried a craft and given it up because they found that, although they could make enough, they could not make more than enough. And more than enough is what they feel they require. A planet on which every inhabitant tries to get more than enough is a planet that is in for a hard time. And in the final reckoning I am sure that having more than enough does not make us more happy. You can definitely have too much of a good thing. What makes a person happy is doing work that he or she loves doing and is superbly good at, being fairly paid for it, and having it properly appreciated.

Apprenticeship

But to become superbly good at one of the crafts is not easy. Many a young person tries it and fails in the attempt. The old-fashioned apprenticeship system was the best system for young people, and for master craftsmen too, that there has ever been. The young person was subjected to fairly rigorous discipline, maybe in some cases too rigorous, but by this he was taught not only his craft but also the habit of hard work and discipline that would, later, enable him to enjoy life and prosper at his trade. For the master craftsman is a happy man. He glories in his skill and his work, drinks his wine or his beer with zest, looks forward to his food and sleeps well o' nights! Boredom he is a stranger to. If he looks back over his life surely he does not regret the hard apprenticeship that qualified him for being what he is? Surely it is better for a young person to be subjected to some pretty hard discipline, and earn low wages, for a few years, and then spend the rest of his life as a respected and self-respecting craftsman, than to tumble straight into factory work. I include the "professions" in my assessment; a good doctor or a good dentist is a master craftsman too and should be treated as one, no more, no less. There is nothing higher on this planet that a man can be.

Interdependence of Craftsmen

During my researches I was struck by the *isolation* of many of the craftspeople I met. When I talked to the old people –

some of whom were in their eighties and still working every day – I had the impression that in their younger days they were not isolated at all. At that time there seems to have been a great interdependence of craftsmen in the countryside. Each craftsman was dependent on his brother craftsmen of different trades in order to be able to carry on his own trade. The fisherman, for example, (and fishing is a fine and ancient craft) was dependent on the farmer who grew the flax for his nets, the net maker who made them, the basket maker to make his traps and pots, the boat builder who built his boat.

The boat builder in turn was dependent on the blacksmith who forged the chain plates, spider-bands, anchors, chains and dozens of other items needed for a fishing boat, the woodsman who felled and carried the timber for the boat, the sawyer who cut it up, the oil-miller who made the linseed oil needed to preserve it, the flax spinners and weavers who made the canvas for the sails, the sail maker who made them, the rope maker who spun and twisted the hemp for the ropes, the iron founder who cast the pigs of ballast for the bilge – and so it went on. All these interdependent craftsmen

knew each other. Each could go to his supplier and discuss with him exactly what he wanted. Each saw the beginning and the end of what he had created and each one of them probably thought of his own contribution as he ate the fish that the fisherman caught. But now such men are isolated. They may be making a good living now, because of the new interest in hand-crafted goods but it is a lonely living.

And what of the few young people who want to enter the noble hand crafts; they too plough a lonely furrow. A hundred bureaucratic rules and regulations have made it almost impossible to find a craftsman willing to take on apprentices. The very few that do manage to learn a trade ultimately benefit hugely, because the products of the hand crafts are becoming scarcer and more sought after as every year goes by. A young man set up as a farrier near where I used to farm in Dyfed. He makes his rounds in a little van with a portable forge and anvil in it and shoes horses. I worked out how much money he must have been making once (it was a simple sum) and was staggered at the amount.

Other young men and women manage to scrabble their way into a craft without undergoing a formal apprenticeship. They are at a great disadvantage but some of them, by sheer determination, manage to reach near perfection in their trade. These are mostly very happy men and women. I believe more and more people will join their ranks and as this happens the world will become a much better place. I believe that as more and more craftspeople fight through, in town as well as country, something like the old community inter-relationships will grow again. A wholesome and whole society will be recreated.

That good craftsman, Eric Gill, once wrote: "leisure is secular, work is sacred. The object of leisure is work, the object of work is holiness. Holiness means wholeness."

It was in search of wholeness that this book was written.

WOODLAND CRAFTS

At one time broad-leaved native woodland flourished in Europe and was used by rural communities to the full. The maiden trees – those grown from seed and intended to reach maturity a century or more later – were hardwood trees and were spaced so their boughs would grow big and wide. Their timber would eventually be cut and seasoned and used by workshop craftsmen. Between and eventually beneath the maiden trees, smaller trees and saplings proliferated and were cut and used every 10 or 15 years. This was known as the underwood, and it was divided into areas called cants and sold to woodsmen who lived by and mostly in the wood. They would cut and sort the wood, use whatever they needed for their own special woodland craft, and sell the rest. In this age of waste big trees are felled and taken to the sawyers, and all their tops and the underwood are piled into great heaps and burned.

COPPICING

I F YOU CUT DOWN PRACTICALLY any well-established hardwood, particularly deciduous, tree just above ground level the stump will not die. Shoots will sprout up and you have perhaps a dozen smaller trees where you had one before – the basis of *coppicing*. If you cut the trees higher up the trunk similar new growth sprouts, out of the reach of cattle and horses. This is *pollarding*, which is practiced where animals have access to the trees or where their appearance is considered important, as in streets or parks. Coppicing is chosen where grazing animals are totally excluded.

Coppicing is the most fundamental of woodland crafts. In Europe the most commonly coppiced trees are *hazel, ash, sweet* or *Spanish chestnut, oak, alder* and *maple*, each of which is made use of in different ways, as will become apparent in the rest of this section on woodland crafts. *Willow* will coppice readily and is used for basketry and sometimes hurdle-making, but it is cut annually whereas true coppice trees have anything up to a 20-year growing span

RIVING TOOLS
Light pieces of wood can be rived with a *froe*, while heavier pieces require a *beetle* and steel *wedges*.

FROE

CLEAVING-BRAKE FOR THIN SECTIONS OF WOOD

BEETLE OR BITTLE

WEDGES

before they are cut back and the wood used. The *rotation* of coppiced trees depends on the size of the wood required. Thus walking sticks grow in five or six years, hazel for spars in eight years, and sweet chestnut for hop poles and ash for hurdles in 15 years. The *stools*, as the cut-over stumps are called, may last a hundred years, although ash stools do not as a rule last this long. When a stool dies another tree should be planted.

Coppice-with-standards is an old and excellent system of woodland management. Here the coppice trees are grown fairly closely together (perhaps every four feet), but other trees or *standards* are interplanted 20 to 40 to the acre and allowed to grow to maturity to be felled for big timber. Oak is the favorite tree for this, although sweet chestnut, ash and larch are often used. Typically the standards are felled after a rotation time of about 10 times that of the coppice; say 120 years if the coppice is cut every 12. Where *grown crooks* (curved boughs) were needed for ship building (see p. 110) coppice-with-standards was a very popular method, for the oaks sent forth side branches which provided the crooks. In the belief that wooden ship building will come into its own again, I am planting some coppice-with-standards near my home.

RIVING
Riving, or splitting wood, is a craft that is harder to master than it looks. A good woodman will rive plenty of straight-grained pieces out of a small tree trunk, where a less experienced person will waste more wood than he rives successfully. The reason for this is that the wood breaks out across the grain and the rive comes out of the side of the trunk instead of running true to the other end of it. The way to rive most coppice wood is to knock a blade into the end grain, and then push the blade while working it from side to side to open the grain.

HURDLE MAKING

HEN I WAS A BOY I WORKED FOR A winter on a farm in the Cotswolds, uplands in the west of England, on which it was my duty to *fold* two hundred sheep behind hurdles. Folding is a sheep-farming technique which involves keeping the sheep within a rectangle made of hurdles, like small hingeless field gates, tied one to the other, on a crop that the sheep will eat. In my case the crop was turnips and rutabagas.

THE BUSINESS OF FOLDING SHEEP

Every day I had to move the sheep on to fresh turnips and, at the same time, shut them off from the land they had already been over. The sheep were enclosed in a square of hurdles and the first day they would happily eat the turnips within their enclosure. The next day I would come along with enough hurdles for another three sides and build an identical square enclosure on one of the sides of the original.

I would then take out one of the hurdles dividing yesterday's enclosure from today's and drive the sheep through on to fresh turnips. From then on, every day I had to take down three sides of yesterday's enclosure, carry the hurdles over or around today's enclosure and build tomorrow's. In this way the flock was directed over the field in an orderly manner and this did the sheep good and the land too: on land where the soil was light, their droppings took the place of the expensive imported fertilizers.

RIVEN ASH GATE HURDLES

The hurdles I had to carry forward so laboriously were made of riven ash. They were expensive to buy new and took a lot of hard wear, so sometime in the spring the old man who was the local hurdle maker came out from the nearby village to go over them all and repair them. I watched him then and I also went with him to his place of work and saw how they were made.

MAKING A GATE HURDLE

If you have ever made an object in wood which is jointed and meant to be square, you will know how skilful it is to put the 14 mortise and tenon joints together that make an ash gate hurdle. An experienced hurdle maker relies solely on his eye and works surprisingly quickly.

1 *The first job is to remove the bark with a draw-knife from the heavy sections of ash set by for the uprights (known as heads). The hurdle maker then points them with a bill.*

2 *He sets each head in the fork of the brake (his clamp), marks the mortice slots, then bores three holes along each slot.*

He bought ash coppice every winter, felled the 12-year-old trees, and sawed them with a cross-cut saw into the lengths he required. Using a froe and a riving brake he rived these lengths into as many members as he could. Back in his little working area he had a *mortising machine*, or mortising engine as he called it. This was simply a chisel blade fixed near the fulcrum of a lever which could be driven downward with great force by depressing the end of the lever. With this he cut mortises, or long narrow slots, in the short thick pieces of wood he had retained for the pairs of uprights, or *heads* of each hurdle. He then took the *bars*, or rails, of the hurdle – fairly light pieces of ash as long as the hurdle was to be wide – and tapered both ends of each with a draw-knife, holding the work in a *shaving horse* as he did so (see p. 25). These ends formed taper-fit tenons that he then drove into the mortises in the uprights, holding them firm with small wire nails. The ash did not split as the nails were driven home because the wood was so green and full of sap. A light upright, not reaching the ground, was next nailed to the

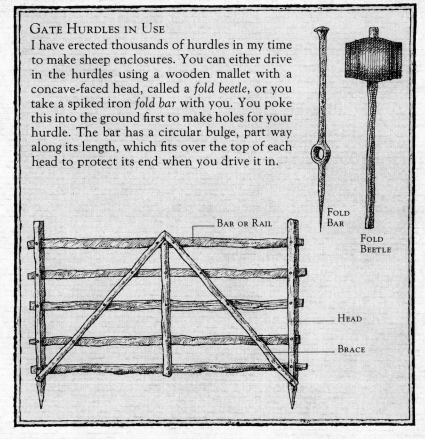

GATE HURDLES IN USE
I have erected thousands of hurdles in my time to make sheep enclosures. You can either drive in the hurdles using a wooden mallet with a concave-faced head, called a *fold beetle*, or you take a spiked iron *fold bar* with you. You poke this into the ground first to make holes for your hurdle. The bar has a circular bulge, part way along its length, which fits over the top of each head to protect its end when you drive it in.

FOLD BAR

FOLD BEETLE

BAR OR RAIL

HEAD

BRACE

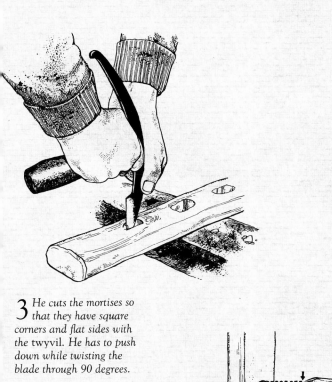

3 *He cuts the mortises so that they have square corners and flat sides with the twyvil. He has to push down while twisting the blade through 90 degrees.*

4 *The bars (rails) are tapered top and bottom at both ends with a draw-knife. This ensures that the tenons push tight into the heads.*

5 *The hurdle maker nails through the heads so that the bar tenons are held firmly in place and then nails braces across the bars.*

middles of the rails and then two slanting braces nailed on with their lower ends near the upright ends and their tops near the top of the center upright. The hurdle was complete and looked very like a narrow field gate. But whereas a well-made field gate would be made in a carpenter's workshop, as I describe on page 140, with its heavy timbers squared, shaved and smoothed, the gate hurdle is left rough hewn and neither head is strong enough to last very long hinged to a gate post.

OTHER MEANS OF MORTISING
Not every hurdle maker has made or inherited a mortising engine, and those that do not, do as I do, and simply drill three adjacent holes with a one-inch bit in a brace and then ream out the long ragged hole with a chisel. A better tool than a chisel for this job is a specially made mortise-knife or a little tool called a *twyvil*. The difference between the tools is that the mortise-knife is two-handled whereas the twyvil has one. Both tools have a pointed blade with one edge straight and the other curved and sharpened on one face only. The blade of either of these will square off the edges of the mortises in the hurdle uprights admirably.

THE GOLDEN RULE OF GATE HURDLE MAKING
There is one trick that you quickly learn when you start making mortised gate hurdles, or field gates for that matter. That is to taper the *tenon* of the rail or horizontal

so that when you drive it in to the mortise the taper exerts pressure up and down and not sideways. If it exerts pressure sideways of course it splits the upright.

Riven ash hurdles are very strong and long-lasting but very heavy. I could carry six of them on my back by pushing a stake through them and getting my shoulder under it, but it was grueling hard work, particularly as I always had to carry them over a rough muddy field and then over a fence of the same hurdles. A disadvantage also of the gate hurdle is that sheep can see through them. We never had trouble with the heavy old Cotswold ewes who would never try to get out, but we also kept some Border Leicester-Cheviots which were mountain animals and could jump like greyhounds. If a sheep can't see it won't go. These sheep, with these hurdles, could see, and they went.

WATTLES
Hurdles which do not have the disadvantage that sheep can see through them are used in the south and south-west of England. These are called *wattles*, and are usually woven with hazel rods, some left *in the round*, meaning not riven, and some riven once. I have seen these made in the West Country, around Dorset.

Wattle making was generally a summer task for which the coppice worker would set aside plenty of hazel of the right sort of thickness, firstly for the *sails*, or uprights of the wattle, and secondly for the long rods used to weave between them. His only

WATTLE HURDLE
The wattle hurdle is woven with hazel rods, some riven and some left in the round. The uprights are also of hazel and consist of two strong end shores with flimsier riven sails in between. When you need to move them, you put a pole through the holes in the middle of half a dozen or so such hurdles and heave them on to your shoulder.

THE MOULD
The wattle hurdle maker uses a mould to hold the shores and sails in place while he weaves the hazel. The mould is slightly curved to produce a weave that tightens when straightened.

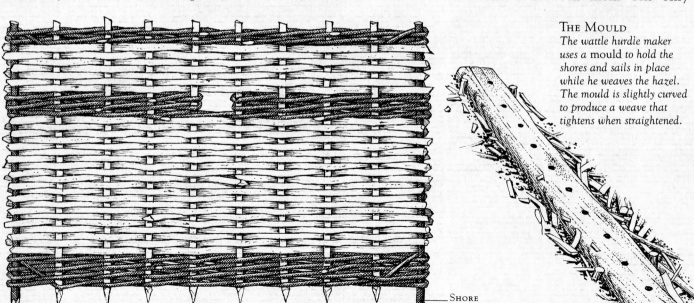

SHORE

SAIL

indispensable tool is a curved billhook. He also makes a rough framework of hazel, called the *gallows*, to stand his bundles of rods against, a measuring pole to keep all the sails to a common height, and a heavy log, riven in two so it will stand flat, used as a stand for the sails during the weaving and called the *mould*. This has 10 holes to take the 10 sails of a true sheep hurdle.

STRENGTHENING DEVICES

Hundreds of years of wattle weaving have produced one or two features that increase strength, given that the hurdler obviously wants to get the most hurdles from the least amount of precious hazel. If you look at the mould closely you will notice it is slightly curved, not because the hurdler had difficulty in finding a straight one, but because he wants a slightly curved wattle. They are stronger this way because stacking them to season will flatten them and so tighten the weave. Look at the hurdle itself closely and you will see that the hazel is left in the round for strength at points of weakness, such as the end sails and the top and bottom of the wattle, while the remaining sails and the bulk of the weaving rods are made from riven hazel.

Most of the wattles made today are not for folding sheep but are used to keep the neighbors from looking into suburban gardens. You can tell a proper sheep hurdle by the little hole left in the middle of the panel for the sheep folder to carry it by, putting a stake through half a dozen hurdles, just like I used to.

MAKING THE HURDLE
Watching a hurdle maker rive hazel with a hook, above, is worrying. It always looks as if he will slice through his hand; but he never does. The first few rows of weave, far left, are of hazel in the round, for added strength. Once the weave is above six inches or so high, the hurdle maker changes to riven weavers, twisting them around the end shores and tucking new rods into the weave, as shown near left.

RAKE MAKING

THE HAND RAKE WAS ONCE SO MUCH a part of the agricultural scene that every piece of lowland coppice would support at least one rake maker confident of the demand for new rakes.

Like so many other useful and pleasing country artifacts, the wooden rake is not difficult to make provided you have the right tools, a knowledge of wood and you know how! I know some people now who make the *tines* (the pegs) of wooden rakes out of machine-cut dowel. They simply buy dowel of the right diameter, cut it into the right lengths and sharpen these lengths slightly with a draw-knife. As most machined dowel is of pretty inferior soft wood the merry snapping sound of tines breaking off accompanies the first attempt to use the rake in a rough field.

MAKING LONG-LASTING TINES

The best material for rake tines is that tough wood, ash, although willow is used in some areas. A seasoned ash pole of about six inches diameter is ideal to start with. You saw the pole into tine-length logs. Each log has to be riven into as many potential tines as possible, and by far the best way of doing this is first to tie a piece of twine tightly around the log, close to one end. You can then put the log on a block and *rive* it in equal parallel cuts one way, and then at 90 degrees, using a froe and mallet (see p. 17). The string holds the riven sections together and you are then left with a bunch of square-sectioned pieces of wood tied together with a piece of string.

There would be nothing to stop you from carving each of these square sections round with a pen-knife, but a much quicker way is to use a *tine-former*. This is a device that can be made by any good metal worker who has a lathe capable of cutting steel. It is a steel pipe with one end sharpened and tempered. The cutting end is as wide as the size you want the tines. The pipe sits in a stand and you place it over a hole in a bench. Sitting astride the bench, with a pile of square-section tines to hand, it is an easy and satisfying thing to place each tine over the sharpened end of the pipe and wallop it with a mallet.

HEADS AND STAILS

The remaining parts of a rake are the *head*, the block that holds the tines, and the handle, called the *stail* or the *haft*. It is in these parts and how they are joined that there are many regional variations depending on the sort of use to which the rake is traditionally put.

Welsh rakes, used on hillsides where you are most likely to come across stones in the hayfield and where a rake is expected to last, are made with heads only some 18 inches or so wide and set at 45 degrees to the haft. The joint between head and haft

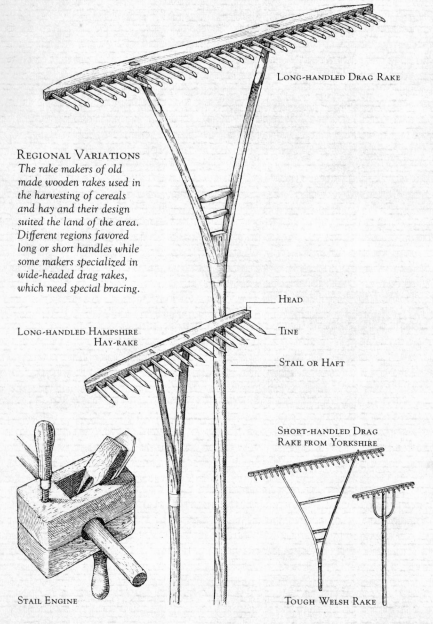

LONG-HANDLED DRAG RAKE

REGIONAL VARIATIONS
The rake makers of old made wooden rakes used in the harvesting of cereals and hay and their design suited the land of the area. Different regions favored long or short handles while some makers specialized in wide-headed drag rakes, which need special bracing.

LONG-HANDLED HAMPSHIRE HAY-RAKE

HEAD

TINE

STAIL OR HAFT

SHORT-HANDLED DRAG RAKE FROM YORKSHIRE

STAIL ENGINE

TOUGH WELSH RAKE

is strengthened with a willow hoop. This is the sort I have used most and it is a different class of implement from most country rakes. These have much wider heads set at just less than 90 degrees to the haft and are made to gather grass which grows to a more luxuriant length. Some large drag rakes for gathering hay and wheat have as many as 30 tines. The epitome of these lowland English rakes is the Hampshire hay-rake, where the haft is split or sawn part way down its length so that it can be divided and joined to the head in two places.

Ash can be used for the head, maple may be better, while elm has the advantage that it will not split. Rake makers of long-standing inherit or make a large upright *brake*, or clamp, to hold the head while it is

shaped and drilled for the tines. All such brakes I have seen use scrap-metal on a chain to weight the jaws and are obviously very effective. The rake maker will wet the ends of the tines before hammering them into the head so the ash or willow fibres swell to a tight fit.

Ash is easily the best wood for hafts. If you can find dead straight poles all the better, but most have to be set straight in the brake after steaming in a chest built over a water boiler. If you have ever used a rake for any length of time you will know how important a smooth haft is. To make the final smoothing there is one of those unique woodworking tools that must have developed over centuries of trial and error. It is called in some parts the *stail engine*, and is a double-bladed rotary plane (see opposite) that you twist down the ash pole.

FIXING THE HEAD
The durability of the rake depends on a good, strong fit between head and stail. Good rake makers bore out the head to take the split haft, judging the perfect, slightly acute angle by eye alone.

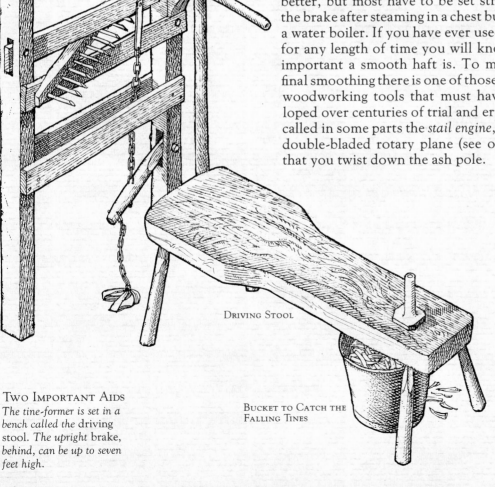

UPRIGHT BRAKE

DRIVING STOOL

BUCKET TO CATCH THE FALLING TINES

TWO IMPORTANT AIDS
The tine-former is set in a bench called the driving stool. The upright brake, behind, can be up to seven feet high.

THE TINE-FORMER
To make perfect little cylinders for tines you take a cleft billet and hammer it into the tube cutter. The second tine in pushes the first out.

FORK MAKING

EARLY EVERYBODY WHO WANTS A pitchfork nowadays goes to the hardware store or agricultural co-op and buys a steel-pronged one. For heavy work, such as lifting hay or straw bales, such instruments are mandatory – a wooden pitchfork would break. But for pitching loose hay or straw the wooden version is ideal, a pleasure to work with and much safer to use when working in stables near horses.

In the Cévennes in France, pitchforks are grown, not made. Little trees are pruned to leave three or four branches, cut when they are ready and taken to a factory near St. Hippolyte du Gard. Here, the handles are straightened if necessary by steaming and then sold to the local farmers. But I am lucky in that the same son-in-law who makes me rakes also makes me pitchforks.

TYPES OF FORK

For light work around the farm, a wooden hay fork can't be bettered. It is a pleasure to use and much safer than a metal tined one. Forks can either be grown, carefully shaping the living tree by judicious pruning, or cut from a straight trunk. To produce the elegant lines of the fork, the wood is first steamed and then placed in a mould for a few weeks.

CUT AND STEAMED FORK

SPACER

WEDGE

GROWN FORKS

JIG

MAKING A FORK

First of all he cuts down an ash tree that has a straight trunk for at least six feet and is about nine inches in diameter. This he rives into halves, quarters and perhaps eighths to produce the right-sized blanks. He then shapes each blank so that the intended head of the fork is wider than the handle. The handle he shapes carefully with draw-knife, spoke-shave and scraper. Holes must now be drilled at the point at which the *tines* (prongs) of the fork will meet the handle and a rivet inserted. His rivets are four-inch nails with a washer next to the head, cut off short so as to leave about quarter of an inch sticking out when pushed through the hole, and another washer popped on the cut end. He spreads the cut end of the nail over with a hammer.

I have known people rive out the tines with a froe but my son-in-law saws them out with a hand rip-saw. He then drills three holes where the *spreaders* are to go before putting the head in his steamer. This is simply an iron pipe propped at a slant with water in it, a plug at the bottom, a rag closing the top and a fire underneath to heat the water. He leaves the fork in for at least two hours, pulls it out and, while it is still hot, drives wooden wedges between the tines. He drives them until the tines are the right distance apart. He makes two, three and four tine forks so obviously he uses different sizes and combinations of wedges.

Using a draw-knife he prepares three rods of hardwood to act as spacers and pushes them through the different series of spacer-holes before pinning them in place with very small nails. The wood, being hot and wet, doesn't split. Now he returns the fork to the steamer, pushing the handle end in first this time, as far as it will go – the splayed-out tines will stop it going right in. After a few hours in the steamer he clamps the handle into the *jig* or mould, which is a standard part of his equipment. The bending, or shaping jig is responsible for producing those beautifully elegant lines of the wooden pitchfork. The work must be left in the jig for a couple of weeks before it is ready. For the last stage the fork is clamped in a shaving horse and the tines shaped with a spoke-shave and the whole fork sandpapered – ready for me to use.

BESOM MAKING

T HE MAKING OF BESOMS, OR "witches' brooms", was greatly simplified with the invention of wire. Or at least, when wire became cheap enough for *broom squires*, as besom makers are called, to afford it.

I watched a besom maker in the south of England. He sat at the end of a shaving-horse in the open right next to a huge stack of birch trimmings which he had cut the previous winter. On a peg stuck into a post near the far end of the horse hung a roll of soft galvanized wire. He quite simply bound up the butt ends of double handfuls of birch using three turns of the wire, each hauled tight against the grip of the horse.

FITTING THE HANDLE
The squire had a stack of handles which he had cut from young ash coppice, selecting them for straightness, and roughly trimming them with the draw-knife to a point. He shoved the point of one of these into the butt end of the wired birch bundle and rammed it hard home. This has the effect of even further tightening the bundle. The broom was done. I think the whole operation took 10 minutes to complete.

OLDER BINDING METHODS
Before the days of cheap wire, *withies* (see p. 156) or hazel wands were used for binding the broom head materials. A heavy clamp with a circular mouth called a *besom-grip* was used, the closing joints crushing the twigs together while the binding was applied. The *bond-poker* was a curved concave blade which was pushed under the binding and allowed the final tying off. As a boy I remember watching an old man using the leg bone of a goose as a bond-poker.

WITHY BONDS
The traditional besom bond of hazel wands or willow rods does not clamp the broom handle quite so tightly as wire. Some squires pre-drill the handle and drive in a retaining peg through the bundle of birch twigs.

FITTING THE HANDLE
If the squire has made a good job of binding the birch twigs, thrusting the point of an ash handle into the middle of the butt ends tightens the bundle to perfection.

BINDING WITH WIRE
The squire I watched had a roll of wire hanging close to the end of his horse with one end passing through the jaws of the clamp. As he closed the jaws with his feet, he hauled backwards to tighten the bonds around the birch bundle.

HANDLE MAKING

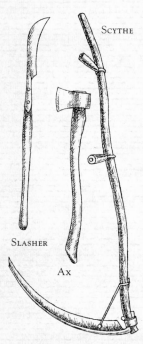

Scythe

Slasher

Ax

Types of Handle
An ordinary stail as on the slasher can be trimmed to shape from a still-green ash sapling. An ax helve is cut from a billet of solid wood that has some curve to the grain, while a scythe snead needs steaming and setting.

Using a Pole Lathe
One of the woodsman's classic tools is the pole lathe (see pp. 33–35 and 96). The treadle is connected by a cord or strap, wrapped around the work, to a springy pole set up to bend above the head of the operator. For turning straight handles, the framework of the lathe must be wide enough to accept the length of the handle. With a pole lathe, you only cut with the chisel while you are pushing down on the treadle. As you let the pole pull the treadle back up, the work spins the wrong way for cutting.

OST TOOL HANDLES ARE MADE nowadays in small factories, or large ones in some cases. Ash trees are cut and brought into the integrated sawmill, billets sawn out with a circular rip-saw and turned on the lathe to make handles. But there are still many country people who make their own handles and they do not, as a rule, have a lathe.

For ordinary *stails* (the country word for straight handles), such as rake and hoe handles and the like, it is often possible to select and cut a straight ash sapling and to trim it down close to the finished shape, while still green, with the draw-knife. To straighten any bends you can clamp the green wood in some sort of holding device. You then leave the handle to season for a year or two, by which time it will have assumed the new straighter shape. After seasoning you can shape it again with the draw-knife, taking the wood down to its final shape and fairing down any irregularities. If the countryman owned, or could make or borrow such a thing as a *stail engine* (see p. 22), his job was a lot easier. But patient work with a draw-knife and fine sandpaper can make a very good job.

Sneads (handles) for scythes have to be steamed and bent, but it is interesting that

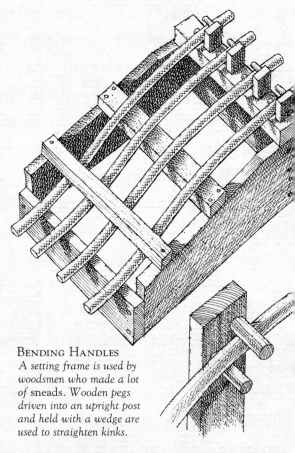

Bending Handles
A setting frame is used by woodsmen who made a lot of sneads. Wooden pegs driven into an upright post and held with a wedge are used to straighten kinks.

English and Welsh scythes have strongly curved handles, while those used in the Alps, for example, have quite straight ones.

The best ax handles, or *helves*, are cut from billets of solid wood riven from a log at least 10 inches thick, which has some curve to the grain that matches the curve of the finished helve. Hickory is the best possible wood, but it is rarely grown in Europe where we "make do" with ash. A good maker lays an existing ax helve sideways on the squared billet and draws round it. He can then clamp the wood and rough-shape the curved profile with a draw-knife before similarly copying the front to back plane. Copying an existing helve only gives you a square guide, mind you, and there is great skill in making the curves just right in the round. Then, if the wood is green, he seasons it for a few months.

After seasoning, the helve can be *fined* right down to the finished shape with a spoke-shave, and then a scraper and fine sandpaper for a glassy-smooth finish. The end that will go into the eye of the ax needs special care as it must be a perfect, cosy fit.

HOOP MAKING

N THE DAYS WHEN ANY AND EVERY-thing was packed in a barrel, the wooden hoops that bound the slack barrels (see p. 94) used for storing dry-stuffs were needed in their thousands. They were a woodland product made by a craftsman called a *hooper*.

Coppice-grown hazel up to eight years old was the best wood for hoops, but chestnut, ash and even oak were used. The wood was cut in spring and soaked in water for a while to soften. It was then riven into 2½- to 14-foot lengths, depending on the barrel size, with a *froe* (see p. 17). To make the hoops easier to bend, the riven side of the

wood was then shaved with a draw-knife leaving the bark intact in a *brake*, or clamp. Willow rods (*withies*) can also be used for making hoops, and my friend Joe Shanahan showed me how. Using an ingenious instrument called a *cleave*, shaped like an egg with three fins carved in its end, Joe took a fairly stout withy and split the withy into three by simply pushing it against the fins. He next shaved the withy with a draw-knife and pushed it through a *bender*, a concave piece of wood with a heavy roller set adjacent to it. The two ends of the hoop were then nailed together to make a perfect circle.

THE HOOPER'S BRAKE
Hoopers had a curious shaving clamp, or brake that allowed them to trim right down the length of a long, whippy rod. This simple device clamped the wood in place by squashing it between a pivoting upright, counterbalanced by a weighted bucket and controlled by the work-man's knee, and a fixed cross member.

A HOOP BENDING EASEL
One method of coiling hoop lengths of riven hazel was to use an easel with six or more crossbars attached to the uprights into which were driven wooden pegs. The wood was simply coiled between the pegs, which were adjustable for different sizes of hoops, until it assumed its new shape.

LADDER MAKING

LADDER TYPES
Fruit picking ladders are generally splayed for extra stability and so you can rest the pointed top against a convenient bough. The pickers' chairs were used among low-growing trees.

RIVEN OAK-RUNGED LADDER

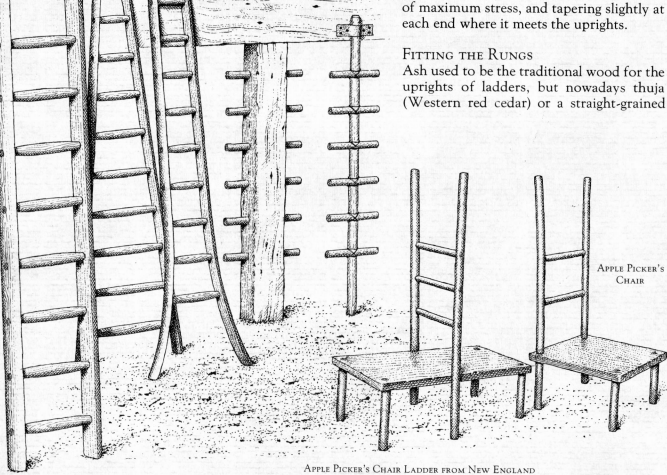

FRUIT PICKING LADDERS

BARN BEAM LADDER

AUSTRIAN HAY-LOFT LADDER

APPLE PICKER'S CHAIR

APPLE PICKER'S CHAIR LADDER FROM NEW ENGLAND

HEN I RETURNED HOME TO ENGLAND after the Second World War, I found a gypsy friend of mine pulling old horse-drawn carts to pieces. The only components he seemed interested in were the spokes of the wheels. Curious, I asked him what he wanted these for, and he said "ladders". He showed me a ladder he was making, using the oak wheel spokes as rungs. I told him he ought to be pulling ladders to pieces to get the rungs out to make wheel spokes, but he did not seem to agree with this at all. "Them things is things of the past!" he said. When one sees the numbers of aluminum extension ladders about today one might be excused for thinking that wooden ladders were also things of the past but, fortunately for ladder makers, this is not quite so.

HEART OF OAK
The only wood fit to be trusted for ladder rungs, in Northern Europe at least, is heart of oak. I shouldn't be at all surprised if hickory is, or has been, used for this purpose in North America. And ladder rungs should always be cleft, or riven, never sawn. Rip-sawing always cuts across some of the grain of the wood, thus weakening it and letting the damp in, leading eventually to rot. Cloven wood, on the other hand, inevitably has the grain running true – for that is the nature of cleaving. Makers of wooden ladders (and any country carpenter can do it) saw heart of oak trunks into lengths a little in excess of the length of the completed rung, cleave the log in half, quarter it, and then cleave it into the three sizes required for the rungs. Then, in the *shaving horse* (see p. 25), each rung is clamped and first trimmed with the *draw-knife*, and then finished with the *spoke shave*. They should be oval in cross-section, so that each rung is strongest in the direction of maximum stress, and tapering slightly at each end where it meets the uprights.

FITTING THE RUNGS
Ash used to be the traditional wood for the uprights of ladders, but nowadays thuja (Western red cedar) or a straight-grained

spruce is preferred as being much lighter. The uprights have holes to receive the rungs drilled out with an auger and in the best ladders these holes are rasped out to give them an oval shape consistent with the oval shape of the rungs. To help ensure the ends of the rungs are all of an identical size, the ladder maker employs a shallow wooden gauge set to the same diameter as the holes drilled in the uprights. Holes and rung ends are so shaped that, when the rungs are driven in, pressure is applied up and down the ladder – that is, along the grain of the side pieces and not across the grain. Thus, the rungs will not split the uprights. This is the same principle that is always applied by woodworkers when driving the end of one piece of wood into another.

Now, trying to put a ladder together is something that can drive you mad unless you know how to do it. The secret is to drive all the rungs in, lightly, to one of the uprights, then to lay this on its side on the ground or, better still, across two tables. Next you take the other upright and, putting it nearly into position, place the first rung into its hole in this second upright. Then tie a piece of string around the two ends of the uprights. You can now engage rung after rung, starting from the first one, until you have all the rungs safely engaged. You are then home and dry and can knock all the rungs fully home using a mallet.

The way a ladder is constructed, it needs no glue, dowels, nails or anything else to hold it together. What it does need, how-ever, is three pieces of wrought iron, threaded at both ends, pushed through small holes in the uprights and held in place with washers and nuts. Commonly, these iron rods are placed out of sight under rungs at the top, bottom and in the middle of the ladder. Now as long as the nuts are kept tight, so as to pull the two uprights of the ladder together, none of the rungs can come out of their holes or work loose. I have also seen ladders made without iron bracing rods but with three or four of the rungs longer than the others, so that they stick out a little. These have holes drilled through their ends and wedges driven into the holes to hold the uprights together.

Less sophisticated ladders can easily be made from a single upright pole to which are lashed simple, unshaped rungs. These are most often found in hay lofts where their light weight makes them ideal for propping in any convenient position.

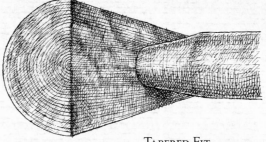

TAPERED FIT
The rungs are tapered at both ends. This ensures that all the joints tighten as the uprights close.

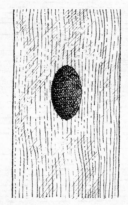

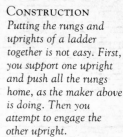

CONSTRUCTION
Putting the rungs and uprights of a ladder together is not easy. First, you support one upright and push all the rungs home, as the maker above is doing. Then you attempt to engage the other upright.

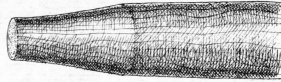

OVAL SECTION
The oval rungs fit corresponding tenons, making the rungs unlikely to split the uprights.

CRIB MAKING

OTHING IS WORSE THAN THROWING loose hay down in a wet field for sheep or cattle to feed on, only to find that much of it gets trodden into the mud. It is surprising how many people do this, and I must admit that I have done it myself.

It is puzzling to think that farmers continue to waste good hay in this manner when hay cribs are so easy to make. I used to make good hay cribs for cattle, and nothing could have been simpler. I simply built a big X shape at each end, forming the feet and the heads of the crib, with cross-pieces joining them and slats at intervals of about four inches. A refinement would have been to have some structure at the bottom between the legs to collect the short bits of hay that fell through, but I never got round to that. This type of crib had a high center of gravity, so needed to be firmly anchored in the ground or the cattle or sheep would have simply turned the whole thing over in their enthusiasm.

COMBINING SKILLS

In various parts of the south of England there is a craft of crib making, and the cribs are strong, good looking and, most important, very serviceable. One might say that this trade is a combination of the skills of the hurdle maker (see p. 18) and those of the basket maker (see p. 155).

The light rods of hazel or willow are bent round to form the ribs. These should be freshly cut and still green to avoid the problem of the wood cracking or splitting. Two long poles (about six to eight feet) are needed to form the base of the crib, drilled at nine-inch intervals. To hold the poles at the right distance from each other, larger cross-members are attached either end and then the bent ribs inserted in the drilled holes. With the basic frame complete it is just a matter of nailing on the long split rods that form the sides, and the crib is made. The farmer simply rolls it over with his foot, stuffs it with hay and turns it the right way round again. This design works fine for sheep, but for larger animals such as cattle a more substantial affair is necessary.

VARIATIONS ON A THEME
For this design of hay crib an old wagon wheel was used as a template. Riven hazel uprights are pushed into holes drilled on the flat edge of the rim and hazel in the round used as the weavers.

SHEEP CRIBS
Fresh-cut willow or hazel rods are bent to form the ribs, some makers shaping the rods so that they bend into a nice bow. Cribs are easy to make, look good, use renewable materials and don't leave rusting scrap in the fields when they finally do give up.

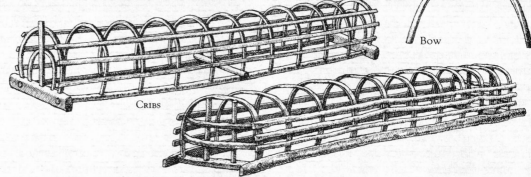

CRIBS

BOW

BROACHES & PEGS

THE ESSENCE OF THE WOODLAND crafts is making the best and thriftiest use of that most precious of raw materials – wood. But every craft – be it hurdle making, chair leg bodging, clogging, ladder or trug making – does generate waste, and so there are craftsmen ready to turn it to their gain.

Mr. Firmin lives in the village of Honing in the Norfolk Broads country and makes his living out of *sways, liggers* and *broaches*, the fixings for thatched roofs. Sways are the hazel or willow poles used to hold the layers of thatch in place. Liggers are almost the same, but thinner and more decorative, and are used on the topmost layer of thatch at the apex of the roof. Broaches are sometimes called *thatching spars* and are used to hold the sways in place.

Mr. Firmin works with his son, and to watch the two of them splitting and shaping broaches is an experience. The broaches are all two feet two inches long and are of riven or split hazel. Chestnut will do for this also and even green elm. Ash, however, cannot be used as it will rot. They each sit down on a wooden *horse*, which has a round piece of wood sticking up through it. They start the rive by knocking an adze into the wood and then shove the split on to the vertical piece of wood so as to widen the split. Very quickly they shove the hazel further and further into the upright wood, guiding the rive with slight twists of the blade of the adze. Out of a small piece of hazel they might extract a dozen broaches.

I tried the same technique with results that seemed hilarious to my teachers. Every time the rive simply split out at the side. I just did not seem able to guide the split straight from one end to the other.

TENT PEGS AND CLOTHESPINS

A gypsy man used to come and sit at my fireside in Wales and drink home-brewed beer and teach me how to make such things as clothespins, tent pegs and baskets. Gypsy clothespins are, alas, almost a thing of the past now – nearly everybody prefers spring pins. The gypsy pins served generations of washerwomen and I can never quite see why they should be unusable now. Perhaps they do not grip so well on plastic wash lines.

THATCHING BROACHES
Broaches are supplied to the thatcher in bundles. It is important to keep them soaking, as above, until they are needed for use because the thatcher bends them into a staple shape. The dampness of the wood helps to stop it splitting, as does a deft twisting action as the bend is made.

BROACHES COUNTED AND READY FOR BUNDLING

TWISTED AND BENT FOR USE

My friend John Jones used to take a stick of willow, cut it into suitable lengths (about six inches – his pins were generous) with sharp blows with a finely-honed hatchet and fashion a head on one of the lengths by shaving the rest of the pin down with his pocket knife. He would then wrap a little strip of tin around the pin at the point up to which he was going to split it and tap a tiny nail through the two overlapping ends of tin and into the wood using the back of his chopper. He cut the tin out of old tin cans with a pair of tin-snips. He then split the pin down from the end opposite the head with the blade of his knife.

Anybody can make a clothespin. But to make them quick enough to earn a living – that's another matter! He used to make tent pegs, too, out of riven hazel. He did all the shaping with his knife (after the initial riving) except for the cut across the grain for the notch which he did with a little saw.

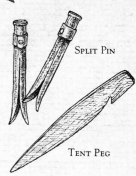

SPLIT PIN

TENT PEG

GYPSY PINS AND PEGS
Split pin and tent peg making has been an important commercial activity of the gypsy community for many generations. The willow wood used for the pins can be found almost anywhere in the country, growing unwanted in swamps or unused ground, and is there for the taking.

CLOG SOLE CUTTING

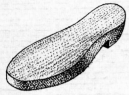

THE CLOG SOLE
Thick, unyielding pieces of alder wood, with shaped sole and heel, once kept the wet and cold from the feet of many farm and factory workers. The clog remains a most practical piece of footwear.

SOLE CUTTING KNIVES
The shaping of an oblong billet of wood to suit the form of the human foot is a skilled business taking many cutting strokes with different shapes of blade. The beauty of the levered knives used for this shaping is that you can exert great force on the blade while being able to move the wood to any angle.

LOG MAKERS WERE SETTLED PEOPLE with their own workshops (see pp 132-3), while *cloggers* were itinerants who lived where their work was – in the woods, in camps among the trees that provided their livelihood. They provided rough-cut soles to individual clog makers, but the bulk of their work went to the clog making factories.

Their raw material was alder, willow, birch, maple or beech wood, preferably alder, since it is a quick growing, coarse-grained soft wood that is easy to cut. It is water resistant and makes a durable barrier against a wet factory floor or a muddy field.

BREAKING UP

The clogger would cut alder trunks up to two feet in diameter, and use it immediately

STOCK-KNIFE

GRIPPING KNIFE

while still green and easy to work. The first operation was to crosscut the trunks into shorter logs of four graded sizes – *men's, women's, children's* and *middles*. These logs were then riven into *sole blocks* with a *beetle* (a heavy wooden mallet) and wedge, then with an ax and finally with a *stock-knife* or *bench-knife* to the rough size and oblong shape of the finished sole. Cloggers called this part of the operation, *breaking up*.

The clogger's stock-knife is about 30 inches long, with a hook at one end which is slipped under a ring on a low bench, and a handle at the other. The knife is slightly curved, and has a lethal-looking blade four inches deep and about a foot long near the hook. By pushing down on the handle, great leverage is exerted on the blade. Grasping the handle with his right hand, the clogger would hold a sole block in his left and with a few deft strokes of the knife cut it out to the right shape, carving out the notch between heel and toe as he did so. Some cloggers went on to use a *hollowing knife*, similar to the stock-knife, to scoop out the instep, and then with a *gripping* or *shaping knife*, to cut the narrow groove around the side of the sole into which the clog maker would later fit the leather upper.

All this would take the clogger very few minutes indeed, for years of practice made him able to build a stack of soles twice as high as a man in a couple of days. He had to work fast to make a living.

Cloggers would work an alder grove until it was exhausted, then move on. Alder is a prolific grower in damp fertile soil so cloggers could follow riverside groves confident that new growth was establishing itself in the groves they had left.

SEASONING
Being a very sappy wood, alder needs to dry out for perhaps nine months before it can be used. The clogger built great conical stacks using the rough-cut soles like bricks, but being careful to space each sole so that there was a good circulation of air throughout the stack.

BODGING

OT SO MANY YEARS AGO, THE beechwoods of England were populous with a class of men known as *chair bodgers*. To call someone a "bodger" in England is to accuse them of bungling, and just how these highly skilled craftsmen came to be called by this misleading title is hard to understand.

Chair bodgers were one of three types of craftsmen associated with the making of traditional country chairs. The bodger was basically an itinerant woodland worker who specialized in the making of the legs and stretchers of the famous Windsor chairs. Even as late as the 1950s there were some chair bodgers, but unfortunately now there are none left. And so a craft going back at least five hundred years is no more.

In their heyday, however, they would purchase a stand of trees, clear a space to set up their temporary living quarters and go about the business of selecting just the right trees from which to make the chair legs and *stretchers*, or braces. Ideally, the beech trees had to be not overly old. They also had to be straight grained and rather

leggy, meaning that they had grown a little too quickly. By only felling the right trees, gaps were left in the wood where new seedlings could grow, and by not cutting trees too young, they could be allowed to grow on and so extend the useful life of that paticular stand of trees. These people had a real awareness of their surroundings, nature if you like, which not many of us are privileged to experience nowadays.

The tools of the chair bodger were few and simple: an ax, draw-knife, saw and some chisels. This helps explain why the life of the bodger was so isolated – with so few tools it was much easier for the bodger to work the trees where they fell rather than haul logs back to a central workshop somewhere in a distant village. As the bodger was responsible for the turned parts of the chair, a lathe was also necessary.

After felling the tree, the bodger would haul or roll the trunk back to his woodland workshop, remove any side branches and saw the log into *billets*, pieces of wood approximately the right length for a chair leg. Next, a wedge was driven into the billet in order to split it into as many pieces as possible without causing undue waste. Depending on the size of the billet, anywhere from four to as many as sixteen legs could be split from the one piece of wood.

THE POLE LATHE

A pole lathe, *below, is powered by a tensioned ash or larch sappling up to 12 feet long secured firmly to the ground at one end and left unsupported at its other end over the lathe itself. Depressing the foot-operated treadle pulls down the pole by means of a piece of cord, or a leather thong, which looped around the work, as the piece of wood to be shaped is called, and twists the work in one direction. This allows the bodger to cut the work with a chisel supported on the tool rest. When the treadle is released, the bodger withdraws the blade as the pole springs back again, turning the work in the other direction. The lathe is adjusted to take different lengths of work by moving the puppets along the bed of the lathe.*

PREPARING THE CLEFT

Once the hewn wood has been sown into billets and then split with mallet and cleaving ax, the cleft can be worked on by the bodger with a side-ax to trim it to the approximate shape of the finished leg.

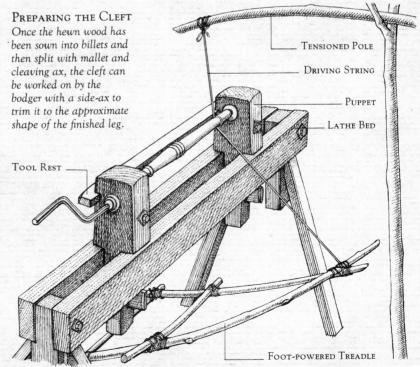

TENSIONED POLE

DRIVING STRING

PUPPET

LATHE BED

TOOL REST

FOOT-POWERED TREADLE

Now the bodger would use his side-ax, which was sharpened on one side only, to fashion the pieces into the approximate chair leg shape. The next refining stage involved the bodger's draw-knife. As with all draw-knives, this was a two-handed affair with handles set at right-angles to the blade. The bodger would draw the blade over the wood with such skill that the shape and proportion of the leg or stretcher were immediately discernible.

The final stage was the turning of the wood on the lathe. Now, despite our modern conception of what a lathe is, simple versions have been in use stretching back probably as far as the Iron Age. And I should reckon that the type used by the bodger would have been recognizable by our Iron Age ancestors. The bodger's *pole lathe* was a simple affair, made entirely from the rough products of the woodland. The *work*, as the piece of wood being shaped was called, was revolved a short distance in one direction by a treadle powered by nothing more than the bodger's foot, and then turned in the opposite direction by the action of a bent ash pole that acted as a spring. This ash pole could be as long as 12 feet. A piece of string ran from the foot treadle to the top of the pole, which was planted securely in the ground and further supported by the wall of the bodger's hut. The top of the pole was left unsupported to allow it to bend and whip back upright again. The pole lathe had one major drawback – the actual cutting of the wood could only be done on the foot-powered turn of the lathe.

From this description it can be seen that the beechwood was cut, shaped and turned when still green. Green wood is not suitable for chair making, so the bodger would stack the finished legs and stretchers beside his hut for weeks until they were sufficiently seasoned. The length of time seasoning took was very much dependent on the weather. When this process was complete, the bodger would transport his work to one of the big chair-making centers such as High Wycombe in Buckinghamshire. Here, the other two types of craftsmen would take over – the *benchman*, who was responsible for all the sawn parts of the chair such as the seat and back, and the *framer*, who would assemble the chair and carry out any of the little finishing details. The framer would also make the steam-bent parts of the chair if this was required.

A Chair Bodger's Camp

Deep in the beechwood forests of England, when there were beechwood forests in England, the quiet was disturbed by the sounds of ax and chisel against wood wherever chair bodgers went about their work. The bodgers traveled light, sometimes alone, sometimes with a workmate, with the few tools necessary for their trade. They would set up camp, making a shelter to work and sleep in through the spring and summer months. The results of their industry were prolific. Cleft wood soon piled up waiting to be cut to shape at the shaving horse, and then to be turned at the bodger's pole lathe. The lathe was made of hewn wood components and designed to be dismantled and carried from camp to camp. The clearing and any shelter would quickly be covered in wood chips and shavings amidst the stacks of seasoning chair legs. Such itinerant work is now a thing of the past, for the last chair bodger left the forest more than twenty years ago, and what woodland there is echoes to very different sounds now.

CHARCOAL BURNING

O MAKE CHARCOAL YOU BURN wood in conditions with insufficient oxygen for complete combustion. In the past I have helped to make charcoal for such diverse purposes as burning bricks and powering a Model T Ford with a *producer gas* engine. In Africa the technique was to dig out a large trench perhaps six yards long, two yards deep and a yard and a half wide, with the *spoil* dug out piled on each side of the trench. You then took an ox wagon load of dry wood, cut it into small pieces and threw it into the pit, leaving a little space at one end for a boy to climb down into to light the fire and then get out pretty quickly!

To stand near the trench soon became well-nigh impossible, but stand there we did holding pieces of rusty corrugated iron until, on command, we flung the iron on to the flames and then shoveled mightily to pile the spoil from the trench on top. A week later the earth would be dug off, the iron removed, and there, in the pit, mixed with ashes and earth would be the charcoal.

THE KILN METHOD

Years later, back in Suffolk, in a wood near Bury St. Edmunds, I came across a more professional way of making charcoal. The charcoal burner, who came from the south of England, was living in a small elderly trailer on the edge of the wood. A great many large trees had been felled in the wood the year before and the *tops*, or branches, left behind. It was these that he was sawing up into quite short lengths with a circular saw driven by an old tractor, and splitting with an ax, for charcoal making. He used a kiln which was formed of steel rings, each about two feet deep and five feet in diameter. He packed one ring with wood and then hauled another ring on top of it until three rings full completed the kiln. He covered it with a steel roof with a vent in it, which could be opened or closed. He lit the fire at a vent in the bottom of the kiln and, when the fire had well and truly taken, closed the vents. It was several days before the kiln was burned out and cool enough for the burner to open and dismantle, raking out the charcoal and throwing it on a coarse sieve to separate it from the dust and ashes. He could then shovel it into bags. He showed me how you could test the quality of the charcoal by throwing a piece down on a board. It should make a ringing sound as it strikes the hard surface.

PRIMITIVE SHELTER
The charcoal burners of old lived out in the woods during the summer months, building their own makeshift shelters. These had a wooden framework, lashed together, which was roughly thatched, as shown right, or covered in turf. Inside, there was room for a couple of improvised bunks above the bare earth.

THE TRADITIONAL METHOD

In the days before the introduction of the steel ring kiln, charcoal burners built their wood into conical stacks, covering them first with straw and then with ashes and earth. The old English charcoal burners were, we are told, a race apart. Before the discovery that you could smelt iron ore with coke made from coal, which happened in the early eighteenth century, these wild men of the woods were the basis of most industry. Their product was used for iron making, glass making, and in gunpowder. All summer (for the burning was done in the summer when winds were not too ferocious) they lived in conical shelters made from sticks with a turf or thatch covering, often far from their homes and in very primitive conditions. They were true men of the woods. They used tools with esoteric names, such as the *mare*, which was a kind of framework barrow for carrying wood. Then there was the *loo* (a country way of saying lee), which was a screen to keep the wind off. The rake used – a curious one – was called the *corrack*, and the long-handled shovel, the *shool*.

The burning took considerable skill and the old charcoal burners were secretive about their methods. It is known, however, that the work started by building a vertical chimney of logs. Around this core a stack was carefully built up of logs (from two to four feet long) up to about the height of a man. This was then covered with bracken, straw or other vegetation and then very carefully covered with ashes and earth to form a *clamp*. Burning charcoal was dropped down the chimney at the center of the clamp, followed by dry tinder on top to ignite the wood. Then, when the fire had spread out through the stack to the burner's satisfaction the hole at the top was plugged with mud. The burner then watched the clamp for about a week. If a strong wind got up the smouldering fire within would *break out*, and if this happened the whole batch was lost. More earth was added to *dress* any weak places.

Nowadays charcoal, made in sophisticated retorts, has a hundred uses in modern industry, but the days of the smoke-blackened men, wise in the ways of the woods, are over. Even so, I saw it made in clamps in Mallorca in 1955 or thereabouts, and it is still being made in this way in Mediterranean countries where much cooking and heating is done with charcoal.

BUILDING THE STACK

The success of the traditional woodland method of charcoal burning depends on the skill with which the stack is built. Too much air circulating in the wood reduces it to ashes, while excluding air completely results in charcoal of variable quality. The way an old woodsman from Sussex used to stack the wood is shown below.

1 *The burner builds a chimney of billets, triangular in fashion, in the middle of the area cleared for the stack.*

2 *He stacks billets against the three sides of the chimney, working out to a circular shape with the clear space of the chimney at its center.*

3 *The roof of billets is added with each billet laid pointing towards the chimney but not blocking the shaft.*

CHARCOAL BURNING IN PORTUGAL
The traditional method of charcoal burning is still alive and kicking in some Mediterranean regions, as this recent picture of a Portuguese clamp shows.

OAK BASKET MAKING

ASKETS MADE OF SPLIT OAK COME IN many different sizes and shapes and are designed to carry a wide variety of produce in countries as wide ranging as England, Scandinavia and America. One such is the Sussex *trug*. The name comes from *trog*, which is an old name for a boat. The little basket is boat-shaped, light, strong and handy, and is ideal for the garden where it can be used for carrying flowers and other long stuff.

The trug is a member of that large family of containers woven, not of round wood, but of flat slats of material. I have seen a group of African women catching tiny fish in a shallow lagoon by tramping forwards in a line, holding baskets below the water. The baskets they used were made just as a Sussex trug is made, with thin slats of wood slightly overlapping and making an escape-proof trap for the small fish.

Making a Trug

The Sussex trug maker takes two straight wands of ash or chestnut and splits them in half. He steams them, then bends them around jigs – both into round-cornered oblong shapes, one with the bark inside the ring and one with the bark outside. The hoops are held with small nails. The two are then fitted together – the one with the bark inside vertically to act as the handle for the trug, the one with the bark outside horizontally to act as the rim. The strips used for the body of the trug are best made of oak, split as thinly as possible. They must then be *faired down* – made wider in the middle and narrower at each end.

Trug Making
To make a trug you need a draw-knife and shaving horse, wood steamer and some improvised jigs. The frame and handle are set in jigs (1), and then tacked together with the main split-oak slat (2). The rest of the slats are filled in and the feet added to complete the trug (3).

The Trug
What I most like about the trug is its boat-like shape. You can fit all manner of long stuff in it, such as cut flowers, green scallions, rhubarb stalks and the like.

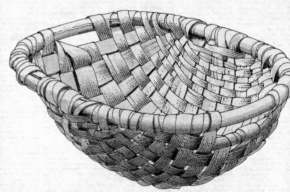

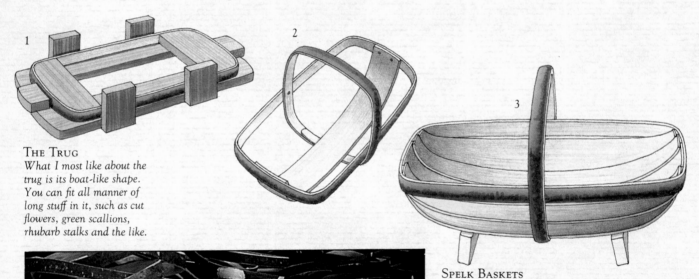

Spelk Baskets
Spelk, or swill baskets, are made by weaving thin slats of oak around a stout hoop or bow of ash or hazel wood. The strips are obtained by boiling oak poles and riving them while they are still hot. You use the stoutest strips for the warp of the basket and save the lighter ones to weave through them. The result is a basket in which you can hold fine materials, even flour.

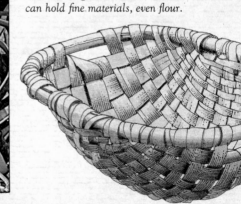

A wider central strip is then nailed to the rim at both ends, being bent round into the necessary boat shape. The rest of the strips are simply bent round and nailed at each end to the rim so that they form the *planks*, as it were, of the boat. Really, nothing could be simpler. The little nails used must, of course, be clenched over. As in so many examples of what I call "engineering in wood", every piece that makes up the trug is under tension – it is *sprung*. And it is this springing that gives the trug its strength.

SPELK BASKETS

These oddly named baskets are true baskets (unlike trugs) in that they are woven with a *warp* and a *weft*. They are built round a hoop (often called a *bow* or *bool* in the north of England) made of ash or hazel. The *spelks*, as the weaving elements are called, are made by boiling oak poles from four to six inches in diameter, and riving them while still hot. The stouter spelks are

nailed to the bow as the warp and lighter spelks woven into them as the weft. These lighter spelks are sometimes called *chisies* or *ribands* in different parts of the country. It is important to keep the spelks soft and so they are immersed in hot water until used so that they will bend without breaking.

If such baskets are to be used for carrying, say, coal, coke or firewood, the warp of the basket is often made with round wood such as hazel. If it is to hold small stuff, both warp and weft are of spelks.

In some parts of Sweden you may be lucky enough to see elaborate split oak basketry. Some of these baskets are made in much the same way as the spelk, with slivers of oak being used to weave a container. Some Swedish baskets have a stiff wooden frame with split oak weaving filling the gaps. In America, too, there is a long tradition of split-oak basket making. Baskets of many different designs were (and still are) made by the Indians.

AMERICAN BASKETS
Most of the baskets from the Appalachian Mountains are made of split oak, some, like the Tennessee-made basket shown below, using white oak colored with vegetable dyes. Regional differences account for the many varying designs and the uses to which the baskets are put.

SWEDISH BASKET
Traditional wooden-weave baskets from Sweden, like the one made in 1866 illustrated bottom, were ornately painted and used to carry gifts of bread and other produce on feast days.

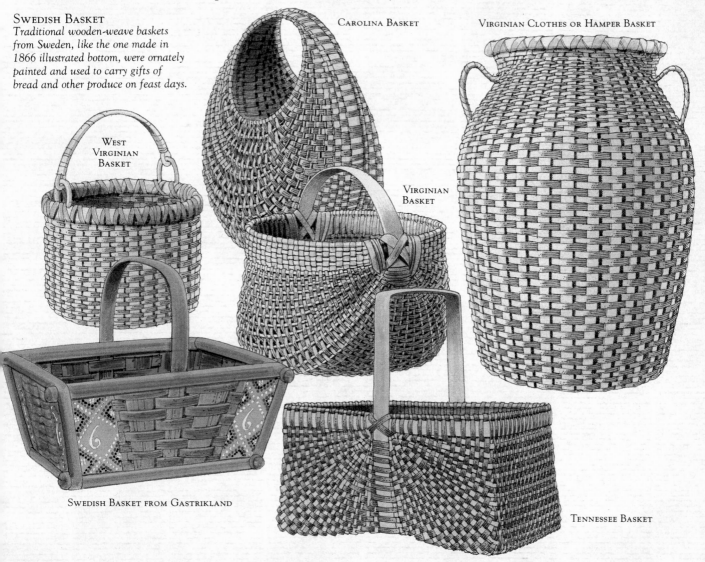

WEST VIRGINIAN BASKET

CAROLINA BASKET

VIRGINIAN CLOTHES OR HAMPER BASKET

VIRGINIAN BASKET

SWEDISH BASKET FROM GASTRIKLAND

TENNESSEE BASKET

BUILDING CRAFTS

A t one time you could walk through an English village and know
in what part of the country you were by asking yourself a few
questions about the type of building around you. Were the roofs
thatched in straw or reed? Were the walls of clay or flint? There
was a usage of local building materials and techniques that you
could depend on. It would have been thought madness to pay for
building materials to be hauled across the country when there
were local materials that could be exploited for nothing but the
sweat of your own brow, or for the price of an honest day's work
by a local craftsman. If there was good stone in an area then houses
were built of it. If timber was plentiful, fine timber homes resulted.
Buildings were then sure to sit comfortably on the land and to
look as if they should be there. Now there is a great uniformity of
building. Materials are mass-produced and concrete reigns
king among them. Local skills required by local
materials are either lost or are now an
expensive alternative.

WOODEN BUILDING

A TYPE OF BUILDING I HAVE HELPED to construct, and have spent many comfortable months in, is what I call the archetypal African hut. In fact, the simple wooden construction is common to many parts of the world.

To build such a hut, you choose a flat site and scribe a perfect circle on the ground by using a piece of string tied to a central peg. You dig a narrow, deep trench around the circle, leaving a section undug for the doorway. Then you stand rough poles in the trench so that they touch each other right round, except for the door. These you lash together at the top with strips of bark or creepers, and then you trample the earth down hard around the base of the poles. This makes the wall, which you finish off by daubing liberally with mud. For the roof you make a circular framework of light poles on the ground nearby. It is best to make a simple cone shape, and this you thatch (see p. 46) and lift on to the circular wall, securing it there with any convenient binding material. A family of Africans can build such a hut in a day. It should last for many years and when it does eventually rot, it only takes another day to build a new one while the old hut makes good firewood. The floor is of beaten earth and sometimes, for real luxury, smeared with cowdung. When a fire is burning in the middle of the floor you cannot stand up with comfort, but the moment you sit down you are below the smoke level, are warm and, most important, free of flies and mosquitoes. They don't particularly like smoke.

On a recent visit to old haunts in Kenya I was horrified to see the good old round hut being replaced by oblong buildings with corrugated iron roofs. They were hot inside, full of mosquitoes and most uncomfortable. Furthermore, the iron costs money that the owners could ill afford and would rust away rather quickly. But they look *modern* and have, therefore, status.

Log Cabins

I once spent a few nights in what the owners claim is the biggest log cabin in the world. It is not, as one might expect, in the Canadian wilderness but in Scotland, at a place called Lothlorien near the Galloway coast. The cabin is enormous and houses a large community, comprising several families, who, despite the physical drawbacks of the construction, find it a pleasant place.

The reason why the community chose logs to build with is because they were offered a large supply of very cheap, extremely long Douglas fir trunks. I personally would not have chosen this method of construction. In the first place it is a very

Log Building in Finland
Finnish or Scandinavian log house builders have always made log homes to last with hard, seasoned red fir or pine. They interlock a number of rooms and the jointing of log to log is traditionally so precise that a thin layer of moss inserted between the logs during construction is all that is needed for a permanently weatherproof result.

lavish use of that splendid material – wood. The same logs ripped down into planks would have provided enough material to build an entire village, and the planks could have been tongued and grooved so as to keep out the wind. As it was, the inevitable chinks between the logs had to be bunged up with mortar (*chinking*, as it was called in the New World), which cracked and fell out at regular intervals.

THE AMERICAN TRADITION

The American backwoodsmen were said to carry their sawmills on their backs. The only tools they carried were an ax, a broadax, a crosscut saw and an auger bit. Together with these they needed a sheet of thin steel, to be made into a stove, and a small sack of nails for fixing *shingles* – the roof tiles made from wood. With this equipment they could build a cabin that would stand up to the fiercest winters. I gather from my early days as a reader of romantic novels that these hardy woodsmen would wait for the first frost and then throw buckets of water over their cabins. The water thus thrown would freeze and seal the building. Well, rather they than I!

The only disappointment with this romantic image is that there is nothing

NOTCHING

The crux of building with logs is to make good corner joints – a process known as notching. *The beautifully intricate joints shown below required a master crafts-man's skill. They are: the* square notch *(A); the* furrow notch, *with inclined side cut (B); the* furrow notch with heel *(C); and the* dovetail notch, *with its impossibly complex angles (D).*

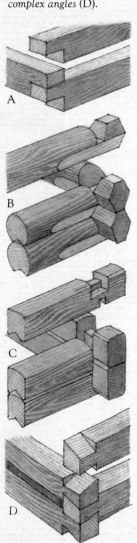

A

B

C

D

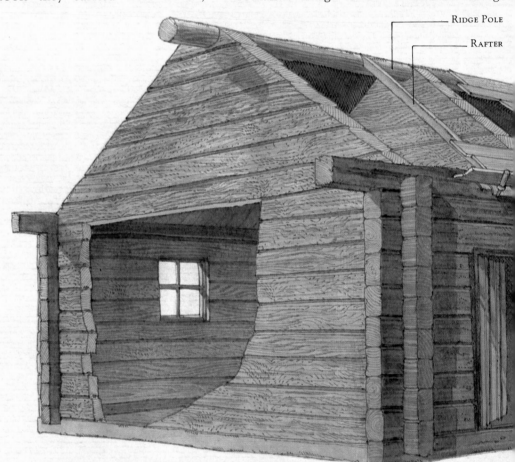

RIDGE POLE

RAFTER

SWEDISH LOG HOUSE

The cutaway illustration, above, shows a standard Swedish log house. It was the model for timber building in America for many settlers but whereas the American version was often seen as a temporary home, the Scandinavian log house was built with great care and expected to last for generations. The logs were split and hewn as smooth as planed boards, and they were grooved so that they slotted together. The two-room plan consisted of the vardagstuga, *the larger living, dining and sleeping room, and the* gang, *used for storage.*

STONE FOUNDATIONS

If a timber home is intended to be permanent, it has to have dry feet. That means having a foundation that lifts the bottom timbers clear of the damp earth that will rot them. You might see a stone plinth used, especially where the cabin is built on uneven ground.

ROOFING
Roof construction was developed to a high degree and included layers of birch bark and moss with an outer layer of riven timber. One side of this layer was allowed to project over the ridge somewhat like a comb.

Moss

Planking

Birch Bank

Eaves Board

Iron Fixing and Peg

Riven Log Outer Layer

MOUNTAIN CABIN
An American log cabin of this type, with a wood and clay chimney, would have been built up to the end of the nineteenth century. The shingle roof (roof tiles of riven white oak) was fixed with nails – a very precious commodity.

CUTTING SHINGLES
I watched shingles being cut from pine and larch in Austria. In America, shingles are still made from white oak and red cedar in the East, and redwood in the West. Some cutters call shingles shakes if they use the traditional method of riving them with a froe, as shown here. The average size of a shingle is approximately 8 by 12 inches.

really unique about the American log cabin. Its origins are very firmly rooted in Sweden and Finland. The first log cabins in America were introduced in the mid seventeenth century by Swedish and Finnish settlers who established colonies along the Delaware. But the proliferation of this type of building is probably due to the more wide-ranging Scots, Irish and German settlers. They built a version of pioneer cabin with an external chimney, made of wood and clay, stone or brick, against the gable end.

Although, theoretically, a log cabin could be built by one man, construction was more usually a community affair. After the trees had been felled they had to be hauled back to the building site and *notched*, or cut for the corner joints of the cabin, before being raised to their correct position. As the walls became higher, logs had to be hauled by ropes and pushed from below, using two other logs as a ramp. Only when the outer shell and roof were complete were the windows and doors cut out.

Contrary to popular belief, the American log cabin was rarely meant as a permanent home. It was often regarded as a temporary shelter until a family became established in its new settlement and a conventional timber or brick house became possible.

WALLING

I N MANY PARTS OF THE WORLD YOU will find houses, from simple huts to substantial and enduring two-story cottages, made from locally available material such as clay and flint.

CLAY LUMP WALLING

Go to most villages in East Anglia and you will see many buildings with what are called locally *clay lump walls*. These are made of clay with a mixture of sand and other components, rammed moist into moulds and then turned out. There are thousands of clay lump houses still standing, none built later than the 1920s. So long as they are kept well covered with rendering and "their heads and feet dry" (that is built on an impervious foundation and roofed) they will stand for years.

COB WALLING

In the West Country *cob* walling is common, using unfired earth as a raw material. Either the walls are built up, a layer at a time, by placing a mixture of mud and straw on the layer below, after it has been allowed to dry, or *rammed earth* construction is employed. Rammed earth techniques require strong wooden shuttering to contain the mixture and heavy ramming from above. The soil used must have the right moisture content—too wet it bulges up each side of the ram, and too dry it does not knit together. Also,

the soil should consist of a mixture of graded particles for best results. Every sized particle from clay through coarse sand to small gravel can be used. All soil is improved for this purpose if five percent cement is added to it. Lime, too, makes a good stabilizer, though not as good as cement. Cob walling makes it possible for people to build lasting houses costing practically no money at all.

FLINT WALLING

Flints washed out of gravel beds or picked up from the beach are either round or oval shaped, they tend to be all about the same size and are a real headache to build with. The secret of success lies in the mortar. Nowadays, cement is used but traditionally it was a mixture of lime, left to mature in the damp for at least a month, and sand. The desired consistency was like butter.

The corners or *quoins* of flint-built houses are always of brick, as are the foundations and door and window surrounds. The flint, in fact, acts as in-filling only. Nearly all the churches in East Anglia are built principally of flint and several are still standing after 700 years. Modern flint building is expensive, but there is a lot of it still done in north Norfolk because this is the *flint coast* and for many miles around all the houses and barns are built of flint. It is a tradition which is being kept up.

Most buildings of flint were built, at least partly, of *knapped flint*. This is flint that has been struck with a hammer to make at least one face of it straight. Many such flints were knapped into cubes. Building with knapped flint is called *flush work* and much of it includes beautiful patterns.

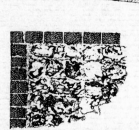

BRICK QUOINS

KNAPPED FLINT

FLINT HOUSES
Brick is used for the quoins or corners, foundations and door and window surrounds of flint houses, since flint by itself lacks the strength for such load-bearing positions and is too random in shape.

COB HOUSES
The walls of cob-built houses are built up of unfired earth layers of clay mud and straw, with chalk and grit added for strength. Each layer is up to two feet high and two feet across, depending on the wall that is being built, and must be left to dry before the next layer is placed on top.

LIME BURNING

IME IS A MOST USEFUL COMMODITY for any rural community, conditioning its soil, whitewashing its walls and mortaring its stones. Every village within easy reach of either lime or coal used to have its own lime kiln, and lime production was once an important rural industry. Nowadays industrially produced lime has replaced locally produced material, but many old kilns still survive.

TYPES OF LIME

There are three types of lime. The first is rock limestone ground up in a mill. Often called *whitines*, it is used for neutralizing soil acidity and improving clay soils. From limestone rock we also get *quicklime*, or calcium oxide, produced by heating up lime in a kiln. This is a pretty ferocious substance and was much used in days of old for disposing of the bodies of criminals and others the authorities wanted to get rid of. If you leave quicklime about in the air for long enough, or chuck water on it, you will get *slaked lime*, or calcium hydroxide. This is quite a harmless and benign substance, but the act of slaking with water causes great heat, and should be done with care.

Slaked lime has been put on the fields of Europe, to *sweeten* acid soil, for at least two thousand years. Added to about three times its volume of sand and mixed with water, it makes a fine mortar which, though not as strong as cement mortar, has nevertheless stood up, in many a medieval castle or other buildings, for a thousand years or so.

Another important use of lime is for whitewash. To make this you merely have to mix slaked lime, very thinly, in water. A hundred pounds of lime will whitewash a medium-sized house. Then you simply slosh the stuff on. The only disadvantage of this traditional whitewash is that it will rub off on your coat if you lean against it.

LIME KILNS

A lime kiln is a huge brick pot with an open top and a hole in the bottom of it. The bottom of the kiln is plugged with brushwood, and then layers of soft coal or, better still, anthracite, and broken limestone are piled on top, filling up the kiln. The brushwood is then ignited, and the thing left alone. Tramps used to love to

sleep on burning kilns in cold weather and occasionally one would be overcome by the fumes and not wake up again. After the kiln has burned out and cooled, the contents are raked out of the bottom hole of the kiln and the lime is slaked with water.

When the cost of imported cement was too high I burned lime in the open, in a heap. You lay brushwood on the ground, maybe two feet of it, then six inches of broken limestone on top, then another of brushwood, then a further layer of limestone, and so on to the height required. The object is to make a neatly rounded stack, which you then plaster thickly with mud, the thicker the better. You need to make a hole at the bottom of the mud on the windward side, and several small holes in a line at the top on the leeward side. The wood is then lit and left to burn and cool.

SRI LANKAN KILN
In Sri Lanka, rural kilns such as the one above, are still used today, This example is roofed against the tropical rains.

LOCATION
Kilns like this were often built next to a waterway for ease of transport.

THATCHING

HE FIRST ROOF ANY MAN SHELTERED under, apart from the roof of a cave, was of thatch. The traditional huts of tribal Africans are nearly always roofed with thatch. The conical framework of the roof is thatched by laying on grass with the heads of the grasses pointing downward and lashing it down with bark strips. At the top the stems of the last round of grasses are tied tightly together with bark to form a sort of top-knot. I never knew one of these huts leak.

Sri Lankans have a magnificent form of thatch called *cadjan*. It is, I suppose, common to all tropical countries where palm trees will grow for it is thatch made from interwoven palm fronds. A good cadjan roof will keep the worst monsoon out.

EUROPEAN THATCH

In Europe we make do with such stuff as grass, heather, straw or reed. Heather was, and is, used to roof the little "black houses" of the Outer Hebrides and other northern isles. In the West of Ireland oat or barley straw is still sometimes used to form a rather primitive kind of thatch. It only lasts two or three years but this is not a drawback when you can re-thatch yourself or when you can get the local thatcher to do it for the price of a bottle of whiskey.

The thatch of northern Germany, Denmark and England differs from African tribal thatch in that the *butts* (bottoms) of whatever vegetable material is used point downward, not upward. As the butts are thicker than the flowering tops, each strand

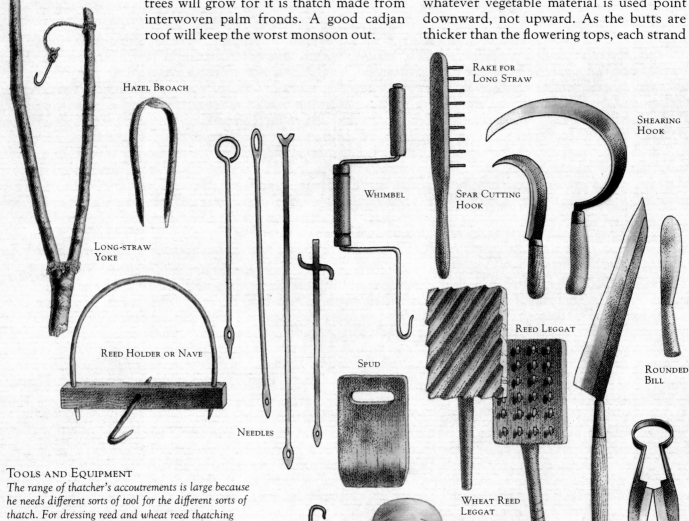

HAZEL BROACH

RAKE FOR LONG STRAW

SHEARING HOOK

LONG-STRAW YOKE

WHIMBEL

SPAR CUTTING HOOK

REED LEGGAT

ROUNDED BILL

REED HOLDER OR NAVE

SPUD

NEEDLES

WHEAT REED LEGGAT

KNEE AND ARM PADS

SHEARS

IRON SECURING HOOK

EAVES KNIFE

TOOLS AND EQUIPMENT

The range of thatcher's accoutrements is large because he needs different sorts of tool for the different sorts of thatch. For dressing reed and wheat reed thatching you need different sorts of leggat, whereas for long-straw thatching you do not need a leggat so much as a rake and a sharp shearing hook for trimming. Then different thatch holders are used for long straw and reed. All thatch is sewn to the rafters at points across the roof, using long needles and twine or straw rope twisted with a whimbel.

of thatch lies closer to the horizontal than you would think and so Northern European thatch tends to be very thick and requires a great deal of material to make a roof, combined with much labor and skill.

LONG-STRAW THATCHING

When I was a boy, in the Essex and Suffolk countryside, every farm labourer could thatch a rick, or a hay stack, and many an older man could, and often had, thatched his own house. The material they used in both cases is called *long straw*. This is simply straw – generally wheat but oats would do at a pinch and rye is excellent – which has passed through a threshing machine. The *drum*, as the old type of threshing machine is called, knocks out the grain and also breaks and mixes individual straws.

Old Bill Keeble, the foreman of a farm on which I worked in Essex, showed me how to prepare this straw for thatching. He

AT THE RIDGE
Whatever the thatching material at the ridge, you have to use a flexible material, such as sedge or long straw, to cap the apex.

LONG-STRAW THATCH
Once you have a little experience of thatch you will recognize the soft finish of long-straw thatching. Hefty yealms, or bundles, of straw are tied firmly to the battens nearest the eaves to start the job which continues up the roof to the ridge. The thatcher staggers the layers of thatch up the roof securing each layer with hazel rods pinned to the rafters with iron hooks.

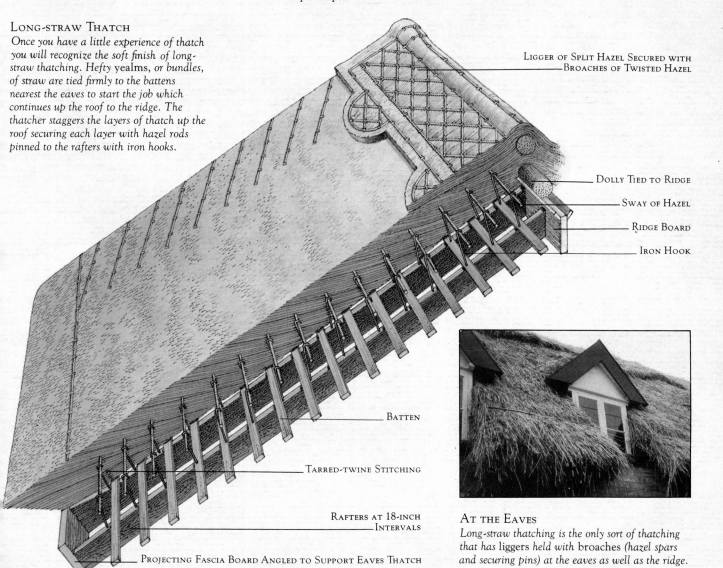

LIGGER OF SPLIT HAZEL SECURED WITH BROACHES OF TWISTED HAZEL

DOLLY TIED TO RIDGE

SWAY OF HAZEL

RIDGE BOARD

IRON HOOK

BATTEN

TARRED-TWINE STITCHING

RAFTERS AT 18-INCH INTERVALS

PROJECTING FASCIA BOARD ANGLED TO SUPPORT EAVES THATCH

AT THE EAVES
Long-straw thatching is the only sort of thatching that has liggers held with broaches (hazel spars and securing pins) at the eaves as well as the ridge.

ANCIENT ORIGINS
The thatch shown here, with its turf ridge, is part of a reconstruction of an ancient Saxon hut. It displays none of the fine finish that a modern thatcher would take pride in, but it shows how thatch has been an effective roof covering since early times.

MORE THAN OLDE-
WORLDE CHARM
The wheat reed thatching, above, is more than just beautiful to look at. You have to live under a thatch to appreciate it fully. It provides excellent thermal insulation and keeps out a lot of noise – not an unimportant consideration in these days of screaming jet planes.

called the process *drawing* but thatchers in other parts of England call it *yealming*. The object is to turn a mass of bent and broken straw, all lying higgledy-piggledy, into orderly bundles of straws all pointing more or less the same way.

We would fork the loose straw into layers. As Bill formed each layer it was my job to fling a bucket of water over it to make the straw less brittle. Then working from the bottom of the pile Bill would pull handfuls of straw out and lay them on the ground. The wet straw would slip out easily and slide straight as each handful was pulled. When he had six bundles he would lay these inside a forked stick which was called a *yoke*. A piece of string closed the mouth of the forked stick to keep the yealms in. The yoke was then carried up the ladder to the top of the hay stack or straw rick that he was thatching.

Starting at the eaves he laid the wet straw evenly on the stack in a layer four inches thick and fastened this layer down by laying a stick along it, midway up the layer, and fastening this stick down by hammering in *broaches* with a mallet. The horizontal stick (often of hazel left "in the round") is called a *sway*. The broaches, also of hazel, are 18 inches long, sharpened at both ends, twisted in the middle and then bent over like hairpins. The two sharpened ends were driven into the stack or rick with the wooden mallet.

Another layer of straw would be laid over the first, slightly higher up but well covering the sways and broaches, and so on, layer overlapping layer. When the ridge was reached bundles of straw would be laid horizontally along it to form a roll and the up-standing straw on one side bent down over it, then the upstanding straw on the other, and on each side of the ridge there would be more sways and broaches to hold these ends down.

Houses can also be thatched with long straw. It is the cheapest method of thatching used in England but even so it costs about £10 a square yard to have it done.

LONG STRAW V. REED THATCH
In the days of cheap labor (or when people had the time to do jobs for themselves) thatching with long straw made sense. It would last perhaps 20 or 25 years and then you could simply put another coat on or perhaps strip the roof and start afresh. If you were a farmer the straw was free: if

you weren't you could buy it for practically nothing anyway. It was the cheapest kind of roof there was.

Nowadays it is hard to get long straw for nearly all straw has passed through a combine harvester which ruins it for thatching. Also, the price of labor being what it is, if a man pays for thatching a roof, he wants it to last a long time. Hence the growing popularity of reed thatching in spite of its high initial cost. And there is no doubt that reed makes the finest thatch in the world, lasting 70 years and maybe 100 years.

In spite of its name Norfolk reed (*Phragmites communis*) is not confined to Norfolk. It grows anywhere where there is enough water, as far as I know. The reeds among which the Marsh Arabs of the deltas of the Tigris and Euphrates live are, I imagine, the same plant. These Arabs build substantial houses, rafts and all kinds of day-to-day artifacts from reeds.

Much of the so-called Norfolk reed used to thatch houses in England now comes from Poland as the huge reed beds of the Biesbos in Holland, the traditional source of reeds, have been largely drained.

CUTTING REED

Plenty of reed is still cut in the Norfolk Broadland country of England. I have known Mr. Russel Sewell for 25 years now. Being eighty-three years old he no longer cuts reeds for a living but he continued to do so until he was sixty-five.

I remember going out with him, when I lived in Suffolk, on a freezing winter's day into the reed beds next to Rockland Broad. The tide had flooded the bed that day and the ice crunched under our rubber thigh boots as we walked. He wore an ancient jacket and the sleeves and body of it were cut and worn by the sharp reeds. His hands must have been like iron for he wore no gloves. You can cut your hands badly on the sharp edge of reed leaves.

It was after Christmas and most of the leaves had frozen and been blown off the stems of the reeds. Russel would sieze a handful of stems in his left hand, cut through them at the bottom with a slice of the sharp hook he had in his other hand, clean the rubbish out of the base of the bundle with a few downward strokes of the hook, and lay the bundle to one side.

When he had a *fathom* of reeds (which is a super-bundle just big enough for a man to clasp his arms round – a fathom, or six feet,

in circumference) he would bind it near the bottom with a piece of string. Before the days of cheap string, reed cutters would use twisted willow twigs and were in the habit of planting the odd willow in the reed beds to supply them. Nowadays you can often see a huge willow tree grown out of control in an old reed bed.

He carried the fathoms of reeds, slish-sloshing through the shallow freezing water, to the side of the *drain* (the name for a drainage ditch or dike in these parts), where lay a long flat-bottomed punt, called a reed-lighter, and into her he loaded his reeds. When fully loaded she had a stack of fathoms in her higher than Mr. Sewell. The latter poled her up the drain to a *staithe*, as small quays or landing places are called in the Broadlands, and there unloaded, to await being taken away to the thatchers, sometimes by Norfolk wherry in those days.

It was Russel who explained to me that if a reed bed is not cut one year the reeds are not so good for thatching the next, and are termed *double wild*. Thatchers at one time would not buy this if they could help it, but when the combine harvester came into the wheat fields and the thatchers could no longer get long straw they were happy to buy double wild reeds and all.

THATCHING WITH REED

Although Norfolk reed is the best roofing material in the world you cannot make the ridge with it. The ridge is either made of long straw, sedge (*Carex spp.*), or sweet grass or rond grass (*Glyceria maxima*). The latter is called rond grass in Norfolk because it can be bent *round*, as over a ridge.

I found Mr. Mindham thatching a house with reeds near Watton, in the county of Norfolk. Mr. Mindham's father was one of seven sons and they were all thatchers. Their father was a thatcher too. Thatchers

DECORATION
Thatchers have always added decorative features to mark their work. The stack ornaments, above, are, like corn dollies, traditional and were once thought to encourage good harvests. The ship's wheel, left, is pure fancy.

FOUR-POLE DUTCH BARN
The permanence of thatch is exploited in the German Dutch-barn structure below. It has a pyramid-shaped thatched roof that can be adjusted in height or removed altogether as the store beneath is removed or replenished. This avoids the need for new thatching every year.

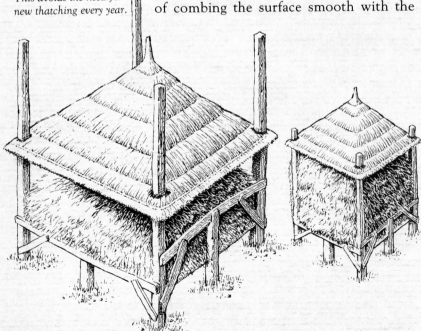

were plentiful in those days and they thought themselves a cut above farm workers and even brick layers. They would cease all thatching after the end of October and go into the woods to cut sways and broaches. After Christmas they would take to the reed beds, for by then frost and gales had defoliated the reeds. About April they would be back on the roofs again.

The technique for reed thatching is different from that for long straw. Instead of combing the surface smooth with the side rake the thatcher bangs the ends of the reeds up from below with the *leggat* – known as *dressing* the thatch. The leggat is a board with a handle on it and old horse-shoe nails driven into it. A reed roof has a severe appearance compared with the smooth, flowing lines of a long straw roof.

Mr Mindham hammered steel hooks down through the thatch into the rafters below to hold the horizontal hazel sways which held the reeds down – one sway to each course, or layer of reeds. Only at the ridge did he hold the sways down with broaches. He kept the broaches either in a bath of water or under damp sacks until he needed them – so that they could be twisted into shape more easily.

WHEAT "REED" THATCHING
There is a third kind of thatching in Northern Europe and that is what the thatchers of the West of England call wheat reed, or combed wheat reed, or Devon reed.

It is not reed at all but simply wheat straw – but wheat straw that has not been through a combine or a threshing machine. This means that the straws are unbroken, unbent and all lying the same way. In the West of England much wheat is grown especially for thatchers' use. The technique of thatching with it is almost the same as for reed and it will last for perhaps 45 years.

SLATE CUTTING

LATE IS A METAMORPHIZED SEDI-mentary rock, such as shale, which has been deposited as mud or silt under water and compressed by subsequent deposits above it into rock. Because this process took place slowly over millions of years rather than violently, as with volcanic rocks, the slate was formed in flat sheets. It can therefore be split into thin slabs – or thick ones if required – with even, level faces, and is very strong. It is a magnificent roofing material and a hundred years ago half the great cities of the world were roofed with it. A great deal of the world's slate was quarried in north Wales, but only a few mines are still working.

Slate generally occurs in thick seams and often slants at an angle into the mountain-side. After the outcrops have been quarried, inclined shafts are driven along the dip of the vein following the walls and roof of *country rock*, the quarryman's term for rock that is not slate. Horizontal tunnels called *levels*, about 50 feet apart, and vertical shafts called *roofing shafts* are then hollowed out from the main shaft allowing access to the slate. The miners leave the hard country rock above their heads for a roof, and 40 foot thick pillars of slate every 45 feet or so to support the levels above. If they don't do this the mountain collapses on top of them.

Slate has a happy knack of splitting in two directions at right angles with each other. The rockmen utilize this habit to break slate out in rectangular blocks of about two tons each, generally blasting it with explosive. These are then taken out of the mine, split into smaller blocks of four to eight inches thick, and are then sawn, by special rock saws, into blocks a little larger than the size of the finished roofing slates.

The *splitter* then gets to work. Seated and wearing a leather apron, he balances a block of slate on his knee, places a chisel precisely in the middle of one edge, and gives the chisel a tap with a hammer. When the chisel has entered the stone he gives it a twist and the block splits in two. Then he splits each half block in two. And he goes on sub-dividing until he has split as many roofing slates as he can from the block, each slate being about one sixth of an inch thick. The splitter's job is highly skilled; one slip and a whole block of slate could be ruined.

FROM NARROW LADIES TO QUEENS
There are many different sizes of cut slate. In North Wales the splitters gave a certain dignity to their slates by ranking them with names of female nobility, from the smallest *Narrow Lady* up through *Princess* to the largest, dubbed *Queen*.

Finally the split slates are handed to the *dresser*, whose job it is to cut the roughly shaped slates to the required dimensions. This used to be done by hand, but for many years a water-powered dressing machine called a *Greaves* has been used.

SLATE DRESSING
Once the splitter has finished his job, the dresser takes over, for while the slates are now the correct thickness, they still need to be cut to the final shape and size and given a chamfered edge. In days of old dressing was done by hand, the dresser laying each slate on a steel anvil and slicing right down the edge of it with a knife called a sax.

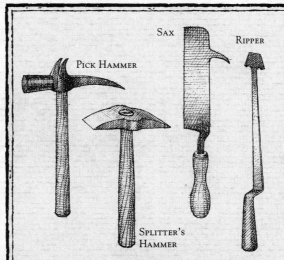

PICK HAMMER

SAX

RIPPER

SPLITTER'S HAMMER

SLATER'S TOOLS
A good slater could split slate accurately using the edge of a *splitter's hammer*, instead of the usual hammer and broad-headed chisel. The spikes on both the *pick hammer* and the *sax* are used to make the nail holes in roofing slates.

CRAFTS OF THE FIELD

Our rural landscapes were once tended by hand: not just the land itself, but also the boundaries that divide it, the ditches that drain it and the pathways that serve it. If it took days and days of hard labor to repair a dry-stone wall, or lay a hedge, that was accepted. Land owners could afford to pay wallers and hedgers for their skills. If such details as stiles were required, they were made with care. Now that the land is largely tended by machines, and labor costs are so high, there is neither time nor money for such things. Those that love the land are the losers as features of the landscape that have existed for centuries tumble into disrepair. In very few years modern factory-farming techniques which, among many other abuses, ignore such details of landscape as hedgerows, have spoiled our countryside.

Let us hope that crafts of the field that have been passed down the generations will never be completely forgotten.

HEDGE LAYING

HE PROPER WAY TO SERVE A HEDGE is to *lay* it, in the winter months. It keeps the hedge thick near its base and so stock proof, and stops gaps appearing. Once layed the hedge may grow unattended for many years.

The first job is to clear dead wood and weeds and to cut back any growth not needed in the final laying. If the hedge runs uphill you start at the uphill end and slash about half-way through each component stem of the hedge in turn. Then, wearing thick leather gloves if the hedge has thorns in it, and leather trousers too if you can get them, you bend each stem over until it is nearly, but not quite, horizontal. You work your way down the hedge laying the stems towards the sunlight and, if possible, away from the prevailing wind so that the part-cut stems have the most favorable conditions for regrowth.

Nearly all we hedge layers half-cut through the small tree stems of the hedge with a downward stroke of a sharp bill hook. Some purists maintain that it should be an upward stroke so as to stop rain water getting in the cut. I have never found this to be the slightest problem, for white and blackthorn, the commonest of hedges, are

tremendously resilient. And I am sure that the up-cutters would be left far behind in any race with we down-cutters, who can manage 60 yards of hedge on a good day.

STAKING AND ETHERING

For a fancy job you save any stems cut out of the hedge, clean off the side growth and use them as stakes to support the laid stems until they grow into place. You drive them in every yard or so, intertwining them with the laid stems. The stakes should be driven down into the hedge so cattle do not use them as rubbing posts and work them loose.

Lastly, for a very fancy job, you *pleach* the stakes with *ethers*. That is, you weave thin, whippy stems, such as hazel rods, into the tops of stakes so as to make a continuous strip of basketry along the hedge.

MAUL

BILL HOOK (KENTISH)

LONG-HANDLED SLASHER

HEDGING TOOLS
You first take a long-handled slasher, and clear the ground up to the hedge and trim back the side growth. The essential operation is to cut partly through the main stems almost to the ground with the bill hook, as in the inset picture above. The maul is the hedger's cudgel for driving in the supporting stakes, which can be seen neatly bound in the main picture.

DRY-STONE WALLING

WHEN I WORKED AS A LEARNER farmer on a Cotswold farm more years ago than I like to think about, I was allocated as an assistant to an old gentleman who came to the farm to repair wall gaps. The two things I remember about this old gentleman are that he had a big white mustache and he was grumpy. Whenever I tried to lay a few stones he would throw them down and put others in. It seemed my duties were to hand him stones and to fill the centre of the wall with rubble. Maybe if I had served him in this capacity for seven years or so I would have graduated to laying a stone or two myself. In fact, there is no great mystery to dry-stone walling. Anyone can learn to do it with practice. It is the endurance of the skilled waller that is so impressive.

To walk over the Pennines, or other northern hills of England, is to be amazed at the distances of beautifully-made walls that stretch over the bare hills, up the steepest slopes, plunging down into deep valleys, clinging to desperate contours. The labor they represent makes the building of the Egyptian pyramids small beer indeed.

Dry-stone walling means building walls of stone without the use of cement or lime mortar. Strictly speaking, if mud or clay mortar is used the process is no longer dry-stone walling, but since building walls with certain kinds of stone required it, such walling can be included here.

TYPES OF STONE
There are as many kinds of stone wall as there are kinds of stone, and these vary enormously. There are, however, two main classifications of all building stone: *free-stone* and *non free-stone*. Free-stone is the quarryman's (and the waller's) word for stone that splits naturally into rectangular lumps. Non free-stone breaks up any-old-how. There is an intermediate kind of stone that breaks into layers so that the top and bottom of each piece of stone are parallel but the sides and edges can be any shape. True free-stone, such as that marvellous Jurassic limestone found on the Isle of Portland in Dorset, can be made into massive walls with vertical sides that will last for ever. Very few wallers have used or will use good quality free-stone, however. Layered stone, such as the Jurassic oolitic limestone found in the Cotswold Hills, is fine to build with but requires more walling skill and, once built, such walls will not last for ever without maintenance. Finally, there are the shapeless, random, uncooperative lumps, often of granite or other igneous rock, that have been dumped by some glacier of a past ice age, which wallers in places such as West Wales or parts of Ireland have the misfortune to use.

WALLS CALLED HEDGES
As a waller, you cannot build a true dry-stone wall at all with stone of the last mentioned kind. Instead you build what in Wales and the West Country is called a *hedge* and in the part of Ireland in which I now live, a *ditch*. It consists of two rough stone walls, leaning in towards each other quite steeply, mortared with earth and with an earth infill between them. Because of all

DIFFERENCES IN STONE
The next time that you are traveling in dry-stone wall country, take the time to look at the quality of stone used by local wallers. It will range from huge interlocked lumps of granite to exquisitely-jointed blocks of limestone.

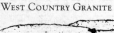
WEST COUNTRY GRANITE

YORKSHIRE GRITS

the earth, grass and other plants quickly grow over the newly-built hedge and it is possible, indeed desirable, to plant a quick-thorn hedge along the top of it. In spite of the thorn hedge, I have never known such a construction that would keep a determined mountain sheep in for more than a few minutes. A tell-tale fence of rusting wire netting along the top of this type of wall gives the game away.

Walling with Cotswold stone, or the carboniferous limestone of the north of England, or the Millstone grits, is a very different matter, and walls constructed with these layered rocks are very effective stock barriers. Indeed, properly maintained, a well-made dry-stone wall is about the most effective stock barrier there is.

Wall dimensions vary according to the type of stone used. With the sort of stone that breaks out of the quarry in layers, such as Cotswold or Pennine stone, it is better to *batter* the walls, that is starting the base of the wall wide and drawing in the thickness to a narrower top. Using Cotswold stone, for example, the batter is traditionally an inch in for every foot of height. A five-foot wall would be typically two feet

LONELY WORK
You need a walling frame to guide the direction, thickness, batter and height of a dry-stone wall. This waller is working in classic fashion, a hand either side of his guide string, plenty of stone led on to the site, but most characteristic of all, he is alone.

EXMOOR SANDSTONE

NORTHUMBERLAND LIMESTONE

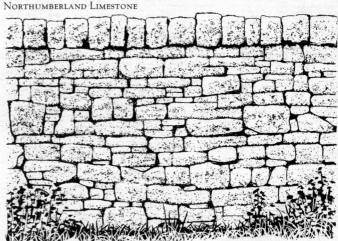

CONSTRUCTING A WALL

In areas of good walling stone you can attempt the sort of ideal construction shown right. The two skins of the wall rise up from the large foundation stones with an even inward lean. The best stone is used for the facing while the middle is packed with small stone debris. Much of the wall's strength comes from the throughbands – flat stones large enough to reach through the full width of the wall about half-way up its height.

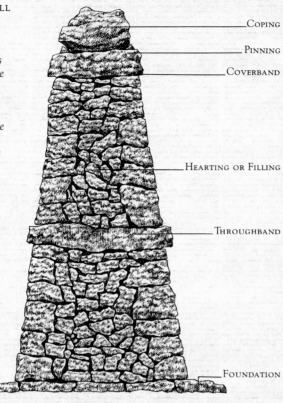

COPING

PINNING

COVERBAND

HEARTING OR FILLING

THROUGHBAND

FOUNDATION

FREE-STONE

INTERMEDIATE

NON FREE-STONE

STONE FOR WALLING

As soon as you start to build with stone rather than just look at it, the very different nature of stones from different regions becomes clear. Good walling stone breaks into lumps with flat faces that stack well. The best, free-stone, breaks cleanly in two dimensions. Intermediate stone gives good flat faces in one plane while non free-stone presents the waller with random-shaped lumps.

wide at the base and about 14 inches at the topmost horizontal course of stones. Such a wall would be considered pretty high and massive though; most field walls are smaller than this, especially where the stone is not so good.

HOW TO BE A WALLER

To build a new wall of this kind you need a template, sometimes called a *walling frame*. This is a simple timber frame and it should have a plumb bob with a lubber-line attached to one of the horizontal members so that the frame can be judged vertical. The template must match the dimensions of the section of the completed wall and is positioned along the line of work as a guide.

The professional waller knows what the dimensions of a wall should be: the amateur has only to look at the nearest professional wall.

The stone is, in farming parlance, *led on* to the site. In the old days this meant

the stone was dragged there by horse and cart or, on steep slopes, horse-drawn sled. It is quite daunting to discover just how much stone is needed to make only a short length of wall. A small mountain of loose stones seems to fit into nothing. It is conversely cheering to find what a lot of stone can be quarried from quite a small hole in the ground. Wallers obviously avoid hauling stone uphill so they always seek their little quarries above their place of work.

When building a new wall a trench is marked with pegs and line and taken out to the length of the section of wall to be built. On uplands only the top layer of turf need be removed to get down to firm subsoil or the rock itself so as to ensure that there will be no uneven subsidence as the living soil is compressed under the weight of the wall. On lowlands, the trench might have to be dug deeper. The trench is cut a little wider than the intended width of the wall.

With the stone on site, the waller lays the foundation first. This may seem an obvious statement but near my house in Ireland there is a small castle on which the authorities have fixed an information notice which tells us: "the top part of the castle was built in the fifteenth century – the bottom part was added in the sixteenth century". Flat stones of even thickness are chosen for this foundation and are laid carefully. If they subside the wall will come down.

The two facings of the wall are then built up, keeping pace with each other with good, big stones at the bottom and the space in between them carefully packed with smaller stones that form the *hearting*. The stones of the facings must break their bonds, as laid bricks must. In other words a waller must "lay two stones on one" or "one stone on two". Vertical joints running unbroken up the wall are anathema.

The smaller and rougher filling stones inside the wall must also be carefully fitted together and interlocked with the facing stones as far as possible. Ideally, the facing stones should be laid so that each one slopes very slightly from the inside of the wall down towards the outside. This construction will ensure that the wall sheds water from its interior in the same way that thatch does. It is water that will eventually bring down a wall, just as the same element will eventually erode Mount Everest.

The art of the waller lies in knowing which stone to lay his hand on next, and how to place it. The best face of a squarish

Walls in Poor Stone Areas
Where the local stone occurs in large, unbreakable amorphous lumps, as it does on the land I farmed in Wales, walls tend to be low and devoid of strengthening details. They need regular maintenance.

stone is put to the outside of the wall. Guide strings on both sides of the growing wall are raised up, course by course, with one end of each string pegged to the last completed section of wall and the other ends fastened to the walling frame.

Throughbands and Coverbands
About half way up the wall is made as level as possible in preparation for *throughbands*. These stones, each a little longer than the width of the wall at that height, are laid with their long axes across the line.

They are vital to the wall's strength. In some areas they are chosen to be considerably longer than the width of the wall so that they project several inches on either side. This can be seen in some of the noble walls of the Pennines. If such long stones are in good supply the whole course will be made of them; if they are scarce, then there will only be one throughband every yard or so with normal walling in between.

With the throughbands laid walling goes on as before with the middle of the wall becoming narrower and the facing stones generally smaller until the wall is once more levelled off in preparation for the *coverband*. This is a layer of flat stones that completely covers the width of the wall. Some wallers nowadays lay these stones in cement mortar. This may sound like cheating but it is a good idea, if the owner can afford the mortar, for it keeps the water out and so prolongs the life of the wall. Some wallers say that the use of mortar is detrimental to a very good dry-stone wall as it takes away the essential flexibility that the wall needs as it settles after construction.

Crowning the Wall
On top of the coverband comes the *coping*, the crown of the wall. This is a row of fine, big flags, or flat stones, set on edge and usually slightly leaning, which gives the wall a crest. Coping stones are chosen with a fairly level edge to sit on the coverband and they are about the same width as the top of the wall. They are jammed and wedged if necessary.

Dry-stone walls may well last centuries if well-maintained. Gaps always occur in old walls and must be built up again before more of the wall goes. Patching up with strands of barbed wire, or wire mesh, always leads to more trouble in the end even if it saves time in the short term. Alas, the few remaining custodians of the hills can hardly manage essential day-to-day farming, and such jobs as wall repairs are neglected. However, with the increasing price of fencing materials, the care of existing dry-stone walls and the building of new ones, may well become a priority again.

Making Good Stock Barriers with Poor Stone
Stock farmers need effective barriers and in areas where there is plenty of stone for walling it makes sense to use it. Poorer walling stones make less effective barriers so in different parts of the world various methods to improve them have been used. These include the Cornish hedge, with its real hedge planted in the hearting soil of a stone wall and the American wall with a rail construction on top.

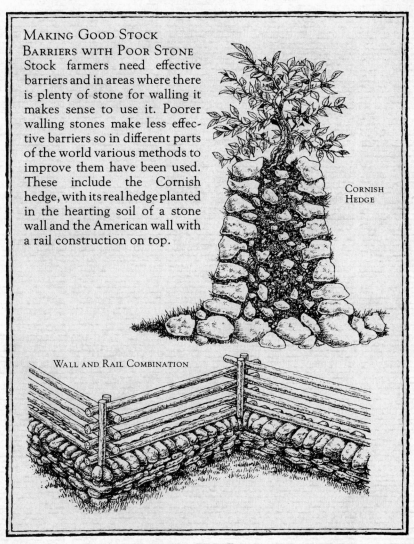

Cornish Hedge

Wall and Rail Combination

MAKING STILES

T IS A REMARKABLE FACT THAT human beings, slow, cumbersome and stupid though they may be, can get their bodies through, over, or under obstacles that defy much livelier animals. In wooded areas, or districts with no suitable stone, estate carpenters in the past have devised various devices, some of them very cunning and some beautiful, to fulfil this purpose of letting *Homo sapiens* out, but keeping *Os domesticus* or *Ovis ovis* in. The commonest of these devices is the *two-step stile*, simple and fool-proof and long-lasting (provided the components are of chestnut or heart of oak), but climbing over it requires a modicum of agility and, in days of long skirts, was considered a little indelicate for ladies. It is conceivable that the escort of one of these delightful creatures might hope for just a glimpse of a trim ankle as his beloved climbed over.

I suppose that the *kissing gate* might lead to some other immorality as its name implies. It is a cunning device consisting of a small gate that swings between the arms of a V-shaped frame. If properly proportioned, and the local carpenter invariably makes sure that it is, the zig-zag gap produced will stop even a Welsh sheep.

FOR THE AMUSEMENT OF SQUIRES
The *collapsing fence stile* works surprisingly well and is a lot of fun. It makes a great clatter as it falls down and poachers are

WOODEN SQUEEZER
This V-shaped gap in a fence allows the passage of human legs, but bars the body of heavy lowland sheep.

CANTILEVERED STEP STILE
Found in the northern limestone regions of England, such monuments to the waller's art defeat the heavy sheep bred in the dales.

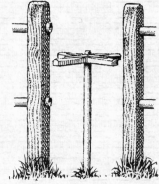

TURNSTILE
Turnstiles were once part of the country scene, simply but attractively made with two wooden crossbars pivoted on a central post.

STONE SQUEEZER OR PINCH STILE
This gap is similar to its wooden counterpart above, but the tighter pinch keeps out more agile mountain sheep and demands more agility of the user too.

CORNISH SLAB BARRIER
This is an unusual barrier consisting of parallel slabs of local stone set apart at distances that make it difficult for stock to traverse them.

wise to avoid it. It is commonly found in large estate parks, where it was built for the amusement of the squire and his guests, and tends to go together with such things as *ha-has*. The ha-ha is a fence built down in the bottom of a deep ditch. Standing only a few yards away from such a fence you do not know there is a fence there and the splendid view is saved.

KNOWING THE TWO-LEGGED BEAST

The best stilemakers not only know the sort of livestock they are trying to keep in, but also the nature of the two-legged beasts likely to be roaming the countryside. A fine example of the sort of ingenuity required is seen in the *bastard stile,* which has a small gate above a stile. It owes its efficiency to the fact that the gate is set at such an angle that gravity always pulls it back into the closed position. There is no need for a latch and the human going through it need not stop to close the gate.

STILES IN STONE WALL COUNTRY

Dry-stone wallers have been similarly clever in their making of stock-proof gaps, not all, I might add, for the use of humans. You will often see a *hare gate* – a hole left in the bottom of a wall big enough to let a hare through but not a sheep. This is no doubt a great convenience to hares, but it is also a convenience to poachers who can set their *purse nets* (see p. 118) across the opening. Lest the landowners be given too much credit here for humanity to hares, let it be mentioned that these holes were made with the ancient sport of *coursing* in view. I have seen my own lurcher dog Esau (a deadly hare catcher) after a hare where there was such a gate; the hare shot through the gate and Esau took the wall at a flying leap.

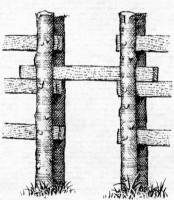

LADDER STILE
Agile stock, such as the Welsh mountain sheep, would be up and over a cantilevered step stile (opposite) in the twinkling of an eye. To keep them in more drastic measures must be taken, such as this tall ladder stile with its very necessary hand rail.

TWO-STEP STILE
Ask someone to describe a stile and they will invariably tell you about the two-step stile – a classically simple design.

BASTARD STILE
This stile and gate combination is a clever product of both the carpenter and the blacksmith. No latch is required.

RAIL-IN-A-FENCE STILE
Where large, placid cattle are the animals to be contained, the human way through can be delightfully simple, such as this rail across a fence gap. You slide the rail aside to pass through.

COLLAPSING FENCE STILE
The product of precise and beautiful carpentry, this collapsing stile masquerades as a normal section of fence.

WELL DIGGING

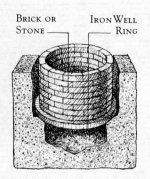

BRICK OR STONE — IRON WELL RING

STEENING
This method of well digging only works in soft ground. The weight of the steen (meaning stone) helps push the iron well ring further into the ground as the spoil is removed from underneath.

WELL HOUSING
The superstructure of this well is very simple: a windlass for the rope and bucket and a little wooden roof. The fencing is to deter man or beast from blundering into the abyss.

ODAY, IF WE WANT WATER, WE simply turn on the tap and out it flows. To extract water from below the land's water table now we use expensive machinery and power and drill for it, just like drilling for oil. But it was not so long ago that every community used to have its own specialist well-digger who not only knew where to find water, but how best to dig a well to get at it. There is nothing miraculous about digging wells: it is simply hard, back-breaking work, and very time consuming too. And I speak with all the authority of an experienced and proficient well-digger.

THE RISKY METHOD

After I left my job working in a copper mine in Zambia, I got employment with another ex-miner sinking a well at Chisamba, just north of the capital Lusaka, in the center of the country. The well was to be sunk in hard limestone rock which luckily needed no supporting but did need to be drilled and blasted, rather than just dug out. Jack and I used to take turns to be lowered down the well very slowly, squashed into a small bucket and hoping that the rope would not slip through the windlass at the top. I had to squat on the floor at the bottom and make shot holes with a hand-held *bit* (like a cold chisel) and a *lump hammer*. You pour a little water into the hole to act as a lubricant, wrap a rag around the drill bit so as to stop the water splashing you in the eye, then wallop the bit, turning it between each wallop to stop it getting stuck.

After drilling about 10 holes like this, each perhaps two feet long, I would ram a stick of dynamite, a detonator and a safety fuse into each hole, light the fuses, stand on the bucket and shout to Jack to winch me up. It used to occur to me at such moments that then was the perfect time for the chap on top to pay off any grudges he held against his partner!

After the blast, we would wait a little time to let the fumes get away – we used to hang a blanket down into the mouth of the well to help this. (The blanket, for some reason, caused a down-draft on one side and an up-draft on the other.) Then one of us would go down the well and shovel the broken rock into the bucket, clearing the well floor ready for the next round of blasting. We were paid 10 shillings a foot for sinking that well, and we earned every penny of that money.

TREAD WHEEL
To operate the bucket of a tread wheel, a man or donkey would walk round the inside tread of the wheel. This 17th-century wheel is housed in a timber-framed and thatched building.

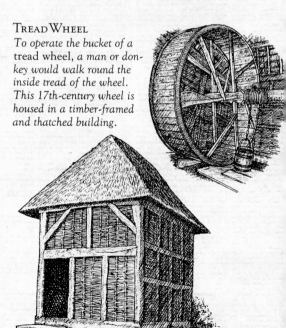

AN ANCIENT TECHNIQUE

Well sinking with the help of explosives might be messy and sometimes dangerous, but at least some of the back-breaking labor has been taken out of the job. But before dynamite and gunpowder, all wells were dug by hand. I once drank water from what are known as the Queen of Sheba's wells at Wajir in Kenya, near the Somalia border. These go down some two hundred feet into solid rock. The only way Her Majesty, or more likely some of her subjects, could possibly have sunk them would have been by the same technique the Romans used for mining. They would light a fire against the rock, and when the rock was hot enough, douse it with cold water, causing it to split. Then they broke up the rock, carted it away, and lit another fire.

LINING A WELL

Not every well is dug in solid rock; some are dug in soft ground, which can just be excavated rather than blasted out. Digging these wells presents other problems though, particularly how to stop the walls of the well falling in once the well is dug and full of water or, worse still, while it is in the process of being dug.

When I was in India, in the Punjab, I saw an ingenious method of overcoming this problem. There they propped up the loose soil walls with timbering until, having reached the bottom, they would build up a lining of bricks, removing the timber as they went.

The method used in England for centuries was to build the brick lining from the top down, not the bottom up. This is not as stupid as it sounds. The way it was done was to first encircle the proposed well hole at ground level with a strong iron hoop and to build a low brick wall on top of it. Then the well would be dug directly beneath the hoop, causing the hoop and its circle of bricks to be undermined. As the well was dug deeper, the hoop would slowly sink to the bottom, and more bricks would be added to the wall at ground level. When the well reached the required depth, and the surrounding wall was complete, the well would be topped with a simple windlass and protected by a tile roof. Elaborate shelters were also constructed around the well head. This method of construction has not changed very much over the years, apart from brick being superseded by reinforced concrete hoops the diameter of

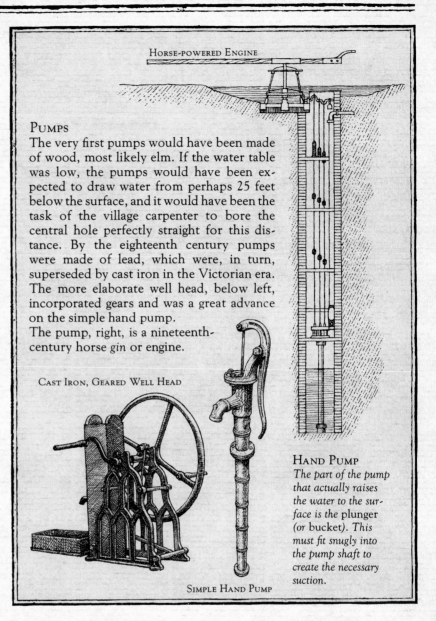

Horse-powered Engine

PUMPS

The very first pumps would have been made of wood, most likely elm. If the water table was low, the pumps would have been expected to draw water from perhaps 25 feet below the surface, and it would have been the task of the village carpenter to bore the central hole perfectly straight for this distance. By the eighteenth century pumps were made of lead, which were, in turn, superseded by cast iron in the Victorian era. The more elaborate well head, below left, incorporated gears and was a great advance on the simple hand pump.

The pump, right, is a nineteenth-century horse *gin* or engine.

CAST IRON, GEARED WELL HEAD

SIMPLE HAND PUMP

HAND PUMP

The part of the pump that actually raises the water to the surface is the plunger *(or bucket). This must fit snugly into the pump shaft to create the necessary suction.*

the well and about five feet high. The hoops are piled on top of each other as the lowest one sinks down the newly built shaft.

DEW PONDS

Not all water has to be drawn up from the depths of the earth, however, and many a downland field has a dew pond nestling in it, providing water for the flocks of sheep and other livestock in need of a drink. These ponds are hollowed out by hand and lined with a layer of *puddled* or kneaded clay up to six inches thick, which serves as a waterproof lining. Over this is spread a layer of lime to set the clay hard, then a layer of straw, and then finally a lining of earth, about one foot of it, to protect the clay and lime from erosion. Such ponds are filled up by rainwater and kept topped up by fresh rainfall and dew.

PEAT CUTTING

HE EXISTENCE OF PEAT THAT CAN be cut for fuel has made it possible for people to inhabit the remoter areas of our countryside. Even today the distant peat beds of Scotland and Ireland are invaded by small armies of diggers, cutting and removing their fuel for the long winter months.

WHAT EXACTLY IS PEAT?

Peat, or turf as it is called in Ireland, is only formed in very damp climates. It is formed, so the scientists say, where wet anaerobic conditions (conditions that exclude oxygen) prevent putrefactive bacteria from decaying dead vegetable matter quickly enough. The slowly decaying vegetation forms a wet, acid mass which, if left to lie where it is, grows to a great thickness. The weight of the turf on top compresses the layers below making them hard and firm. Subsequent

growth on top of the mass dies in its turn, adding to the turf below. These beds can be up to 20 feet deep, the bottom layers browner and lighter in consistency.

RAISED BED AND MOUNTAIN FORMS

In the western and northern parts of the British Isles, peat occurs in two forms, as *raised-bed peat* and *mountain peat*. The former, seen in vast deposits in the bog country of central Ireland, has built up since the Ice Ages into huge masses acting like giant sponges, retaining the rainwater that falls in the winter and releasing it into the atmosphere later in drier weather. The mountain peat is found in small irregular beds on mountain sides, wherever the configuration of the ground has allowed it to form. Luckily, the giant machines that are greedily eating up the raised bed peat cannot manage the more inaccessible and

HOT SUMMER WORK
It is only possible to cut and carry peat when it has lost some of its water, and therefore weight, in the heat of summer. A family can provide itself with winter heat for a week's toil in the sun.

PEAT CUTTING TOOLS

Diggers arm themselves with a marking iron, for making vertical cuts through the grass layer into the peat; the paring iron, to expose the peat; and the slane, for cutting out the peat bricks themselves.

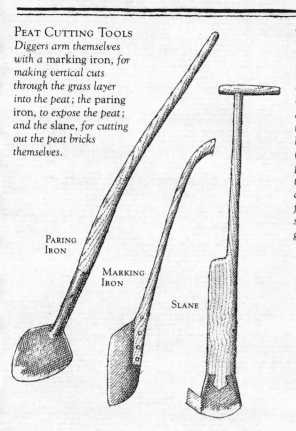

PARING IRON

MARKING IRON

SLANE

TRANSPORTING THE PEAT

The means of transporting the treasured fuel reflects the nature of peat country— wet and boggy. Wheeled vehicles would sink to their axles in an instant so their place is taken by the hand barrow and the sled (see pp. 104–105). Most peat regions also have traditional wooden, peat-carrying boats ranging from the small vessel shown here, to larger sea-going varieties.

HAND BARROW

SLED

IRISH PEAT BOAT

difficult mountainous areas, so there will still be enough mountain peat left for those adventurous enough to exploit it.

You can only dig by hand in summer when the peat has a chance to dry. Wet peat is far too heavy to transport, and too soft and boggy to travel over.

THE PATTERN OF WORK

Almost invariably the people work on the edge of an existing pit, a pit which has been worked for perhaps hundreds of years. Each family or worker has their own front line allotted and works up on the high peat near the edge of the pit, paring and then digging down strip after strip, each strip being nine inches or so wide. When it is too far to lean down with the *slane* (above) the digger simply marks out another strip and works that one.

Soon he can climb down into the second cut to go on working the first cut at a deeper level. Probably his wife and children back him up by picking up and carrying away the turfs he has cut. Each turf is about 10 inches long by four inches wide and deep, although in some parts of England the peat is cut into cakes, or *mumps* as they are called in Somerset. These are the length of the blade of the slane and then cut again into three blocks when drier. Depending on the depth of the turf and its condition, a man can cut an area of turf about 10 by 40 yards a week if the weather stays fine.

STACKING THE PEAT

The turfs are piled up to dry in *windrows*, which look like low, loose walls, and then *ruckled*, or gathered into pyramid-shaped heaps. The shape of these piles of turf varies in different districts, some looking like giant beehives, others more like haystacks, but provided the air can get through them the shape does not matter very much. After drying, and this can be a long, slow process in a wet summer, the by now lighter peat can be transported.

Small sleds are sometimes used, as are wheelbarrows with special bodies and very large, wide wheels, hand barrows and, where there are water-courses, shallow-draught boats. Once home, the turf must be well stacked, and covered somehow to keep out the rain. Wet turf will not burn.

Peat cutting is a time consuming and laborious business, but the smell of a peat fire and the warmth it gives off makes all the effort worthwhile. But it leaves its mark on the countryside as vast swathes of land are cut up and taken away for burning. The Norfolk Broads in the east of England and many of the meres or lakes that surround Amsterdam and Delft in Holland are the flooded remains of ancient peat diggings.

PEAT RUCKLES

The sort of drying heap, or ruckle, shown here, is used in Somerset. It must be contructed to allow a good passage of drying air between each of the mumps, as the peat bricks are called in that part of the world.

WORKSHOP CRAFTS

While sitting in the town workshop of a local basket maker recently, I learned much more than the intricacies of basketry – impressive as these are. During the course of the day several people dropped in, fellow townsmen and women who had ordered, or were ordering, baskets, and other people, friends of the basket maker, who just came in for the chat. In a rural community with its share of local craftsmen, workshops can be convening places where you go to discuss your needs, and where the craftsman meets the customer. In this way the artifact you end up with is not just any kitchen chair, any 20-foot boat, any saddle, it is your chair, your boat, your saddle, made with only you in mind and incorporating any subtlety you want. If the craftsman is also your neighbor, the transaction is the beginning of a relationship. Your payment helps to keep your neighbor. If there is any hope for the rural community, workshop crafts must prosper.

CHAIR MAKING

CLOSE FRIEND OF MINE, JOHN Brown, makes quite the most beautiful chairs I have ever seen. He draws his inspiration from very early Windsor chairs and from the colonial tradition of North America. Besides making chairs he runs a small farm and he is the only carpenter I know who works in Wellington boots.

John cuts all his wood from trees he has felled himself. He cross-cuts the trunks into suitable lengths and rives these into the pieces he needs. The seats are sawn from inch-and-a-half, well-seasoned elm planks and then beautifully shaped to fit the average posterior with an adze and draw-knife before being finished with a cabinet scraper, in a process known as *saddling*. He chamfers wood from lower edges of the seat to give an impression of lightness to the wood.

The legs of his chairs he makes from oak and shapes them perfectly round with his draw-knife. Unlike the *bodgers* of old (see p. 33), John does not use a lathe for legs and spindles, preferring the appearance of hand-shaped wood. He does not fit *stretchers* (leg braces) either as he thinks the legs should be strong enough without them. The holes he drills in the seat for the legs must be angled just right so that the front legs end up at a small angle to the seat while the back legs splay out at a greater angle.

Once the legs are in place it is time to make the *spindles*. These are the rods that hold up the back and arms of the chair, and oak is his favorite for this. If he is making the Welsh traditional Cardiganshire chair, he will need eight 30-inch spindles for the back. Each has to be half-inch in diameter at the ends, increasing to five-eighths of an inch about 12 inches from the seat. And each spindle he shapes by hand, as he does for the 12 shorter arm spindles.

Two Arms in One

When the spindles have all been set in place John then turns his attention to the arms. He makes them from one piece of inch-by-inch ash, steamed in a *steam chest* to wrap around the back of the sitter. Each end

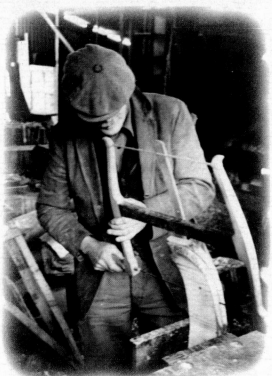

Carpenter's Tools
The chair maker's set of tools is common to that of most country carpenters. Chair makers still favor the spoon bit *for boring. The* trying plane *is the second longest of traditional planes, its length spanning bumps and hollows for a level finish. Decorative mouldings were once planed using concave and convex pairs of planes called* hollows *and* rounds.

Cutting a Comb
This is John Brown, country chair maker, cutting out a curved comb *for one of his chairs using a bow-saw. After hours of labor, the comb will form a silky-smooth shoulder support in a beautiful-looking chair.*

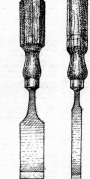

FIRMER CHISELS

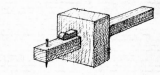

MARKING GAUGE

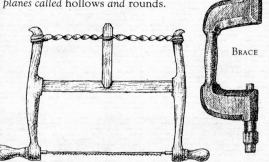

BRACE

TRYING PLANE

SPOON AND CENTER BITS

PAIR OF HOLLOW AND ROUND PLANES

BOW-SAW

makes an arm. John's steam chest is a piece of iron pipe, closed at one end, tilted at an angle, with water in it and a small fire underneath. He puts the wood to be steamed inside the pipe, plugs the open end with rags and leaves it to steam for at least two hours. Over the years he has made all the *jigs* he needs. These are the shaping devices made of scrap wood around which he bends the steamed wood. When he thinks the wood has been steaming long enough he hauls it out and, working with gloves on because the wood is hot, bends the wood round the jig. An assistant then drives wedges in to hold the wood in place. The wood is left on the jig for at least a day, taken off and a piece of string tied across it to prevent it opening again.

He next drills the arms to take the spindles, shapes and surfaces them with a spoke shave (to remove staining caused by the steam) and finishes them carefully with a cabinet scraper. To get the arm to fit, there is considerable twisting of spindles. At this point you realise that every piece of wood in the chair is under some sort of tension and from this it gains its strength.

The Comb

John cuts the ends of the arms to taste, and then makes and fits the *comb*. This is the curved piece of wood that goes along the top of the back spindles. Sometimes he cuts this on the curve from the solid wood – sometimes he steam-bends it. Sometimes he carves a design on it. Whatever the shape, it must please both himself and his customers. Glueing the spindle ends and malleting home the comb again slightly distorts the spindles, adding to the overall tension within the chair, and thus strengthening it.

In the early days, Windsor chairs were often painted red, green or black. Now they are usually stained and polished, revealing the different colors and grains of the wood. The wood can be oiled with linseed oil for a different effect.

That Indefinable Thing

Whatever country chair you want John will make: there is only one stipulation – the chair must please him. If it pleases him it will also please you. There is that indefinable thing *quality* about his work – perfect form and line and proportion. No computer could work out what this quality is nor could any mechanized production line ever hope to reproduce it.

The Carpenter's Shop

The art of working with well-seasoned hardwoods is now all but restricted to the making of very fine (and very expensive) furniture. Most jobbing carpentry today deals with laminates and reconstituted timber and the village carpenter's shop is largely forgotten. If you can find country chair makers at work, like those shown here, you are lucky indeed, especially those skilled enough to use the full set of carpenter's tools. Two of the traditional range of wooden-bodied planes lie on the bench in the foreground. The smaller, coffin-shaped smoothing plane is kept very finely set for cutting a very fine finish after the wood has been trued by other planes. The larger jack plane gets its name from the expression Jack of all trades, and is, as you would expect, an all-purpose plane used for the first leveling off.

Eric Thomas

FOUNDING

NEEDED A TON OF BALLAST FOR MY new boat *Dreoilin*. I intended to have iron ballast as it can be shaped to grip the keel so that it stays put if the boat lies over in a breeze.

Luckily for me the little town near where I live happens to have a four-man foundry in it run by Sonny Power, known as "Slasher" to his friends, and his three sons. Reiner, the builder of my boat, had made me two wooden patterns of the ballast from which we were to make eight castings, each about 150 pounds. These I took to the foundry where they were carefully laid in a square iron-framed *casting box*. Sand, and it has got to be just the right sort of sand, mixed with a little coal dust to give it cohesion, was tightly packed round the patterns to take an impression of one side of them. Another iron box was laid over the bottom box, two pins engaging in two sockets so as to position it correctly, and

IRON CASTING
Pouring the red-hot molten metal into a mould is a dangerous business that requires great strength and precision if an accident is to be avoided. Speed is also essential for the iron cools and solidifies rapidly. The metal must be allowed to cool before the sand boxes can be opened up and the object inside inspected. Then the stem caused by the metal solidifying in the pouring hole can be removed and the finished piece is smoothed up on a grindstone and polished.

more sand was rammed in to take an impression of the other side. The top box was then lifted off, ever so carefully so that the sand did not fall out, and runnels were cut in the sand of the top box through which the metal was to be poured. My wooden patterns were taken out, oh so gently, and the top box was then replaced on its partner.

The Powers spent a week *laying down*, as they call it, about 30 items in sand boxes, eight of which were my ballast pigs. Then the great day dawned when my ballast was to be cast. The *cuplo*, as the blast furnace is known, is as high as an average room and perhaps four feet in diameter, standing in its glory among piles of scrap iron, coke and broken limestone. This is needed as a flux and to purify the iron. A fire of sticks was lit in the bottom of the cuplo and a lot of old boards and firewood were then flung in the top. When a strong fire was going, in went most of the coke.

A centrifugal wind blower, driven by an electric motor and attached to the cuplo by an old rusty pipe increased the draft. Bits of rag were tied round to plug any holes in the pipe: the whole arrangement would have been thought worthy of Rube Goldberg in his more ingenious days.

In a surprisingly short time the fire was hot enough and a hole was poked into the clay bunging up the flow hole. Out came a little trickle of red-hot molten iron. Now there were a number of buckets with long iron rods fastened to them, and these buckets, lined with clay, were placed under the spout to catch the molten iron. The first sample was not hot enough so was flung back into the cuplo, but after not very long the iron was judged fit to cast and Mr. Power himself filled the first bucket. He carried it into the shed and carefully poured the molten iron into a sand box. Many little cones of clay lay at hand and each time a bucket was filled one of these was shoved into the flow hole to restrain the iron until the bucket was ready again.

Then, spectacularly, one of the boys flung buckets of water on the cuplo and vast clouds of hissing steam obscured the scene. The pouring was over, and all I had to do was to wait until the next day before opening up the moulds and inspecting the work. And that was how my ballast was made.

BLACKSMITHING

REMEMBER, IN THE VILLAGE NEAR the east coast of England where I was brought up, going often to the village blacksmith shop (no trace of it left now) and being entranced by the scene: whiskery old horsemen with their corduroy trousers tied beneath the knees with pieces of string, holding their huge gentle horses, or lounging about in the shop, their faces lit red by the glare of the forge fire, a boy about my age working the long wooden handle of the bellows. How I used to envy him. The music of the hammer on the anvil was beautiful to me. The fierce hissing as the blacksmith pressed a red-hot shoe into the horn of a horse's hoof and the smell of burning horn were magic. The old horses seemed to enjoy it all, as did their masters, and the place was like a club.

THE MAGIC OF THE ART

Later, when I went to agricultural college, the only useful thing I learned was blacksmithing. I didn't learn very much of that,

THE BLACKSMITH'S TOOLS

The blacksmith is in a unique position as far as tools are concerned. Understanding the strengths and weaknesses of metals, and how you *temper*, or regulate the hardness of steel, he can make his own. Working metal involves cutting, shaping and punching it, when it is cold or, more commonly, when it is hot. You need tools of different tempers for hot or cold work and you never mix the use of the two for risk of badly blunting the hot tools on cold metal, or changing the temper of cold tools on hot metal. Generally, hot tools are longer so the smith can keep his hand away from the hot metal. There are cold and hot chisels, grasped and struck, for cutting. Cold and hot *sets* are for heavier cutting, having handles and being struck by an assistant wielding the sledge hammer. Some shaping tools come in two halves: one fits into a hole in the anvil, the other has a handle and is positioned over the lower half with the work sandwiched between. The top half is struck to shape or flatten the work. These include *swages*, *fullers* and *flatters*. When the blacksmith was also the farrier, he would also require a set of tools for shoeing.

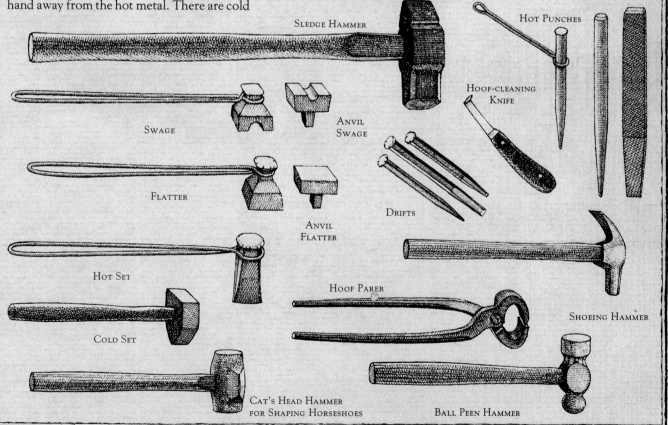

SLEDGE HAMMER

HOT PUNCHES

HOOF-CLEANING KNIFE

SWAGE

ANVIL SWAGE

DRIFTS

FLATTER

ANVIL FLATTER

HOT SET

HOOF PARER

SHOEING HAMMER

COLD SET

CAT'S HEAD HAMMER FOR SHAPING HORSESHOES

BALL PEEN HAMMER

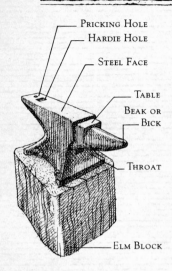

- PRICKING HOLE
- HARDIE HOLE
- STEEL FACE
- TABLE
- BEAK OR BICK
- THROAT
- ELM BLOCK

THE ANVIL
I learned some smithing on an anvil just like this one, with a step down, called the table, just before the beak. It is not surfaced with blister steel like the main face, and here you cut iron without blunting the cold chisel. You punch over the pricking hole while the hardie hole accepts the square end of fullers and similar tools, especially the upside-down chisel, called a hardie.

THE SMITHY
To this day I can't walk past a smithy without looking in, hoping for such a scene as this. Farriery tools, such as rasps and paring knives, are collected in a work tray on the floor in the foreground. Next to it is the tripod sometimes used to support a weighty horse hoof. Behind the tray, on an elm block, is a swage block, with its multitude of recesses and holes used to guide hot metal into shape. The array of tongs, skirting the forge, were all made by the smith himself for grasping every different size and shape of hot metal. The work in hand proceeds at the anvil, the smith shaping iron strip with one of the many different weights of ball peen hammer he has always to hand.

but I did learn how to make a chain out of a wrought iron bar, and this involves the business of *welding*, one of the blacksmith's basic skills. It depends on bringing the two ends of wrought iron to a white heat, so that sparks just begin to fly from the iron, then hammering the ends together fast and furiously. If you fail to raise the two ends to welding heat they will not unite; if you make them too hot they will simply burn away. No doubt there are scientific explanations as to why wrought iron will weld together when it reaches a certain heat, why cast iron will stand high temperatures and not melt or burn, why steel can be made hard by getting it very hot and then cooling it very quickly, or soft by heating it and cooling it very slowly, but I do not know them. I prefer that they remain part of the mystery of blacksmithing. My tiny bit of knowledge about working with iron or steel has been very helpful during my life, particularly in areas where blacksmiths were few and far between. And I can understand why the first metal workers were counted magicians among their stone age fellows and guarded the secrets of their craft.

REPAIRING AN ANCHOR
George Whelan is a blacksmith friend of mine. He claims he is retired, but I seldom go past his shop without hearing the sound of the hammer. His shop is a long, rough building with a forge in one corner of the biggest room, an anvil by it, a trip hammer which tends to go wrong so that he has to rake somebody in to wield the sledge hammer in the old-fashioned way, a power drill and what may look, to the ignorant, like an indescribable muddle everywhere. But out of this muddle he finds, in a miraculous way, every bit of iron, steel, chain or other oddment that he needs for whatever job he has in hand. He told me that, at one time, the then local priest used to come into the forge and fish out all the odd bits of iron from under his bench with his walking stick – just to try to guess what they were.

I met George, as I have met many other craftsmen, because of the need to fit out my wooden boat *Dreoilin* (see p. 106). I needed anchors and, because *Dreoilin* is built in the traditional way and is to be fitted out traditionally, the anchors have to be traditional too. I had bought a fine big *fisherman* anchor from a gypsy friend in Wales, but it lacked a *stock* (the cross member that runs at ninety degrees to the shank). I took

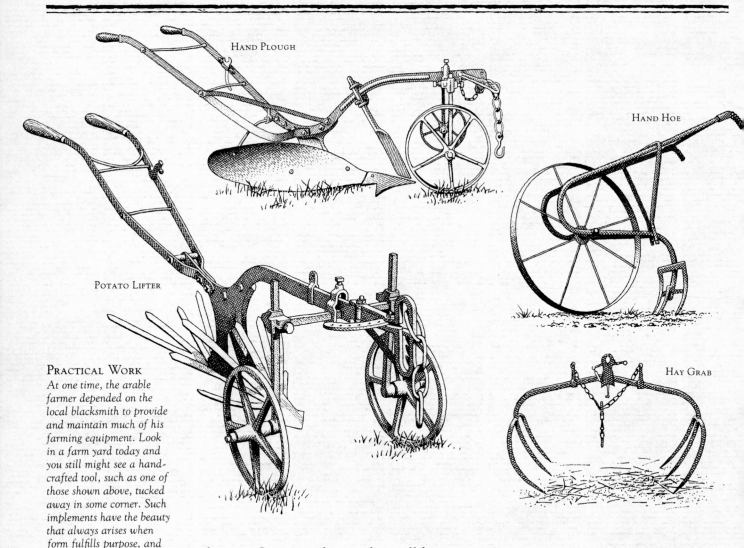

HAND PLOUGH

HAND HOE

POTATO LIFTER

HAY GRAB

PRACTICAL WORK

At one time, the arable farmer depended on the local blacksmith to provide and maintain much of his farming equipment. Look in a farm yard today and you still might see a hand-crafted tool, such as one of those shown above, tucked away in some corner. Such implements have the beauty that always arises when form fulfills purpose, and they last much longer than mass-produced equivalents

it along to George and started to tell him exactly what I wanted. He cut me short very quickly, telling me that he had made plenty of stocks in his time.

He took my anchor, found a suitable bar of steel and, shaping the curving end of the stock in the forge fire, he quickly fitted a traditional stock. This lies flat along the shank when the anchor is not in use so that the anchor can rest flat on the deck. In use, the stock is held in position with a steel wedge or *cotter*, which hangs on a chain.

HOW THE BLACKSMITH'S CRAFT HAS CHANGED

George's history is typical of many blacksmiths. He told me how he was the last in a long line of blacksmiths in his family, how throughout the Second World War there were horses to shoe by the thousand and how four men could hardly keep pace with the work. There were also wheels to *shoe*, or tire (see p. 84), and a hundred other blacksmith's jobs to keep the farms of the countryside running smoothly. There were

no electric arc-welders available then and so it was all forge work. After the war tractors came in, horses went out, and, worse still for the blacksmith's trade, every other farmer bought an electric arc-welding set. So many farmers can now do welding for themselves that blacksmiths, including George, are left with shaping work. Shaping steel or iron into intricate designs still has to be done with forge and anvil. The last time I went into George's shop he was forging 130 ferocious-looking steel hooks, each about a yard long, with barbed points, looking exactly like giant fish-hooks. George was taking them out of the fire and holding them on the anvil, while his son – back for a few days from college where he is learning industrial chemistry – walloped the iron with a sledge hammer. George would indicate the position and direction of the sledge with a tap on the anvil from a hand hammer. If I had had to guess the purpose of these ferocious-looking instruments I would still be guessing now. They were for sticking into the bottom of a lake. If there is any

DECORATIVE WORK

Fine decorative shaping has always been an element of smiths' work, but as electric arc-welding has superseded fire-welding techniques for mundane metal-work, more smiths now specialize in decorative work, such as gates.

MAKING SCROLLS

Scrolls are an obvious feature of much decorative ironwork. Various stages in making three sorts of scroll are shown right, and some of the tools used by the smith appear below. You pull the hot metal around a template called a scroll iron, using scroll wrenches. Effects such as the leaf and the snub end require the crimp and the halfpenny scroll slotted into the anvil.

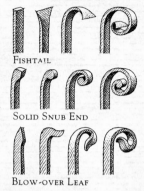

FISHTAIL

SOLID SNUB END

BLOW-OVER LEAF

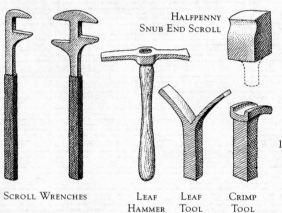

SCROLL WRENCHES

HALFPENNY SNUB END SCROLL

LEAF HAMMER

LEAF TOOL

CRIMP TOOL

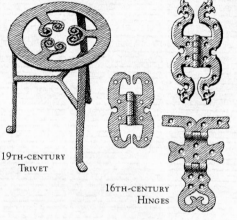

19TH-CENTURY TRIVET

16TH-CENTURY HINGES

18TH-CENTURY WEATHER VANE

body of water in Ireland with salmon in it there will be poachers trying to get them out. I pity any poacher who dips a net into those waters.

George is still called upon to make harrows, for the hand-forged job is far better than the machine-made article. He specializes in what he calls the Scotch harrow, or S harrow – a series of S-shaped pieces of steel with spikes bolted into them. The spikes are graded, with the longest ones at the back. This causes the harrow to dig in at the rear keeping the spikes to the ground.

THE DEMISE OF WROUGHT IRON

Wrought iron is the blacksmith's metal *par excellence* and all the really fine examples of the ornamental blacksmith's art are made of it, welded and shaped by the heat of the forge alone. But wrought iron has been wholly superseded by mild steel, and modern steel will not weld well using traditional forging techniques. Steel is stronger, but it rusts and does not last as long as wrought iron. George uses steel

mostly, but he still has a supply of wrought iron obtained from the iron fencing that once surrounded the many large country houses that pepper the Irish landscape. He uses this precious stuff for special jobs that need to last, such as boat fitments. Ornamental work made in mild steel welded by the electric arc method (and most is nowadays) is nothing like as beautiful as traditionally forged wrought iron.

TEMPERING BLADES

The official way to temper an edge, such as a chisel blade, is take the blade to blood red, quench it in water, then take back the heat by laying the blade on a special steel block which is hot. Various colors creep down the blade: light straw, dark straw, blue, brown and a bee's-wing color. When that last color comes you quench the edge in oil. However, no village blacksmith would do it that way. He would heat the blade, cool the edge, then let the colors grade down, quenching when the edge gets to the right bee's-wing color.

IRONWORK OF EXCELLENCE

Ironwork at its best is a lasting joy to me. The examples above are all English and I know that the decorated hinges in particular were made by Suffolk smiths.

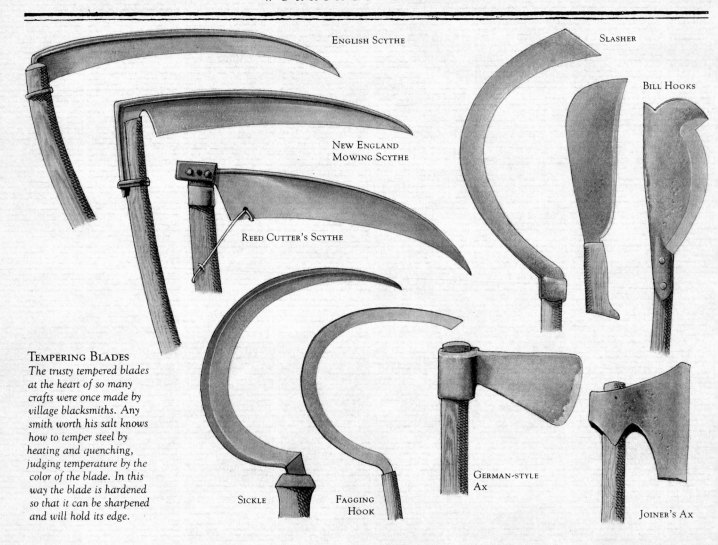

ENGLISH SCYTHE

SLASHER

BILL HOOKS

NEW ENGLAND
MOWING SCYTHE

REED CUTTER'S SCYTHE

TEMPERING BLADES
*The trusty tempered blades
at the heart of so many
crafts were once made by
village blacksmiths. Any
smith worth his salt knows
how to temper steel by
heating and quenching,
judging temperature by the
color of the blade. In this
way the blade is hardened
so that it can be sharpened
and will hold its edge.*

SICKLE

FAGGING
HOOK

GERMAN-STYLE
AX

JOINER'S AX

FORGING COW-BELLS
A smith in a cattle-farming area might well
be called upon to cut out and forge cow-
bells like the one shown below. The exact
shape is dictated by local tradition and the
whim of the smith himself.

In former times, particularly when good
steel was in short supply, George Whelan
used to forge all sorts of blades for farm
implements from the spring steel of old car
or truck springs. I have a Gurkha *kukri*
which is probably made of such steel and its
edge is both hard and sharp, and it keeps its
edge. George said that a blacksmith relation
of his used to make up a mixture of white
and yellow clays and water, and mould the
block of clay into the shape of the blade he
was to temper. Using this the whole length
of the blade could be tempered at exactly
the same time.

If you temper light sheet steel, such as is
used for spades – particularly turf-cutting
slanes (see p. 62) – you have to keep the
quenching water spinning to stop the blade
from buckling as the water vaporizes.

FARRIERY
When the horse was part of everyday life,
shoeing them was a major part of every
blacksmith's work. As horses became
fewer and more widely scattered, the farrier

THE TINKER

THE WORD TINKER WAS ONCE APPLIED TO AN honorable group of men and women who traveled the roads, in Scotland, Ireland and other parts of Europe, performing the most necessary task of making and supplying goods made of copper, tinned plate and, sometimes, sheet iron. Tinkers could also *tin* copper vessels by melting tin and coating the inside of the vessels with it.

Tinkers did what work there was to be done and then moved on. When they returned some years later, the tin or copper goods they originally supplied would have worn out and there was another spate of work for them.

Tinkers would most likely join two sheets of metal by lapping them, that is folding the edges of the sheets into a joint. This was done so well that the folds in the metal met perfectly and objects like those at the bottom of this page are still perfectly watertight years after.

Another method of joining metal used by tinkers was riveting and I have watched them make rivets. You cut a little triangle of metal from an old tinned can, roll it into a cone, place it, point first, in a suitably sized hole in a bar of cast steel and hammer the cone to form a flat head. The piece of cast steel with the hole in it, which in fact had up to six different-sized holes in it, was called a *nail tool* and was one of three portable anvils forged in mild steel for tinkers by village blacksmiths. The other two were the *stake* and the *hatchet stake* (below). With these, a hammer, a pair of tin snips and soldering iron a tinker could make any useful artifacts.

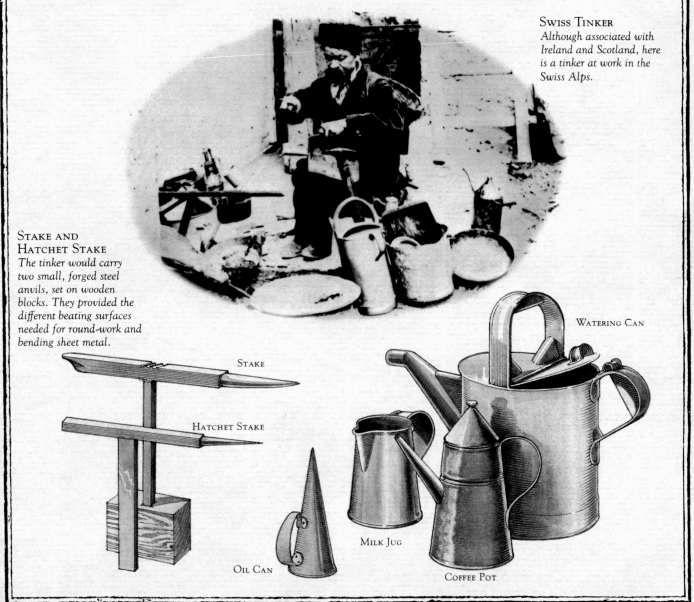

SWISS TINKER
Although associated with Ireland and Scotland, here is a tinker at work in the Swiss Alps.

STAKE AND HATCHET STAKE
The tinker would carry two small, forged steel anvils, set on wooden blocks. They provided the different beating surfaces needed for round-work and bending sheet metal.

STAKE

HATCHET STAKE

WATERING CAN

OIL CAN

MILK JUG

COFFEE POT

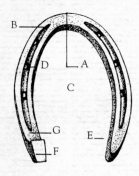

PARTS OF A HORSESHOE
A TOE CLIP
B FULLERING TO RECESS
 NAIL HEADS
C FROG OF HOOF
D NAIL HOLE
E HEEL
F CALKIN
G BRANCH

became a separate craftsman and he now travels to the horses with an anvil, a small forge, an electric air pump, his tools and blank shoes all in the back of a van.

The old-fashioned European farrier worked in his forge and horses had to be taken to him, but then there was a smithy in every hamlet and no horseman had far to walk. Jack Turner was such a farrier. He is 76 years old and his hands and wrists are scarred and discolored by the red-hot scale that landed on them at the forge. He can show you a big toe completely flattened by a heavy horse. The weight of "them horses", and the unremitting toil expected of a country blacksmith in his younger days have also ruined his heart. But his spirit is unbroken and when he talks of his life of toil he can still laugh out loud.

Jack worked with his two brothers and his father and they had two main classes of customer. There were the farmers. "We looked after about seven hundred horses of farmers I suppose and shod them all every three months." And there were the lightermen. Traveling the labyrinthine waterways of the Fenlands, near the central eastern coast of England, was a strange race of men called the *Fen lightermen*. As the few locks they had to pass through were small they had small *lighters* (flat-bottomed barges), and to make a living they used to work these in pairs – the two vessels being pulled by a horse. When the wind was fair they would set a square sail on the leading lighter and the horse would jump aboard the following one and have a rest.

The lightermen would draw up at the pub that adjoined Jack's forge, leave their horses to be shod and stabled, fill themselves up with beer, and then stumble aboard their lighters to sleep. Jack remembers many a night of fun with these wild men.

Jack's forge was cut off from some of the local farmland by the wide River Ouse. Horses would be brought to the far bank and Jack and his family would row over, carrying ready-forged shoes and their hand tools, and shoe the horses cold – that is, without first applying the shoe hot to make a slight impression on the hoof to see if the fit is perfect. With hot shoeing, the smith can still alter the shoe slightly at this stage. With cold shoeing, the shoe has to fit exactly first time. Jack came to know all the horses he shod.

A man can shoe 10 heavy horses in a day and that is all. When you pick a horse's leg up it is inclined to lean a lot of its weight on you and a big cart horse weighs a ton. Not that I have ever shod a horse – I feel that to drive those nails in, knowing that you could ruin the animal for life by driving one at the wrong angle, is just too much responsibility for me, but I have removed many a shoe, and trimmed many a hoof, and know that to pick up a horse's hoof and work on it is back-breaking work. And horses can go mad while they are being shod. Jack told me of one which reared up and rolled down the river bank and into the river when he was trying to shoe it. They only saved the horse from drowning by getting a rope round it and hauling it out.

HORSESHOE TYPES
When you look at horseshoes closely, what strikes you is how far from "horseshoe-shape" most are. The farrier has to modify the shape of every shoe he makes to suit the unique shape of every hoof. Good farriers become skilled in making shoes that help a defect of gait, or an injury, and the more extreme of these shoes are referred to as veterinary shoes.

OTHER SHOES
Horses are not the only beasts that smiths might be called on to shoe. I have picked up little sickle moon-shaped ox shoes in the Namib Desert, made in pairs for cloven hooves. Mule and donkey shoes are shaped like magnets.

REAR SHOE WITH
FEATHERED BRANCH

FEATHERED FORE SHOE

MULE SHOE

FORE SHOE
WITH CALKIN

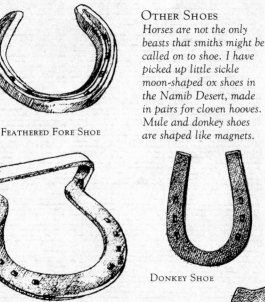

VETERINARY SHOE
WITH MERGED BRANCHES

VETERINARY SHOE WITH HEEL BAR

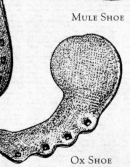
DONKEY SHOE

OX SHOE

KEEPING SATAN AT BAY

Such were the economics of the Great Depression in England that shoeing 10 horses a day was not enough to earn a living and nor was getting up at three in the morning to shrink on a dozen wheel tires. Jack Turner's papa was a good man to have around at this time. Like every other master blacksmith in the days when people really had to work for a living, he subscribed to the belief that "Satan yet finds work for idle hands to do" and was determined that his sons, and others under him, should offer no chink for the Evil One to creep in. If there were no horses to shoe at any one moment, or tires to shrink on, or chain harrows, or potato-lifters, or reapers, or other machines to repair, he set the family of forgers to making spike harrows, for there was always a sale for these. Nothing was wasted. Old Turner would buy stuffed horse collars and forge the iron fittings for them. Old iron cart tires, too worn to be used again, would be cut into strips and these strips made into horse shoes. Scythe blades would be bought from Sheffield and handles from some place in Norfolk and the two married together by forging fittings to hold the blades in place. They forged most hand tools and mended all farm machinery. "My father could work with two of us striking – he could turn the iron over while we were striking and we'd never lose a stroke."

Such was the hard old life of a real blacksmith. His skill in shoeing horses was important, but it was his skill in the forge that he liked to demonstrate most.

HOT SHOEING

Horseshoes have to fit perfectly, there are no two ways about it. A farrier usually leaves the shoe he has shaped hot and uses it to burn a slight impression in the hoof horn, to make sure that the fit is correct, as below. Slight adjustments can be made before the final nailing.

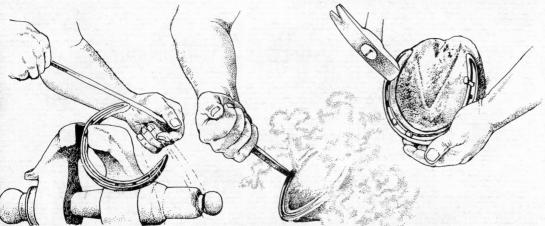

NAIL HOLES

Nowadays, the farrier will buy shoe blanks in various sizes, ready for fine shaping to the hoof. Once he had to bend the shoe for himself. The farrier above is punching nail holes in a part-bent shoe which is being made in the old way.

WHEELWRIGHTING

IT WAS IN SOUTH WEST AFRICA (now Namibia) that I fell in love with wooden wheels. In that vast, empty, desert and semi-desert territory the classic vehicle was then the ox wagon. The early Dutch and English settlers had used it to drive their way north from the Cape deep into the hinterland of Africa. In my time there, I joined in an expedition with the wagon of an Afrikaner to see what lay west of the settled country out toward the Namib Desert. His wagon was pulled by 10 oxen. If it had been loaded it would have needed 20, but all we carried was two huge drums of water and some food. The wagon was 18 feet long and could carry eight tons. Such was the standard South African wagon: a mighty ship of the veld.

Nothing would stop the great wooden, iron-shod wheels. They would smash small trees, crash and crunch over rocks and boulders and plough through the soft sand of river beds.

The front pair of wheels was smaller than the rear pair so that the turn-table on which they were fixed could turn under the front of the wagon. Even so, they were massive and of great weight. The rear wheels were huge, for the bigger a wheel is the easier it runs. The *nave*, or hub, spokes and *felloes* (the rim components of a wooden wheel and pronounced "fellies") were made of exotic hardwoods like stink-wood, or sneeze-wood.

The iron tires were massive: perhaps four inches wide and three quarters of an inch thick. The weakness of these wheels was that their wood shrank in such a hot and dry climate. No matter how well-seasoned down near the coast, up in the desert under the tropical sun the wooden wheel parts had to shrink some more. The only prevention was to keep the wheels wet. Whenever we reached a waterhole, or a steel windmill over a well on some out-lying farm, or a river that actually contained pools of water, our first consideration (after quenching our thirsts and the cattles') was to soak the wheels. If we were able we would support the wagon on blocks, take the wheels off and lay them in the water. When we emptied the dregs of our coffee mugs it was over the wheels. If we had to relieve ourselves, we did so on the spokes.

THE WHEELWRIGHT'S SHOP

When you know how subtle a thing a wooden wheel is, it is natural to look for clever devices in the wheelwright's shop. The truth, as you see, is that he relies on beautifully simple woodworking tools and home-made measures, such as the spoke set gauge bolted to the wheel hub in the foreground. You might note the boxing engine, with its T-shaped handle, leaning against a splendid old lathe behind the wright's bench, the neat stack of embryo rim parts (felloes) on the floor and the spoke dog that the wright is using.

The Geometry of a Wooden Wheel

I began to study the *rationale* of the wooden wheel. It looks so simple but is, in fact, subtle and complex. That this piece of engineering in wood and iron, without nail, bolt or glue to hold it together, could take the force of carrying two tons over the bare, hard rocks of the veld, was a wonder to me.

I noticed that the ends of the steel axles that carried the wheels were not straight but inclined downwards. This caused the wheels to be slanted out at the top and in at the bottom. Wheelwrights call this inclination of the wheel the *hollow*, or the *dip*.

Another most noticeable thing is that the wooden wheel is *dished* – shaped like a saucer with the hollow side away from the wagon. This dishing counteracts the hollow of the wheel to bring the working spoke (the spoke that is carrying the weight of the wagon at any particular time) more or less vertical but not quite. The working spoke only becomes absolutely vertical when the wagon is running along the contour of a slope when the wheel will come under the greatest sideways strain. The angle formed by the inclination of the spoke to the vertical on level ground is called the *strut*. The combined effect of the hollow and dish strengthens the wagon wheel against lateral movement, especially the normal side-to-side movement caused by the walking pattern of the draught beast. Flat, vertically-set wheels, such as those on an Asian ox cart, are not so strong.

Another subtlety of the wooden wheel is that the metal rim – the tire of the wheel – does not run at right angles to the spokes. If it did the rim would only run on its inner edge. Nor does it run at right angles to an imaginary straight line between two opposite points on the rim of the wheel. If it did, the tire would run on its outer edge. The rim of the wheel is in fact cut to a precise *bevel* so that the whole width of the rim runs in contact with level ground. Every angle of the wooden wheel has to be exact and they must match those of the other wheels in the set. If any angle is wrong, the wheel will neither run nor stand up to heavy treatment.

Wagon wheels are massive things and give an impression of brute strength despite their careful construction. It was only when I returned to Britain and saw light carriage wheels, and in fact owned some, that I realized the importance of the wheel's

A Hollow
B Dish
C Strut
D Bevel

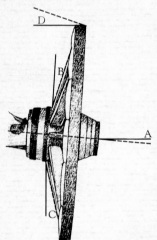

Fitting Felloes to Spokes
If you think of the radiating nature of spokes you will realize that the ends of the spoke tenons are too far apart to engage the holes in the felloes. The wright has to wrench the spokes together temporarily and he uses a lever called a spoke dog (see also p. 82). He puts his weight on the lever as he drives each felloe home.

ANATOMY OF A WAGON WHEEL

THE HEART OF A HEAVY WAGON WHEEL, THE hub or *nave*, is turned from well-seasoned elm to a barrel shape that will accept two iron *stock hoops*, shrunk on hot. The nave is set in a cradle and the spoke mortises marked, drilled and cut. You have to use an existing spoke to mark the mortises around the nave. The mortises allow for the tapered fit and angle of dish of each spoke. The spokes, always of oak that will take the heavy shocks from the weight of the load, have square *feet* (the tenons that fit into the hub) and round *tongues* (the tenons that fit into the felloes, or rim parts).

There are always two spokes to every felloe. These are of ash (preferably grown curved) and are sawn out with a bandsaw to match templates that are seen hanging in every wheelwright's shop. An adze and a curved plane might be used for the shaping. The felloes are joined with strong oak dowels. The tapering joints of the wheel only come together completely under the pressure of the iron tire (dished to match the bevel of the rim) as it cools and shrinks in the tiring process.

The nave is precisely bored with the boxing engine (see overleaf) to receive a cast iron *box* or *metal*, which is driven in hard and is a bearing for the axle arm. The wright has to remove a piece of the nave so that you can get to the *linch*, or *cotter pin*, which holds the wheel to the axle, when you partly remove the wheel to grease the axle.

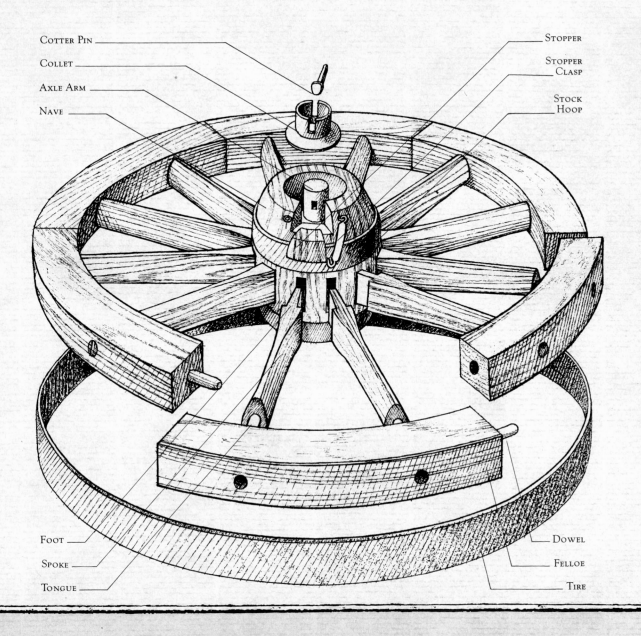

COTTER PIN
COLLET
AXLE ARM
NAVE

STOPPER
STOPPER CLASP
STOCK HOOP

FOOT
SPOKE
TONGUE

DOWEL
FELLOE
TIRE

subtle angles. Such delicate objects can only stand up to rough roads if every aspect of their construction is perfect.

Is it to be supposed that the people who made such artifacts were skilled geometricians? Strangely enough the answer is no. I would guess that until a hundred years ago most wheelwrights could neither read nor write: but they knew how to make a wheel. And wheelwrighting is not a modern science. A dished wheel of the first century BC has been dug up on the Isle of Anglesey.

A Little History

The wooden wheel is a link with our most ancient rural history. Before spoked wheels there were solid wheels that were either hewn from a single piece of wood or made up of several planks joined and braced. Archeological finds prove that the solid disc wheel was certainly used by 3500 BC and its use has been preserved in out-of-the-way places until quite recent times, especially for carrying heavy loads. An example that comes to mind is the Welsh truckle cart, which was particularly used on the Gower peninsula on the south coast of Wales. This is a very simple horse-drawn vehicle which is very like a simple sled on a pair of small, solid wooden wheels, each usually made up of three planks of wood and no more than two and a half feet across. The Irish have a similar traditional vehicle, but I have not seen it in use. I would not be surprised, however, to see a bullock cart with solid wheels today in parts of Asia. Even the spoked bullock cart of India seems to be half-way to the solid disc. When I look at it closely I can see little of the subtlety of construction that has so attracted me to the European-style wagonwheel and to the wrights who made them.

The Wheelwright

There are very few active wheelwrights left, certainly very few who have complete

BOXING ENGINE

FRAME SAW

BRACE

SAMSON

SPOKE DOG

SIDE-AX

SPOKE SHAVE

JARVIS

TIRING PLATFORM

TRAVELER

BEVEL

DRAW-KNIVES

OUTSIDE CALIPERS

SPOKE SET GAUGE

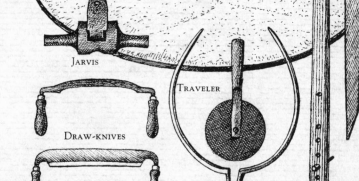

The Wheelwright's Tools
I have not come across a wheelwright who has not inherited the majority of his tools — very beautiful examples at that. New versions would certainly have to be specially made, probably by the wright himself. This, however, is not the tall order it might seem as the specialized tools are quite simple, considering the subtle uses to which they are put. The tools for measurement, such as the traveler (used to measure the circumference of the rim), the spoke set and bevel gauges, are crude devices that require the wright's eye and experience for accuracy. The levers and cutting tools needed are similarly simple but effective in skilled hands.

knowledge of making a wooden wheel, from choosing wood while it is still growing to fitting the finished wheels to the wagon, cart or carriage and watching them roll out of the yard. Moreover, the wheelwright was often the village wainwright too (see p. 98), providing the whole range of wooden-wheeled agricultural vehicles, from wheelbarrows to huge farm wagons. In the heyday of horse-drawn transport the cart or wagon was the work of a team of craftsmen – wainwrights concentrating on the body of the vehicle and blacksmiths forging the necessary ironwork. But the wheelwright's magic was always at the heart of the work and when business was not so good he could undertake most of the work in making wheeled vehicles himself. In fact, a good wright could turn his hand to most things. If your eye is good enough and you have spent perhaps 10 years perfecting the art of making a wheel that runs, there is little you cannot do with wood.

Before the First World War there was need of a wheelwright in every village. After it, the horseless carriage quickly started to remove the demand for wooden wheels and wrights became jacks-of-all-trades or went out of business. Those very few wheelwrights who have survived have recently experienced a surge in demand because, perversely, horse-drawn vehicles have become the rich man's interest.

KNOWING WOOD

True wheelwrights develop an uncanny feel for wood. The wheel's strength depends on the natural characteristics of different woods – elm for the nave because it will not split, even with twelve spoke mortises cut from it, oak for spokes because of its strength and ash for felloes because of its flexibility combined with toughness. Beyond this the wright would get to know the wood growing in his area and would buy it for future use. In England he would find that wych-elm was probably the elm least

ADJUSTING THE BOX
The final balancing of a wheel, so that it runs perfectly smoothly, involves hammering hard oak wedges into the nave to adjust the position of the box – the metal bearing. The wright runs the wheel on a fixed axle to test it and cuts the wedges flush.

SORTS OF WOODEN WHEEL
The bullock cart wheel with its heavy members contrasts with the light handcart wheel which shows the elegance and strength the wright can achieve. His skill is most severely tested by the accuracy demanded in making the smallest barrow wheels.

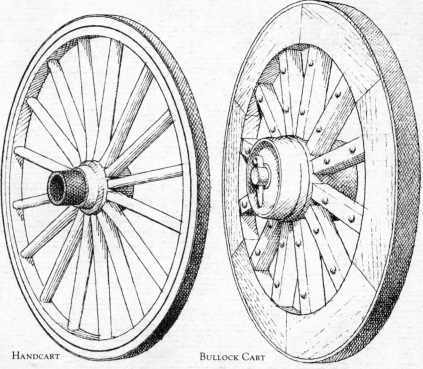

BARROW   HANDCART   BULLOCK CART

likely to split if he could find it and that ash from a hedgerow was probably the toughest and best for his use. I have heard that a good wright would spot the right ash on his travels, noting its natural curves, or *crooks*. He would buy the tree, then cut it and probably leave it lying at the roadside for anything up to two years before using the wood. Long but very necessary seasoning times apply to all wheel wood. Nave blanks need to stand stacked for five years or so, oak billets for spokes for at least four years.

Constant Checking for Accuracy

There is no room for error at any stage in the process of making a wheel. When a hub blank is turned at the lathe, for example, the wheelwright checks size and shape continuously with large, curved calipers. The slightest mistake and the precious hub blank is lost. Marking out and cutting the spoke mortises is particularly critical. With the nave gripped tightly in a cradle, he marks and then cuts, first drilling out much of the waste with a brace and bit. The final dish of the wheel is created by the slight angle of cut at the front and back of each mortise and the wright uses a very simple gauge – the *spoke set* gauge – to guide him.

This is a batten of wood temporarily bolted to the exact center of the nave like the hour hand of a clock. A bone peg is set in the batten the length of the visible part of a spoke from the wheel's centre and projecting from the batten to describe the circumference to which the spokes should be angled. The wright turns the gauge to each spoke position as he cuts each mortise.

How the Wheel is Held Together

It is the fact that iron or steel expands when it is hot and contracts when it cools that holds the wheel together. The tire is forged so that it is a little smaller in circumference than the circumference of the wooden rim of the wheel.

When this tire is heated to a dull red it will expand an eighth of an inch for every foot. Traditionally the tire is heated in a circular fire and then rushed to the wheel, which is clamped in position on a tiring plate. The hot tire is fitted over the wooden rim of the wheel, banged home with sledge

Heating the Tire
Some wrights have a purpose-built oven for heating tires on edge, but most build an open, circular fire. The fire is stocked up with wood shavings to give a fierce heat and the tire is set in the middle of it.

Tiring the Wheel
1 *With the wheel clamped firmly to the tiring platform and assistants ready, the red-hot tire can be lifted from the heat, carried across and dropped on to the rim. Once the tire touches the wood it will start to singe so the tire has to be lowered carefully with the tongs.*

2 *As soon as the tire touches the rim, there is a flurry of hammering and levering (with tire dogs) to position the hot metal evenly around the rim. As soon as it is in place, water is poured on to start the quenching.*

hammers and immediately quenched with water before the wood begins to burn. The subsequent shrinking of the iron or steel compresses all the wooden components of the wheel, crunching it together. The hissing of singeing wood and water on red-hot metal, together with the speed of the operation, make tiring a dramatic part of the wheelwrighting process. Again, measurement and craftsmanship are critical. The wheelwright entrusts his precious wheel to the experience of the backsmith. If the tire is too big, it will fail to clamp the wheel and will soon run off the rim. If it is too small, it will distort the wheel, or even break it.

Iron tires for working carts are commonly four inches wide and three-eighths of an inch thick. A tire for a large wheel needs 15 feet of iron strip and weights 100 pounds. For a century or so blacksmiths have had the use of tire-bending machines – simple sets of rollers so placed that when you push a hot strip between them, and turn a handle, the strip emerges bent to a perfect circle. A few old blacksmiths can remember bending tires without such a machine. They would heat the iron strip to cherry red and poke it through the fork of a tree and gently bend it into a curve.

The only other metal components of a wagon wheel, besides the tire, are the two hoops which are similarly shrunk on to the nave to stop it from splitting.

LASTING QUALITIES

A well-made wooden wheel has an indefinite life, as it can be repaired and retired if necessary. On my farm in Wales I had a *gambo* (a traditional two-wheeled cart of the locality) which was at least a hundred years old. Not only were the wheels wooden but so was the axle. Indeed, it was the wooden axle that dated the vehicle. Alas, a disaster befell it. One of the shafts broke when I was coming down a steep hill with a load up and an uncertain horse. The horse reared and plunged and the cart was badly smashed. The wheels, however, were still perfect and so was the axle.

If I could have found a good wheelwright at the time the gambo could have been rebuilt as good as new around those wheels. Much of the village wheelwright's work was repair work, especially through the agricultural ploughing, sowing and harvesting seasons when farmers would bring in repairs left over from the previous year.

It would be during the quieter times of winter that the wright would make most new wheels and fulfill special orders like making wheelbarrows. Not the unpleasant but efficient modern excuse for a wheelbarrow, but the traditional all-wood barrow that lasts a life-time or more.

The little wheelbarrow wheel with its four opposing spokes, one to each felloe, has the reputation of being the most difficult wheel to make. I have been told of one old wheelwright in his eighties who, although his eyesight is not so good now, has recently made two old-style wheelbarrows. Once you have spent years developing the skill of making a wheel that runs true, it must become ingrained.

STRAKES
Sections of iron, called strakes, were sometimes fitted to wagon wheels as an alternative, or as well as, a continuous iron tire. The wright could fit strakes on his own, beating them on hot using big, square-headed spikes and quenching each strake as he went. He would use the samson (see p. 82) to pull adjacent felloes together before fitting each strake.

3 *As the tire cools and contracts it crunches the joints of the wheel tight. The dish of the wheel can be made more pronounced at this stage, if need be, by loosening the tiring platform clamp and letting the nave rise up to it. This platform has a tank beneath it and the wheel can be plunged into it for final quenching.*

COOPERING

COOPERING BIDS, ALAS, TO BECOME a lost art unless circumstances change somewhat. This is very sad because the cooper's craft is truly an art, extremely difficult to learn and one requiring long experience and great skill. You can get a pilot's licence to fly an aeroplane in the United Kingdom after 40 hours' flying time. To learn to make anything like a good barrel will take you an apprenticeship of four years (not long ago it was five). And at this moment, as far as I can find out, there is not one apprentice cooper in the British Isles.

It is interesting to speculate how man first discovered that you can store liquids inside vessels made of slats of wood. My own feeling is that coopering is an offspring of boatbuilding: if you can keep liquids out of a vessel then, surely, keeping them in is a logical step.

The secret of a barrel's tightness is its shape. It allows iron binding hoops of fixed

IRON AND ASH-BOUND SLACK BARRELS

COMPONENTS OF A CASK
Over hundreds of years the parts of a cask acquired traditional names that are now part of the cooper's mysterious language. The names of the sections of the top or bottom of a cask – the heads – and of the hoops, are shown right.

MIDDLE
CANT
QUARTER

BULGE HOOP
QUARTER HOOP
CHIME HOOP

THE VARIETY OF USES
The wooden cask can be made in a great variety of sizes and of different resiliences from tiny portable carriers to the Great Tun of Heidelberg.

TRADITIONAL CAPACITIES
In cooper's language, a *barrel* is a cask that holds 36 gallons. Smaller casks are the *kilderkin*, the *firkin* and the *pin*. Larger casks are the *hogshead*, *puncheon* and *butt*.

BUTT 108 GAL	PUNCHEON 72 GAL	HOGSHEAD 54 GAL	BARREL 36 GAL	KILDERKIN 18 GAL	FIRKIN 9 GAL	PIN 4½ GAL

THE COOPERAGE
The fully fledged cooper takes great pride in his dexterity combined with strength and speed. With more than one cooper at work the cooperage becomes a hive of noisy and productive activity. Here a cooper drives on a permanent chime hoop.

sizes to be driven towards the widest part, squeezing the slats, or *staves* as they are known, together – impossible with a cylindrical shape, for example. Another advantage of the barrel's peculiar shape is that, if you know how, you can handle a very heavy barrel with great ease. A weight that would be impossible to carry, lift or drag if it were in the shape of, say, a box, can be rolled by a small child if it is a barrel. A barrel can be "trundled", that is tilted on to one of its rims and spun along; it can be rolled as it lies horizontally; and it can always be hoisted from the horizontal to the vertical by rocking it through its longest axis and then finally heaving it upright.

If you examine a barrel stave you will see why a barrel is a very difficult thing to make. The stave is hollowed out on the concave side, rounded somewhat on the convex side, tapered at each end and, finally, its two long edges are cut on a chamfer. Now if you consider the geometry of a barrel, it is obvious that all the staves in it must be exactly the right shape in order that, when the hoops are driven on, all the staves fit their neighbors exactly. If one stave is out of shape by the slightest degree the barrel will leak. I don't know if any mathematician has ever worked out the ideal shape of a barrel stave (I doubt it), but someone who has done his cooper's apprenticeship can

THE COOPER'S TOOLS

IN MODERN COOPERAGES the drive for maximum efficiency has led to the development of power tools to take some of the effort out of the cooper's craft – steel power grabs to force the iron hoops on to the barrel for instance. But such tools are newfangled and are no real substitute for the traditional set of cooper's tools, shown below. The cutting tools are particularly specialized, their curved blades and bodies betraying the curves of casks they fashion.

The short handles of the heavy-headed tools, such as the adze and side-ax, are characteristic.

They are made for accurate one-handed use so that the other hand is free to support the embryo cask. There is little room for swinging long-handled tools.

Hammer and driver are never far from the cooper's hand. Most coopers make their own driver with its grooved, wedge-shaped piece of iron that engages the edge of the iron hoop being hammered on to the barrel. You might see a cooper's driver without a groove, but this would be an ancient tool used when stout ash hoops were used to bind casks for liquids.

DOWELING STOCK

SIDE-AX

BICK IRON

ROUND SHAVE

TOPPING PLANE

CHIVE

CROZE

BUNG-HOLE BORER

HAMMER

INSIDE SHAVE

SWIFT

DRIVER

DOWNRIGHT

FLAGGING IRON

BUZZ

ADZE

DIAGONALS

HEADING KNIFE

JIGGER

HOLLOWING KNIFE

achieve it in a few minutes, just by eye, and get it right ninety-nine times out of a hundred. When the iron hoops are driven on the barrel the staves will come together like loving brothers.

The Rise and Fall of the Cask

Barrels are mentioned in the Old Testament, are supposed to have been used in Classical Greece (although the use of so many *amphorae* argues that there were not many), and were certainly used by the Romans. There were coopers' guilds in England in the early Middle Ages. A London Livery Company was formed in 1502 and the Coopers' Guild that still operates (or would do if there were any coopers left) was founded in 1662. The cooper's trade was organized in Dublin earlier still, the Dublin Guild being founded in 1501. The Dublin Guild was wound up in June 1983. The sad end of a long story.

The demise of British and Irish cooperage is due to a number of factors, some of which have been operating for a long time. One of the oldest is that British Isles oak does not seem so suitable for cooperage as the imported varieties, which have fewer knots. Staves have been imported from Russia and the other countries linked by the Hanseatic League since the Middle Ages, Eastern European oak being found most suitable. Then, as early as the seventeenth century, American white oak started to be imported for the making of barrels.

A severe blow was dealt to the native industry by the eighteenth-century propensity of the English gentry to drink foreign wines, in particular ports and sherries. These, of course, came in foreign barrels and it was not worthwhile returning the empties. So the spirits trade in these islands came to rely entirely on recycled barrels from the Continent.

A Strange Thing About Bourbon

The next blow, similarly severe, came in the form of an American law. This originally stipulated that bourbon had to be matured in new oak casks only. True, this has since been modified to allow distillers of certain bourbons to use a cask twice, but nevertheless an enormous number of American whiskey barrels have been made redundant and have since flooded the market.

It might be wondered why, if American distillers cannot use a maturing barrel more than twice, Scots and Irish distillers are able to mature what they (and I) would claim to be far superior whiskey, in second or third-hand barrels? The answer is that bourbon must draw certain substances (mainly tannic acid one suspects) from the virgin oak in order to mature properly, whereas the Scots and Irish versions do not need these particular substances.

Used American barrels originally arrived in the form of *shooks* (barrels that have been knocked down and the staves packed in bundles), but now, more and more, distillers are importing complete barrels. This means no work for British and Irish coopers. In Scotland, some whiskeys may still be matured in home-produced sherry casks, but even there distillers increasingly turn to the American 108-gallon butt.

What About Beer Barrel Making?

There was always beer to be stored, however, and indeed brewery coopers held out much longer than the distillery ones, but then the *coup de grâce* fell on them in the shape of that horror of our age of mediocrity: the metal cask. Metal casks can be made by machines minded by unskilled

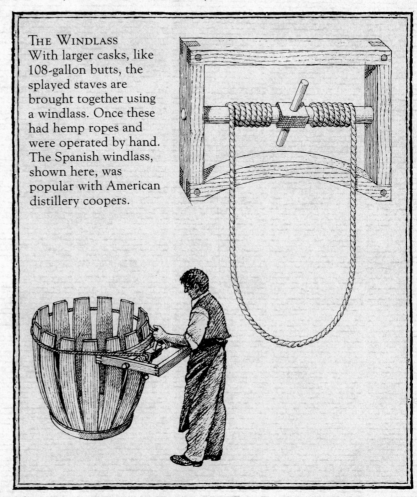

The Windlass
With larger casks, like 108-gallon butts, the splayed staves are brought together using a windlass. Once these had hemp ropes and were operated by hand. The Spanish windlass, shown here, was popular with American distillery coopers.

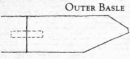

OUTER BASLE

INNER BASLE

THE HEADS
The top and bottom of a cask, the heads, are measured and marked on boards that have been doweled together. The radius is exactly a sixth of the circumference of the groove in the cask waiting to accept the head. Each head is cut out with a bow saw then shaved smooth, allowing for the squeezing of the joints once the head is in the barrel. To ensure a tight fit, the edges of the heads are beveled with a draw-knife, making the inner and outer basle.

labor, whereas wooden barrels have to be built by craftsmen. With the advent of the metal cask, filled with its characterless fizzy liquid, not only was the taste of a famous beer-drinking nation corrupted, but a great tradition of craftsmanship was finally knocked on the head. A faint glimmer of hope is held out by the gallant enthusiasts of various "real ale" societies in the British Isles. Unfortunately, there are still enough old casks in circulation.

WHY USE WOODEN CASKS?
Many attempts have been made by the men in white coats to find a way of maturing spirits without using oak casks. They have even put planks of wood or shavings into stainless steel containers. So far, thank Bacchus, to no avail. Distillers of whiskey, brandy and gin still find that there is no substitute for a good oaken cask. The oak "breathes", allowing some exchange between the spirit and the air outside. A small percentage of the contents is lost by this exchange, but the remainder is far better for it. In Great Britain and Ireland whiskey must be matured in the cask for three years by law. Much of it is matured for twelve years or even longer.

Beer barrels are smaller, but much stouter, than the casks used for maturing whiskey because they have to withstand the pressure of gas given off by the fermenting liquid. A man who worked most of his life coopering for a brewery told me that in the old days beer was much stronger and, therefore, kept much better in the wood than the weaker stuff does now. In fact, the old beer coated the inside of the barrel with a crust, like that of old port. Weak ale eats this off, "the weak feeding from the strong" as they say in brewing circles.

TALKING TO A WORKING COOPER
In Cork, Irish distillers still make whiskey barrels. Most of the work consists of re-making American barrels, but the coopers there can still make barrels from scratch if need be. Mr. Joe Foley showed me how.

Joe had started work as an apprentice at 14 years of age, as had all the men working in the cooperage, including the manager. Joe has been in the coopering trade for 32 years. As he said, he is one of the "last of the Mohicans", for when his generation retires it will mark the end of coopering in Ireland. Joe was jolly and good-natured, and everything he did he did at astonishing speed

making it difficult to follow his movements. His speed of action did not prevent him from keeping up an unbroken stream of Irish raillery.

A WORD ON STAVES
I have seen staves cut in Spain. First, a large, straight, clean-boled oak was felled and crosscut sawn into lengths a little longer than the staves were to be.

These sections were then riven in halves, quarters and then into smaller fractions, until the staves remained about an inch, or slightly more, thick. By riving them out along the radius of the oak (see diagram below) at least one medullary ray of the oak grain remained in each stave. Sawn-out staves might only have part of a medullary ray in them and these would make a barrel that would either break during its making or soon after. A very big oak will yield two rings of staves. The very heart of the tree and the outer sapwood are not used.

Joe started at the beginning by selecting blank staves for his cask. These were

STAVES
Tree trunks have ribs of strength running out from the heart to the bark. These are called medullary rays and, through trial and error, the cooper has learned to cleave oak trunks so that these rays remain unbroken and make liquid-proof staves.

Each oak plank is turned into the stave shape, shown right. One side is rounded, the other hollowed out. The edges are first tapered and then beveled.

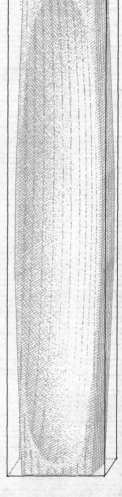

PATTERN FOR CLEAVING STAVES FROM A TRUNK

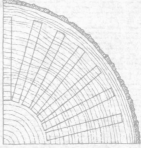

ordinary looking planks of oak a little longer than the height of the finished barrel. He examined the grain of each blank carefully before beginning to shape, or *dress* them, as the coopering expression goes. If you look at the diagram of a stave, left, you will see the subtle shaping required. Each stave is clamped into a device called a *horse*. This is made of steel, but works in the same way as the wooden shaving horse shown on page 25, although Joe worked at the horse standing up. He told me that coopers who make the smaller barrels for beer use a similar clamp, but it is worked at sitting down and is called a *mare*. Others simply clamp the stave under a hook on the chopping block, pressing it against their stomachs. Using a draw-knife with a convex blade called a *hollowing knife*, Joe hollowed what was to be the inner face of the stave, then turned the stave over and changed to a concave knife to *back* the outer face.

Taking the stave to an ordinary chopping block, he took a crude-looking ax, with a huge head and a short handle (the *side-ax*, so called because its blade is sharpened on one side only, like a chisel), and cut the edges of the stave so that each end tapered. In an operation that would have taken me an hour to spoil, Joe *listed* the stave (the cooper's expression) with a few deft strokes in perhaps a minute. To me this was the most

impressive exhibition of skill in the whole performance. He used no gauge, no measure, no template; merely his eye. The list of each stave will give the cask its belly.

The stave was then taken to a giant inverted plane. It was perhaps five feet long and set at a slant with one end on a stand and the other on the floor. This he called the *jointer* and instead of running the plane along the wood he ran the stave along the plane, beveling its long edges. The bevel on each side of each stave will ensure the circular shape of the barrel. Given that each stave can be of different width, it is a wonder that Joe could judge the right bevel, but of course he did.

Raising-up the Cask

You can see how a master cooper constructs a cask on pages 92–93, but, like a novice apprentice, you need to know more than your first study of the process reveals to understand exactly what happens. Talking of novices, I have seen an amateur start to construct a cask and the result was hilarious with staves falling all over the place. To see an expert cooper make the same start, catching all the staves in an end hoop (the *raising-up hoop*) is like watching a piece of legerdemain. A slight pressure on the last stave in keeps enough pressure on all the others around the circle. Joe simply

Dressing Staves
The physical process of dressing a stave to the correct shape is wondrous, because no prior measurement is made. The cooper selects exactly the right number of stave blanks, considering variations in widths, and shapes them all to fit one another by eye only.

The picture, above left, shows the concave hollowing knife being used, while the picture above shows the final beveling of a stave on the cooper's jointer.

pushed the iron hoop down with his hands to effect the first tightening of the staves. This, the *raising-up* stage, is completed by driving another hoop down over the staves, this time using a hammer and driver.

FIRING DIFFERENT SIZES OF CASK

You will have noticed that I started talking about "barrels", but now the barrel is a "cask". The reason is because a cooper is very particular about volumes. His skill is not so much that he can make a watertight wooden container, wonderful achievement though this be, but that he can ensure that any of his containers holds a specific, time-honoured quantity. These are in gallons and have marvellous old names, only one of which is "barrel" (see p. 86).

There is another thing to know about types of cask; some are *slight* and some *stout*. Slight casks have staves of less than one and a half inches thickness, while a stout one has staves thicker than this. Both of these factors, size and thickness of stave, have given rise to different ways of bending the staves to the correct barrel shape. This part of coopering is called *firing* because the village cooper damped the staves well, then stood the cask over a cresset of burning shavings to soften the staves enough for bending. Stouter casks might be put in a steam chest or soaked in boiling water before bending. Whatever the preparation, the shaping is a dramatic affair with plenty of shouting and hammering and steam and smoke. The longer it takes the harder it is to bend the cooling wood. A thick truss hoop is hammered down towards the splayed end of the barrel, then a smaller one follows until the original falls away. Then over goes the barrel, splayed end up, and then wallop, the cooper hammers one side of the truss hoop back towards the belly of the barrel, pulling the staves together until a smaller truss hoop can be caught on to the splayed stave ends above.

FITTING THE HEADS AND FINISHING

It is in the fitting of the top and bottom (the *heads*) into grooves cut into the inside face at the ends of the cask and in the finishing of the cask that the cooper uses most of his specialized tools. Each process in the mystery has its name.

Joe showed me how the cask is *chimed* by cutting a bevel around the top and bottom of the staves with a small hand adze; how the *sun* or *topping* plane evens off the stave

CONSTRUCTING A CASK

The cooper divides the making of a barrel into distinct stages, of which preparing the staves is the first. This complete, the cooper then proceeds with the construction. To understand the process you first need to know that the hoops the cooper uses to shape a cask are not the hoops that will finally bind it. The shaping hoops are of standard sizes and are part of the cooper's tool kit. He has *raising-up hoops* that contain the required number of staves to start the various sizes of cask, and for every raising-up hoop, a *dingee hoop* that closes the cask at the opposite end. The bending of the staves is brought about using *truss hoops* which are thick and made to take a deal of beating. These were once made of ash, but those you see now in use are likely to be of iron. Similarly strong *chiming hoops* are needed to support the ends of the cask while they are being shaped.

After raising-up, the cask has to be *fired*, that is the staves softened by heat or steam, and then curved so that they come together into the dingee hoop and can cool and set to become a *gun*, as the cooper has it. Then there is *heading* – the fitting of the two cask lids and finishing the outside of the cask prior to the making and fitting of the permanent iron bands.

1 *With all the staves dressed, the cooper gathers them one by one in a raising-up hoop.*

5 *The cooper makes the permanent metal hoops using dished steel strip. The strip is offered to the cask and he holds his thumb at the point where he must rivet the ends of the hoop on the bick iron.*

6 *Each head is made by doweling four or five planks of wood together and cutting a circle from the result. The cooper saws out the circle, then uses the adze and the heading knife, above, to cut the basle around the upper and lower edges.*

2 He uses truss hoops to shape one end of the cask, then wets the staves and heats them over a burning cresset. Smaller truss hoops bring the now malleable staves together until the cask can be upturned and the splayed staves closed with truss hoops driven from the opposite direction.

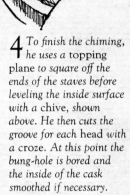

3 When the cask has cooled and set (it is called a gun at this stage), the cooper cuts the chimes, or ends of the cask. He replaces the raising-up hoop with a chiming hoop and leans the cask against the block. He uses an adze to cut the bevel.

4 To finish the chiming, he uses a topping plane to square off the ends of the staves before leveling the inside surface with a chive, shown above. He then cuts the groove for each head with a croze. At this point the bung-hole is bored and the inside of the cask smoothed if necessary.

7 To fit the heads, the cooper releases the chiming hoops, slackening the staves. He taps home the back, or bottom, head first from inside the cask, forcing flagging into the groove. He pulls the top head into place using a heading vice (a metal handle) screwed into the hole made in the head for the tap.

8 With the permanent chime hoops in place, the cooper removes the remaining truss hoops and smooths the outside of the cask with a downright plane, followed by a buzz – the cooper's curved two-handled scraper.

9 The cask is finished by fitting the remaining permanent hoops using a hammer and driver.

SLACK COOPERING

Slack coopering is the term given to the making of casks that do not have to hold liquid. These were made of much lighter wood and were bound with willow or hazel hoops, twisted and nailed (see p. 27). I remember when many perishable items, such as fruit and shellfish, traveled in slack casks. They were non-returnable, on the whole, and provided the cooper with batches of less-exacting work.

ends; how the inner surfaces are prepared for the heads using a curving, 90-degree plane called a *chive*, then grooved with the similar looking *croze* with its two steel teeth, one called the *hawk* and the other the *lance*.

Joe revealed another secret when he showed me how the cooper checks the capacity of the cask he is making using a simple pair of dividers called the *diagonals* before cutting the second groove. He can adjust the capacity slightly by altering the exact position of the groove.

The heads are beautifully made from oak planks dowelled together with *flagging*, or rush, between the joints. Traditionally, they are rough-shaped with the side-ax or cut out with a bow saw before being worked at with a draw-knife.

The cask is complete when it has been smoothed down with a *downright* followed by a *buzz* (both concave-bladed planes), and the permanent dished iron hoops have been prepared and driven home.

WHITE COOPERY

White coopery is a branch of the craft concerned with the making of liquid-tight wooden vessels, either iron or brass-bound, other than casks for spirits, wines or beer.

When I was a boy on the Essex-Suffolk border, every cottager I knew, without exception, had a *back'us* as they called it: a back house. Every farm had one too and in it the *back'us boy* used to have his being. Hanging on the wall of the back'us there was always a *piggin*. This was for a multitude of uses – anything for which a water-holding vessel was needed but it could not, of course, be boiled. Wooden buckets, with *grommets* as the hemp handles were called, were still in common use and you would see one hanging down the well.

Dairying had already passed beyond memory in most parts of East Anglia, but when I moved to Wales I found that every small farmhouse still contained dairying implements. There was always one or more *slates*, which were slabs of slate, troughed out on top, about three feet by five feet, with a hole bored in them. You bunged up the hole with a stick and poured milk into them. It was allowed to settle, then the stick was withdrawn and the skimmed milk ran down into the *buck*, which was a wide shallow tray made by the white cooper, leaving the cream adhering to the slate to be scraped off.

The cream, when taken off, is allowed to sour a little before it is churned. The older type of churn is the one at the bottom right hand corner of this page – the *plunger churn*. The stick coming up from it has a plunger on the bottom of it and it is pumped up and down. By far the best kind of churn, however, is the end-over-end-churn. This is a very beautiful artifact and perhaps represents the peak of the cooper's craft.

The buck (see above) was also used in that most hallowed art, practiced throughout the world, brewing beer. The boiling *spree*, which is what the beer is called before it is properly made, is allowed to run into the buck to cool quickly before the *balm* (yeast) is put in. The successful brew has often been quaffed from fine mugs – further examples of the white cooper's craft.

Let no one underestimate the wooden cask. It is a masterpiece of craftsmanship and an object of beauty. One of the Spanish stave makers I watched told me that there was many a barrel still holding Cognac after a hundred years' use.

END-OVER-END BUTTER CHURN

COAL SCUTTLE

SCANDINAVIAN ALE VESSELS

PIGGIN

BUCKET

DOMESTIC KEG

BUTTER CHURN

TURNING

THE FINANCIAL REWARDS FOR A woodturner today are not what they might be. Wood for turning is hard to come by and expensive. The attractiveness of turned objects lies very largely in the revealing of beautiful patterns of graining by the cutting and polishing of the wood. Elm, yew, apple, pear, cherry and walnut are all suitable. When you buy such wood it is almost certainly unseasoned, which you have to do yourself, thereby tying up your capital.

The woodturner's reliance on making objects of beauty to sell to people who appreciate them is a new thing. Traditionally, woodturners were fully engaged in making things of strictly utilitarian value, the beauty of which was of the type that attaches to all honest objects made well for a good purpose. Years ago I remember meeting Mr. Ellis of Boston, Lincolnshire,

who earned his living as a woodturner there. He made things he called *working women's pianos*, which were also called *dolly-pegs*. These were for women to stir their washing with in the *dolly-tub*. He also made *wringer-rollers*, which were the rollers made of maple for fitting into mangles, and *yokes*, which are the things eighteenth-century dairymaids always carry in paintings, their wooden buckets full of frothing milk. Mr Ellis told me he didn't like making yokes because it was "not strictly a turner's job. They entail a lot of wood carving, too." They were very wasteful of wood because they had to be cut from a big chunk of it. Mr Ellis made them not for pretty dairymaids but for fishermen who, in the Wash (which is what the sea in that part is called), carry large baskets of cockles or mussels across the sand or mud at low tide.

CAREFUL SEASONING

Phil Leyton, my son-in-law and woodturner, fells his own trees whenever possible. He *rips* them (saws them along the grain) into inch, two inch or larger planks with a double chain-saw he has fitted to a frame. He stores the planks, held apart by slats of wood to let the air through, in a shed or in the open if he has to, for several years. Then, if making bowls, he cuts a plank into square sections and roughly cuts these round on a small circular saw. He then sticks a small square of waste wood on what is to be the bottom of the bowl and puts the roughed-out wood near the stove in his house to season even further. Many

BOWL TURNING
A bowl, like the one you can see being turned below, starts out as a large lump of wood, which accounts for the high price of the finished work. Here, the turner is using an inside knife to remove the bulk of excess wood from what will be the inside of the bowl. An adjustable rest helps to support his left hand at the right height.

TOOLS OF THE TRADE
The wood turner uses an assortment of differently shaped tools depending on whether he is working on the outside or inside face of the bowl. The cutting edges also differ. The long handle (up to two feet including blade) provides great leverage and allows you to hold the cutting edge of the blade firmly against the turning wood.

INSIDE AND OUTSIDE HOOKING KNIVES

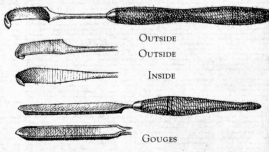

OUTSIDE

OUTSIDE

INSIDE

GOUGES

turned wooden objects today are not seasoned sufficiently, which is why they warp, crack or do other horrible things.

Phil owns an ancient treadle lathe, which is powered by the craftsman's foot. This is a technical advance on the old pole lathe (see p. 35) where when the treadle was depressed the work was turned towards the gouge, but once released the work spun the wrong way for cutting and the turner had to wait for the next change of direction before cutting again – a very tricky operation to perfect. Phil's treadle lathe has a crank and heavy wooden flywheel and gearing to transmit the movement of the treadle up and down to turn the work continuously in the right direction.

I only once saw Phil use the treadle lathe, when he had an order from a wheelwright to turn some elm wagon-hubs that were too big for his electrically driven lathe. Because of the large diameter of the hubs it took three of us to work the treadle while Phil held the gouge – but it worked and the hubs were produced on time.

TURNING A BOWL

Now, to get back to our bowl. Phil, or his apprentice, screws the piece of waste wood previously glued to the roughed-out wood to the *head* of the lathe, which is the part that spins round. Older turners were apt to cut their bowl blank out of a thicker piece of wood than necessary and leave a *pillar* of wood to screw to the head. The pillar was later cut off. But this is too wasteful now that wood is at such a premium. Taking the appropriate gouges or chisels the turner then sets the lathe spinning and, holding the tool against a rest, starts to remove wood. Very quickly he has his bowl shape on the outside at least. Then, using a different-shaped gouge, he removes the wood from the inside. The actual turning takes very little time. Next, the turner applies sandpaper to the spinning bowl. When it is sufficiently smooth, he applies such things as beeswax to give it a deep, rich shine and to fill the pores of the wood. Any excess is taken off by holding clean shavings up against the spinning bowl.

WOODEN SPOON CARVING

In Wales, the traditional *cawl* spoon and bowl are still in demand. Cawl is a kind of broth that the Welsh people consume in large quantities and it is my belief that nobody but a Welsh lady can make it properly. The broth I feel sure would not taste the same out of an ordinary china soup-plate, and the traditional wooden bowl keeps it hot much longer. Also, the cawl should be eaten with a wooden spoon.

Both cawl spoons and bowls should be made of maple wood felled in winter time. For the 10-inch long spoons, maple logs are sawn into 12-inch lengths and split in half with an ax, and split again to blanks about the size for a spoon. Then, with a small, very sharp ax, the blank is roughed out to the outward shape of the spoon. The bowl of the spoon is then cut out with what the Welsh call a *twca cam*, or bent knife. Spoonmakers I know use ordinary kitchen knives that they have bent over themselves.

The Welsh *love spoon*, now sometimes produced in terribly debased form to sell to the tourists, is properly only made by young men as tokens of their affection for their sweethearts. These articles are very beautiful, most inventive and elaborate, and quite useless. Some have balls carved inside wooden cages and others have wooden chains hanging from them, or hearts and other motifs.

HOOKED KNIFE

TRIMMING KNIFE

ADZE

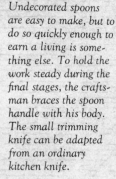

SPOON CARVING
Undecorated spoons are easy to make, but to do so quickly enough to earn a living is something else. To hold the work steady during the final stages, the craftsman braces the spoon handle with his body. The small trimming knife can be adapted from an ordinary kitchen knife.

CARVER'S TOOLS
For a ladle, a little adze is used to shape the bowl. This is refined using a long-handled hooked knife and finished with a trimming knife.

WAINS & COACHES

I F YOU HAVE EVER HEARD AN IRON-tired wagon or carriage being drawn along a modern metaled road surface, the din might make you think that there will never be need of such vehicles again, and that they must have been a terrible trial when they were the only means of carrying a load. But then if you had ever seen the same wagon or carriage being driven along a cart track across country you would realize just how marvelous a means of transport they can be. Big iron-shod wheels were made for coping with rough ground and tracks with ruts worn in them perhaps two feet deep. I have

talked elsewhere (see p. 78) about the giant ox wagons I traveled in across the African plains and how their wheels made light of the roughest countryside. Before that time, in England, I remember the farm wagon as part of daily life. Up until the Second World War there was an unbroken tradition of making mostly wooden horse-drawn vehicles that stretched back to the invention of the wheel. It was a tradition that became highly developed in England.

Every county of England had its own style of wagon that had been slowly developed among its wainwrights and was handed down from master craftsman to apprentice over hundreds of years. The wainwright was probably the village wheelwright. Making the wheels was the most difficult part of the process and it was the wheelwright who held the key to the successful geometry of the wagon, so he was at the centre of operations. If need be he could make the whole wagon himself, otherwise he was foreman to a smith and wrights who specialized in making the undercarriage frameworks and the bodies of the wagons. Working on his own, it would take a wainwright several months to

Barge Wagon
The barge wagon comes at the end of the long tradition of wainwrighting, this example from Oxfordshire being made at the turn of the century. Its details in wood and iron are far simpler than the box and bow wagons.

The English Bow Wagon
The peak of the English wainwright's craft was the bow wagon, a wagon designed for hilly areas. It was called a bow wagon because the raves or sideboards were hooped so as to clear the back wheels, and the body of the wagon was waisted, that is it narrowed behind the front wheels to allow them a greater lock.

CONSTRUCTION OF A SUFFOLK WAGON c1880

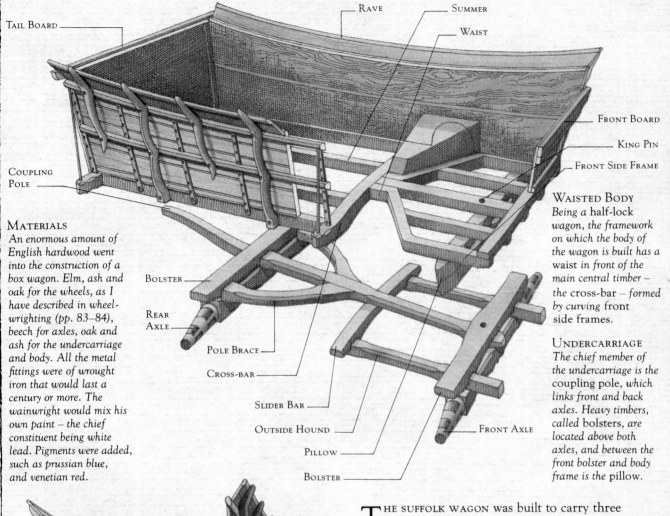

TAIL BOARD

RAVE

SUMMER

WAIST

FRONT BOARD

KING PIN

FRONT SIDE FRAME

COUPLING POLE

BOLSTER

REAR AXLE

POLE BRACE

CROSS-BAR

SLIDER BAR

OUTSIDE HOUND

PILLOW

BOLSTER

FRONT AXLE

MATERIALS

An enormous amount of English hardwood went into the construction of a box wagon. Elm, ash and oak for the wheels, as I have described in wheel-wrighting (pp. 83–84), beech for axles, oak and ash for the undercarriage and body. All the metal fittings were of wrought iron that would last a century or more. The wainwright would mix his own paint — the chief constituent being white lead. Pigments were added, such as prussian blue, and venetian red.

WAISTED BODY

Being a half-lock wagon, the framework on which the body of the wagon is built has a waist in front of the main central timber — the cross-bar — formed by curving front side frames.

UNDERCARRIAGE

The chief member of the undercarriage is the coupling pole, which links front and back axles. Heavy timbers, called bolsters, are located above both axles, and between the front bolster and body frame is the pillow.

THE SUFFOLK WAGON was built to carry three or four tons of grain across flat country. Huge wheels (six feet in diameter at the rear) made traction easy despite the weight of the wagon itself. It is a fine example of the *box wagon* — the square, high-sided vehicles favored in the east of England. This example has planked sides and paneled ends, or *front board* and *tail board* as they are known. The high-sided body adds to the massive quality of the wagon but as you study the nature of construction through the body framework and undercarriage you will see that all of the timbers are weighty. The *cross-bar*, for example, the main timber of the body framework, is about 10 inches deep! Smaller and lighter wagons, particularly the *bow wagons* of the Western counties (see the Oxfordshire wagon overleaf), would have lighter timbers and more of them, in a more complicated arrangement. The red color of the undercarriage and wheels is common to all wagons that you might see. The blue of the body is traditional to most East Anglian wagons.

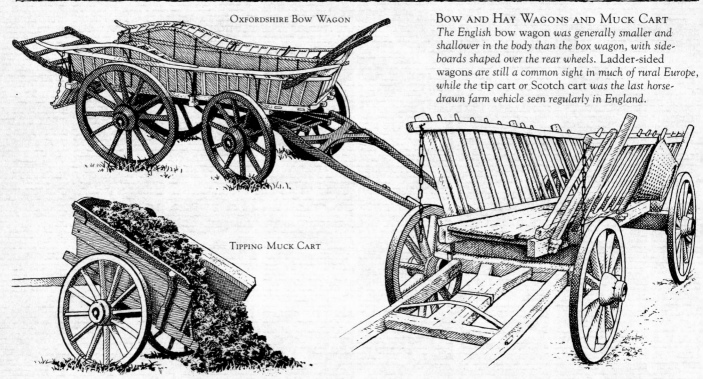

OXFORDSHIRE BOW WAGON

BOW AND HAY WAGONS AND MUCK CART
The English bow wagon was generally smaller and shallower in the body than the box wagon, with sideboards shaped over the rear wheels. Ladder-sided wagons are still a common sight in much of rural Europe, while the tip cart or Scotch cart was the last horse-drawn farm vehicle seen regularly in England.

TIPPING MUCK CART

FRENCH LADDER-SIDED WAGON

build a wagon and in the 1930s he would have charged about £30 for his finished work, painted and standing in all its glory.

WAINS

Such a wagon was for load carrying – as much as four tons of wheat. It would have massive wooden axles sawn out and hewn to a hair's breadth accuracy to complement the complexities of the wheel geometry. The axle arms would be made with a deliberate forward cant (*forehung*) so that the wheels ran very slightly together. This counteracted the tendency for the *dished* and *dipped* wheel to run off its axle.

The front axle was made to turn in a framework about the *king pin* – a central iron post. How much it turned is one of the features that points out the origins of a wagon. There are *quarter-lock* wagons, in which the front wheels can only turn as far as the straight sides of the wagon. Then there are *half-lock* wagons, where the body of the wagon has been given a *waist*, a recess on each side into which the front wheels can turn. With *three-quarter lock* wagons, the front wheels can be turned underneath the body of the wagon as far as the *coupling pole* (the main member that joins the front and rear axles). Finally, the *full-lock* wagon has front wheels small enough to turn right under the wagon floor. Generally, the wagons with more lock were made in

hillier areas where the wagon was likely to encounter restricted and twisty routes.

There was also a great variety in the sorts of wagon body that sat on the undercarriage. Some were square and business-like, such as the Suffolk wagon, others had curves like Rubenesque women, such as the wagons from Devon and Somerset. The plainer sorts were broadly termed *box wagons*, whereas curved ones were called *bow wagons*. You could fit *ladders* or *gates* front and rear, which were frameworks that overhung the ends of the wagon to give it more carrying capacity. Side rails, called *raves*, *lades*, *raths*, *shelvings* or *surboards* (there are almost as many local words for the same part of a wagon as there are types of wagon) similarly increased the capacity widthways.

The finished wagon would have chamfers cut from most of its edges, not just for decoration (and some were very elaborate) but to lighten the construction. Paint was a protection that it paid farmers to preserve. Every part from undercarriage to raves was painted in colors traditional to the area. Blue above with red for the wheels and undercarriage was fairly common. And painting, fine craftsmanship with plenty of *stringing and lining* (the painting of fine lines along the body of the wagon) brings to mind the skills of Colm Breen, a wheelwright and coachbuilding friend of mine who is a master with the brush.

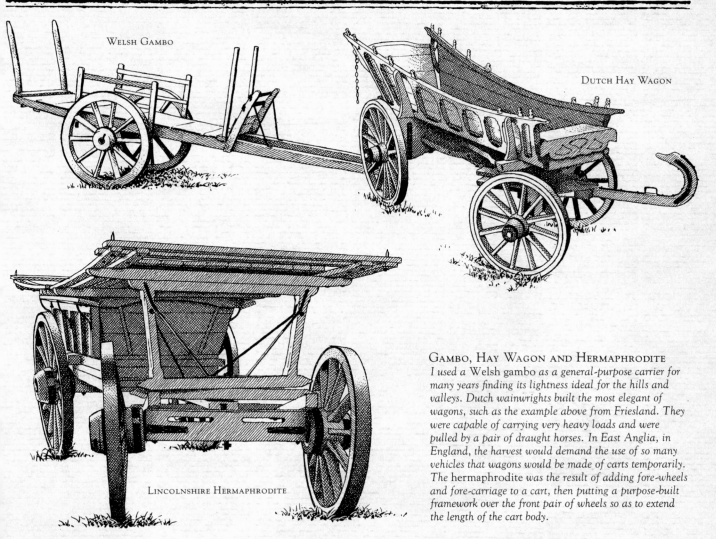

WELSH GAMBO

DUTCH HAY WAGON

LINCOLNSHIRE HERMAPHRODITE

GAMBO, HAY WAGON AND HERMAPHRODITE
I used a Welsh gambo as a general-purpose carrier for many years finding its lightness ideal for the hills and valleys. Dutch wainwrights built the most elegant of wagons, such as the example above from Friesland. They were capable of carrying very heavy loads and were pulled by a pair of draught horses. In East Anglia, in England, the harvest would demand the use of so many vehicles that wagons would be made of carts temporarily. The hermaphrodite was the result of adding fore-wheels and fore-carriage to a cart, then putting a purpose-built framework over the front pair of wheels so as to extend the length of the cart body.

I have talked so far of the truly forgotten art of wainwrighting, but Colm's craft is making the most exquisite of sprung vehicles, made for those who want the real joy of being pulled by horse today (and their numbers are swelling).

Colm Breen is a dapper man, smallish but obviously physically very tough, generally smiling or laughing, taking his trade so lightly that it is difficult to extract information from him: he prefers to tell funny stories of which he has a limitless fund.

ALADDIN'S CAVE
Wandering around Colm Breen's large workshop is like wandering in some strange Aladdin's cave. The bodies of the carts and carriages are so varied that it is impossible to describe them. There is a very pretty little *dog cart* there that has just been built. In days of old there was a box under the driver's seat for the carrying of terriers to the hunt. This box had louvers, or ventilation slits, in its side. Colm now paints

WAGON ACCESSORIES
You would find a *rope roller* at the rear of a wagon. When loading you would pass the binding ropes through the roller and tighten it with levers. Both the *drop chain* and *dog stick* stopped a wagon rolling.

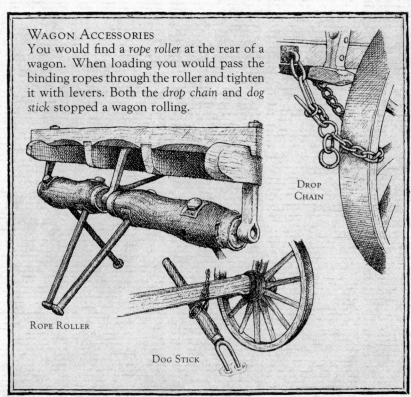

DROP CHAIN

ROPE ROLLER

DOG STICK

WAGONS FOR EVERYDAY USE

It is very easy to forget just how complete and how recent was the demise of horse-drawn transport. I can remember when elegant sprung wagons were the most common of everyday sights. These two examples are from the United States. You can tell this from the style of springing. Single elliptical springs set transversely, along the line of the axles, are an American practice which was never popular in the United Kingdom.

BUTCHER'S WAGON

COUNTRY WAGON

louvers on the sides of the seat box, although no dogs are ever kept there any more.

The curved panels, of which so many small cars and larger vehicles too are made, were moulded in steamed ash. This was a very specialized calling and there were large factories which did nothing else. The curved sheets had to be seasoned, after bending while quite green, for several years and so these big bending factories had piles and piles of them, of all shapes and sizes, stuck away to season. No ordinary coach-builder made his own. Colm still uses existing ones of which there are plenty, but when the crunch comes, he will have to start making his own again.

The *shafts*, which are linked to the horse's harness, often used to be of lance wood (which was a wood of Asian derivation from which the weapons of – for example – the Bengal Lancers were made) but now, with this unobtainable, they are of ash. They can be steamed to shape, but often a composite construction is used: sections of wood glued together, for

CONESTOGA WAGON
The Conestoga wagon was a mighty cargo carrier that once plied the freight routes of the Eastern seaboard of the United States. It was named after the Conestoga Valley in Lancaster County, Pennsylvania. The deep sides are reminiscent of the English box wagon, but this was a giant, to be pulled by a whole team of horses, oxen or mules.

FEED BOX

IRON HASP

CONSTRUCTION
The Conestoga wagon combines very high ground clearance with simple, strong running gear.

FINE FINISH
Despite the size of the Conestogas, the craftsmen who built them paid great attention to detail and the finish of their wagons. There would be a feed box at the rear of the wagon and a tool box with finely wrought iron fittings.

TOOL BOX LID

WAGONETTE

BROUGHAM

COACH BUILDING

I came across the two carriages shown here in the workshops of an Irish master coachbuilder. His business encompasses fine carpentry, elegant iron-work, patent wheel hubs, opulent upholstery and paintwork with a finish like glass. Some of his customers want him to refurbish carriages like the enclosed brougham, which was once one of the most common vehicles about town, while others want him to build new vehicles like the wagonette for the now-popular sport of driving teams of horses. A few, like myself, want him to build vehicles for the sheer joy of using them.

strength. Lance wood was fine and springy when it was new but Colm showed me some old broken lance wood shafts: they splinter into needle-sharp points which can go right through the side of a horse.

The *perch* (the main longitudinal member that underlies a carriage), *bolsters* (transverse members) and all such timbers are made of straight-grained heart-of-oak. Colm finds all the timber he needs of any sort within a few miles of Enniscorthy in Ireland.

Colm still trades with tinkers sometimes (see p. 75). He still occasionally paints their traditional barrel-topped living wagons. He told me that a tinker in a remote part of Ireland would hand his wagon over to another man who would pay him the price of the wagon and drive it as far as, say, Dublin. At Dublin he might hand it over to a third party who would have to pay him for it. This man would bring it to Colm who would paint it. The man would then collect it, drive it back to the man in Dublin who would pay him for it (plus a commission for doing the job). That man would in turn get his money back, plus a commission. No-body had to trust anybody that way!

In coachbuilding you could never be bored, because there is such a great variety of jobs to be done. As Colm himself told me, a coachbuilder has to be master of several trades: wood turner, wheelwright,

blacksmith, carpenter, upholsterer and painter. And the last of these trades is the peak of the art of the brush, for the delicate *lining-out* performed by coach painters is a miracle of skill which involves putting thin, razor-sharp lines of paint along parts of the carriage and the spokes of the wheels.

He told me that some Germans came over to take delivery of some carriages that he had built and he entertained them – and they entertained him – exceedingly con-vivially. The vehicles had to be loaded on trucks at six o'clock the next morning. At half past two in the morning, after they had certainly each consumed a bottle of whiskey, Colm told them that he had got to leave them – he still had two hours work to do on the carriages. He went down to the factory and finished lining-out. The paint he used was quick drying and when the truck came, an hour and a half after he had finished this careful and skillful operation, they could be loaded straight into the truck and they caught the boat for the continent. If that is not professionalism I don't know what is!

I first went to see Colm Breen because I am thinking seriously of going in for horse transport again. I have traveled across southern England in a *governess car* and know the joys of driving horses for pleasure. I want Colm to build me a fine *gig* one day, although he does not know it yet.

SLED MAKING

I N TIMES BEFORE WHEELED VEHICLES became the universal form of transport, sleds, sleighs or sledges (the names are interchangeable) provided the best method of moving heavy loads. To the present day there are a number of terrains in which the wheel is almost useless, and the sled comes into its own, whether there is snow on the ground or not.

In very hilly areas, for example, sleds are ideal. The reason for this is that a horse, or any other draught animal, does not enjoy being pushed from behind and it is only a very steady horse that will hold back the weight of a laden cart, with no brake to its wheels, down a steep hill.

SIMPLE SLEDS

On my own farm in Wales I used my *gambo* – a fine cart of local design with no brake – wherever I could, but on the steepest fields I preferred to use a sled that I assembled, quite simply, from oak and ash I cut on the farm. This sort of sled will not slide downhill without a little pulling and, therefore, the horse is not worried by having to hold it back. I did not even use shafts with it: it was simply pulled by *trace chains* attached to the horse's collar.

A sled very like mine is shown opposite – its basis is a forked branch stripped of its bark and protruding branches, and fitted with a platform of planks. Such sleds are common throughout northern Europe and parts of Africa.

HARVEST SLED CONSTRUCTION

Throughout mid and north Wales sleds, like the one shown opposite top, are built for use at harvest time. They consist of two long side pieces of solid timber, measuring up to a couple of yards in length, mortised together with eight or more cross members. Front and back are tail ladders to hold the bails in place, each ladder up to a yard high with horizontal rails. Side rails run the

TYPES OF RUNNER
Sled runners can be effective on mud and grass as well as on snow and ice, the basic requirement being a curved-up front achieved by steaming in the case of wooden runners. A broad section is best over soft mud or snow, but thinner iron-faced runners are much better for ice.

SAPLING

HALF-ROUND RIVEN POLE

BEECH SAPLING RUNNER ON HICKORY

IRON RUNNER ON ASH

MUDFLAT TRANSPORT
On the vast mudflats off the coasts of South Wales and Cumbria, a rare breed of fisherman exists. He follows the tide out on to the wet mud using a strange sled to support himself and the cockles he rakes. He half lies over the sled and propels himself with his feet.

length of the sled and are pegged at each end to the tail ladders and supported with vertical spindles. These sleds are tilted forward on their runners, making the sled a deadweight which will not slide down a slope unless pulled. But in some places the steep mountainsides defy even the best built of sleds to remain still, so two horses are used – one to pull from the front, and the other to act as a brake at the back.

Wheeled Sled Combinations
Welsh farmers have always made use of wheels as well as runners, ingeniously combining the two to produce a vehicle with wheels behind and sled runners in front. This gives a fairly easy pull uphill or on level ground but, with the weight thrown forward when coming downhill, the runners slow the wagon and spare the horse.

Sleds are particularly suitable when loads have to be brought downhill but no load taken up again. It is a very common sight in the Alps to see a farmer or his wife coming downhill with a small, hand-pulled sled, called in the French-speaking part of Switzerland a *luge*, with one or two churns of milk on it. The churns will be empty on the way back so that the sled will not be too heavy to pull. Such sleds work very well on snow as well as on the bare grass in summer.

Unusual Mud Shoes
A specialized use of runners, as shoes, is on tidal mud. When I was a boy I used to shoot duck among the tidal backwaters of estuaries on the east coast of England. Some of the mud was so soft that it was dangerous to go out on it in our usual waders. We used to construct mud shoes called *plashers*, which we laced to our boots. Some people made them out of old barrel staves. You could, if you were used to it, walk about on the softest mud with these; if you were not you could go sprawling.

The Drag
Drags or drogues are slip-on runners that were carried chained to the back of wagons and were slid under the rear wheels for going downhill. They converted the rear wheels into a pair of runners and saved the horse.

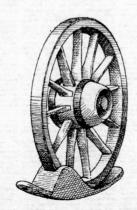

Types of Sled
Sleds are constructed in many ways because of the very different uses to which they are put, and the different craft traditions they come from. The "working" sleds, used on the land for carrying of all sorts, would either come from the wainwright's shop or be constructed by the farmer himself. The elegant ice sleds that glide across the snow scenes painted by the Dutch masters of the seventeenth and eighteenth centuries are beautiful examples of the blacksmith's art.

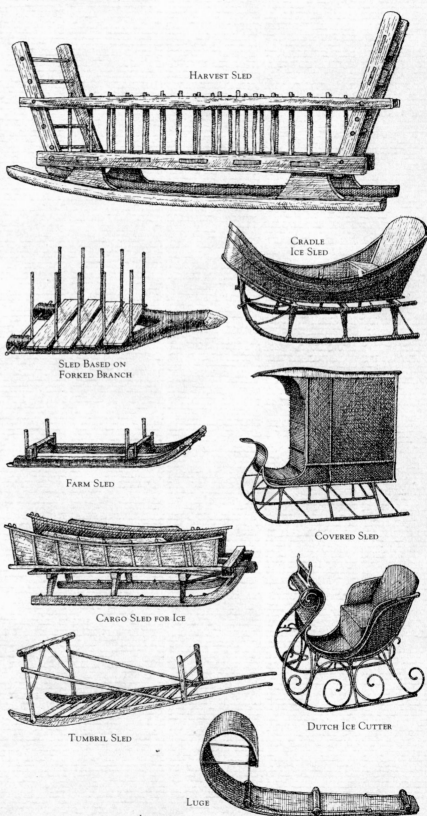

Harvest Sled

Cradle Ice Sled

Sled Based on Forked Branch

Farm Sled

Covered Sled

Cargo Sled for Ice

Tumbril Sled

Dutch Ice Cutter

Luge

BOATBUILDING

HE FIRST BOAT I COMMISSIONED TO be built in England was a 14-foot sailing dinghy. Mr Harry King was a magnificent-looking old gentleman and was known to be by far the best boat builder on the east coast of England and I had to woo him like the suitor of a particularly wealthy princess. At first he would not even speak to me, but I managed to get him round in the end and he built me a beautiful boat in which I sailed all over the Thames estuary, up to Lowestoft and I would have sailed to Holland if I had had the time.

The boat was *clinker* built, meaning the planks (or *strakes* as they are called) of her hull overlapped each other, as did the planks of Viking boats. The method of construction was to lay the strakes first, fixing them together with copper rivets, then to add the *frames* (what landlubbers call ribs) later. The shape of the strakes determined the final shape of the vessel and these were softened in a steam-chest until they could be bent to the shape that Harry King knew instinctively. The thin rock-elm frames were also steamed and then bent into place within the hull and riveted.

CARVEL-BUILT BOATS
There is another ancient wooden boat building technique which is the opposite of clinker building. With *carvel*-built boats the frames are built first and the strakes fastened to them. The strakes do not over-lap, as in clinker construction, but are butted together edge-to-edge.

If you are at all interested in boats (and here I must admit to one of my life's passions) you will notice that every type of waterway or coastline has produced its own ideal vessels, whether for fishing or cargo. Most of the larger boats are carvel built.

On coming to live by a river in Ireland I found a small local, carvel-built boat called a *prong* (see p. 109) very useful. She has an exactly semi-circular section and curves up to both stem and stern. Thick strakes of pine are simply nailed edge-to-edge on to heavy semi-circular frames made by bolting several pieces of curved wood together. Now the river by which I live is very tidal and has sloping mud banks at low water. When my prong is left by the high tide at

THE BOATBUILDER'S YARD
To wander into a boatyard where wooden boats are still made is a rare experience today. Most boatbuilding is now a matter of fibreglass and ferro-concrete. But you might still find a workshop, or the corner of a bigger yard, where traditional vessels are being made in wood – and these are likely to be small and clinker-built. The boat in the foreground of this scene is such an example and shows the overlapping strakes, or planks, all copper-riveted together. The wooden boatbuilder is both the master of the wood he cuts and bends to the subtlest of lines, and a man of the sea, who knows how to make an efficient and sea-worthy vessel that will last.

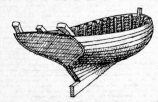

BUILDING DREOILIN
My boat Dreoilin *is half-decked, 25 feet long, with a wide beam (extreme breadth) at the water level and a steeply raking stern. In the method of building employed – carvel construction – the frames, or ribs, are built first and the strakes, or planks, are fitted on to them, butting together.*

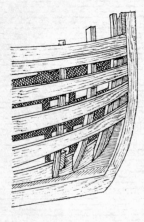

PLANKING THE HULL
The builder of Dreoilin *employed the French method of planking the hull, fitting each alternate strake to the frames and then filling in the gaps. Each strake must be individually sawn to the correct curve and flare, and must fit its neighboring strakes exactly.*

the top of this mud I can board her, let the *painter* (mooring rope) go, and she will toboggan down the mud at high speed and hit the water with a splash! It is possible, when coming in at low tide, to haul her up the mud using a capstan. You could not do these things with a flat bottomed boat – nor with a keel boat: both would stick.

Useful as this little boat has proved, my love of boats has since been directed towards the Galway hooker family of boats. The Galway hooker is quite a large carvel-built vessel, up to 40 feet long. It is half-decked (with a decked-over fore-deck but open aft) and cutter-rigged (with one mast with fore and aft sails). These boats were used, and some still are, to carry cargo between the mainland of Ireland and the islands off the west coast, notably the three Aran Islands. They also double as fishing boats. There are two smaller versions of the hooker. The smaller is the *puchan*, a mere sliver of a boat of 16 to 18 feet, but still capable of sailing the Atlantic rollers. Between the puchan and the hooker is the *gleoiteog*, which is between 23 and 28 feet.

THE GLEOITEOG
Like the other two, the *gleoiteog* is half-decked. There is room under the fore-deck for two bunks in which her crew can sleep. The open aft of the *gleoiteog* is traditionally for the easy loading of turf (peat) to be carried to the turfless islands, and cattle to be carried back.

One day while I was thinking on these matters and wishing that I had the money to buy a *gleoiteog*, I saw a young man with a pack on his back approaching my home. His introduction, believe it or not, consisted of:

"I have read your book about sailing the north German coast and I am going to build you a boat."

"What sort of a boat?"

"A *gleoiteog*."

"I have no money, no money at all," I said.

"I still build you a boat" he insisted.

And he did. When I first saw his work I realized that this determined stranger was a superb boat builder in the traditional style – one of the few remaining who are schooled in the art of building in wood.

Reiner Schlimmer bound himself apprentice for three and a half years to a boat yard in northern Germany and learned how to build traditional wooden fishing boats. Having served his time, he built himself a yacht on Norwegian fishing boat lines, and sailed off to Ireland.

DESIGNING THE BOAT
Building a new boat on traditional lines is a matter of copying the lines of the best examples of the type. Reiner had to draw the lines of the boat and then to make *patterns*, or templates, of each of the frames. He knew of an existing *gleoiteog*, noted for speed and seaworthiness, and took the lines of my boat from this.

Reiner then made the patterns from his drawings, cutting them out of hardboard. The 25-foot hull would have 13 frames and each would be of a completely different shape.

PRIMITIVE BOATS

Y INTEREST IN TRADITIONAL BOATS HAS been fueled throughout the world. When I went to Africa I soon became acquainted with dugout canoes. The finest ones that I came across were those made on the Upper Zambezi by the Balozi people. Called *makoros*, they are slender and graceful, square in section, rising slightly to both stern and bow, and propelled by standing up in the stern and using a very long paddle. I owned one and believe I was one of the few Europeans to master the rather delicate balancing act involved. When mastering it I had the strong incentive of knowing that the Upper Zambezi is full of crocodiles.

The makoro is made with an adze, hollowing out a suitable tree and setting light to it to help the process along. The builders are adept at getting the hull very thin without breaking through to the outside.

On the Zambezi I was introduced to another kind of craft, known locally as *barges*. These craft are completely flat-bottomed, with no keel, the sides and bottom made of thick regular planks hammered over a simple framework. The ends come up at a slight angle and it is on these ends that the paddlers stand.

When in India, I voyaged in the beautiful *wallam* (below), the workhorse of the Malabar coast. Built in much the same way as the Zambezi barges, they have curved *chines* (the angles where the bottom meets the sides of a boat) and beautiful stern-post and stem-heads.

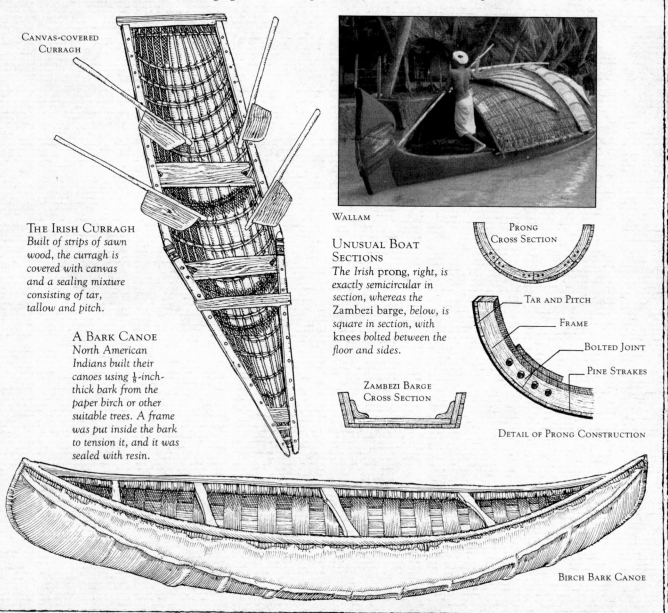

CANVAS-COVERED CURRAGH

THE IRISH CURRAGH
Built of strips of sawn wood, the curragh is covered with canvas and a sealing mixture consisting of tar, tallow and pitch.

A BARK CANOE
North American Indians built their canoes using $\frac{1}{8}$-inch-thick bark from the paper birch or other suitable trees. A frame was put inside the bark to tension it, and it was sealed with resin.

WALLAM

UNUSUAL BOAT SECTIONS
The Irish prong, *right, is exactly semicircular in section, whereas the Zambezi barge, below, is square in section, with knees bolted between the floor and sides.*

ZAMBEZI BARGE CROSS SECTION

PRONG CROSS SECTION

TAR AND PITCH
FRAME
BOLTED JOINT
PINE STRAKES

DETAIL OF PRONG CONSTRUCTION

BIRCH BARK CANOE

CONSTRUCTING THE FRAME

Once the keel of Dreoilin was laid down, work started on constructing the frames of the boat. Each frame consisted of five pieces of wood, the middle piece, or floor timber, lying directly on top of the keel and jointed to it with a deep mortise. To hold each frame firm until the planking was applied, a donkey, made from a rough larch pole, was rigged up in the rafters of the shed, parallel to the keel. Slats of rough pine were attached to the donkey and each of the frames in turn.

DEADWOOD   DEEPLY-MORTISED FLOOR TIMBER

STERN POST

CHOOSING TIMBER

Ordering timber is a very important step in wooden boatbuilding and in itself a forgotten art. Reiner's first requirement was for oak and very special oak at that. Most of the wood in a boat is curved and, while you can bend oak after steaming, it is impossible to bend very heavy pieces and over-bending weakens lighter pieces. So ship builders have always valued *grown crooks* – oak that has grown crooked. One of the reasons why so many park trees were planted in England and Ireland in days gone by is because an oak growing crowded in a forest will grow up straight and clean with few of the treasured crooks. An oak growing free in a park sends out huge branches and these twist about and have plenty of crooks in them. There are very few boat builders left who can select such crooked pieces of timber that can be sawn out into the required shape with the grain running along the curve of the wood.

Larch for the planking had to be straight-grained but it also had to be in long pieces and at least one and a half inches thick.

In addition to the frame members, there was timber to find for the stem post, the false stem, which is peculiar to hooker-type vessels, the apron, or dead wood, and the massive stern post (see the diagram above right). Most boats of this size have a stern post made of several pieces of wood scarfed together. Reiner insisted on one piece with the grain running true through it. Nor was the keel easy to find. Again, the general practice is to scarf two or more pieces of wood together, but Reiner looked until he found one piece that was straight-grained,

three inches wide, 10 inches deep and 20 feet long. It had a very slight bend in it but Reiner corrected this by hauling it straight by tackles and driving posts each side of it to hold it as it was *laid*, or set in position.

JOINING THE FRAMES TO THE KEEL

Reiner lashed a rough larch pole in the rafters of the boat shed above and parallel to the keel and called it the *donkey*. As each frame was built up of its five curved timbers, it was connected to the donkey by two slats of rough pine.

He made the floor timber (the bottommost member of the five pieces forming each frame) very deep, so that he was able to cut a deep notch, or mortise, in it to engage the keel. This is by no means common practice: many builders merely lay the timber on top of the keel and bolt it.

SETTING THE SHEER OF THE BOAT

The keel had been purposely laid on a slight slope, raking downwards aft, while

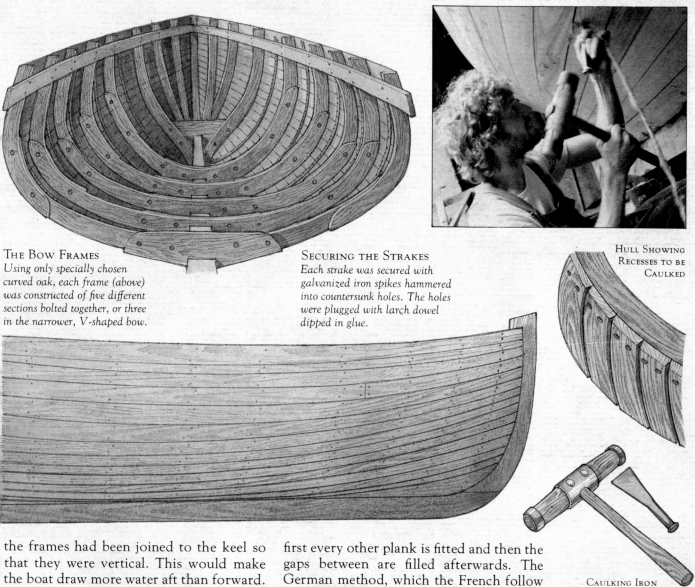

THE BOW FRAMES
Using only specially chosen curved oak, each frame (above) was constructed of five different sections bolted together, or three in the narrower, V-shaped bow.

SECURING THE STRAKES
Each strake was secured with galvanized iron spikes hammered into countersunk holes. The holes were plugged with larch dowel dipped in glue.

HULL SHOWING RECESSES TO BE CAULKED

CAULKING IRON AND MALLET

the frames had been joined to the keel so that they were vertical. This would make the boat draw more water aft than forward. He made a spline of very thin deal, perhaps slightly longer than the length of the boat. This he tacked along the outside top edge of all the frames. The master boat builder can stand back and look at this spline and adjust it by eye until he has created the sweet, sheer line of the boat – the line that the planking of the side of the hull will follow. This is one of the operations that demands that the builder be not only a craftsman but an artist. By measuring from the correctly positioned spline, he marked how much should be cut from each frame top to make it the right height to initiate that beautiful sheer, and then the outside edge of each frame to give the necessary bevels for a snug fit to the curving planks.

PLANKING UP
Reiner, being German, planked up according to the French method. In this method,

first every other plank is fitted and then the gaps between are filled afterwards. The German method, which the French follow of course, is to start at the bottom and work upwards leaving no gaps to be filled. Why it is that the Germans use the French method and the French the German, I have no idea.

Planking up is not just a matter of banging straight planks on to the waiting frames. Each plank has a flare – it has to be sawn into a curve and the curve must be exactly right. Each plank is quite different from its neighbours and before being fitted it is put in the steam-chest. The nails used to hold the plank initially are temporary. The permanent fastenings are galvanized iron spikes, heavily countersunk into holes drilled deep into the planking so that the outside of the hull can be planed.

Reiner turned a thousand little plugs from offcuts of larch planks. These were dipped in glue and driven into the holes to protect the iron spikes from corrosion.

CAULKING THE HULL
Since the hull of Dreoilin is curved, only the inner edges of each plank butt together, leaving V-shaped recesses between the planks on the outside of the hull. These gaps had to be caulked with oakum – a teased out hemp rope – banged in hard with a caulking iron and mallet. When the vessel was put in the water, all the planking swelled, making the caulked joints even tighter. My painstaking boat builder had to do this laborious job by hand – and often in the most uncomfortable of positions.

Some boats and ships are copper fastened. Copper practically never corrodes but it is very expensive and nothing like as strong as iron. A boat builder never mixes copper and iron as the two metals set up an electro-lytic reaction and corrode each other. Most working ships are iron fastened and, if the iron is galvanized and protected, it should last for at least a century. I know a sailing barge from the east coast of England that is 180 years old and her iron fastenings are still sound. The fittings are, however, of wrought iron, which is very long lasting.

With alternate planks fitted, Reiner was left with the small task of fitting, and fitting absolutely exactly, the remaining planks to fill the gaps. He made more thin, flexible splines of wood and pinned them between the planks already attached. He then worked along each spline from stem to stern, attaching little pieces of wood to the

spline at right angles and exactly fitting the gap. They were templates for the cutting of the intermediary planks.

LAST CONSIDERATIONS

When the planking up was completed, Reiner had the laborious job of *caulking* to do, filling up the U-shaped recesses between the planks with hemp. He then went to the additional trouble of fitting steam-bent oak frames between the grown-oak frames for extra strength.

Two very heavy, horizontal *knees*, or supports, fitted on each side of the boat between midships and the stern (the quarter) further strengthen the aft section.

Finishing of such boats includes giving the inside of the hull a few coats of paint above the bottom boards and a thick coat of tar below them. The outside of the hull is heavily tarred, except for the rubbing strake which will be painted white.

When I first visited the shed where Reiner was starting work, a wren was nesting in the rafters. My *gleoiteog* is now called *Dreoilin*, which is Irish for wren.

THE COBLE

Dreoilin is not the first of my boat-building dreams come true. Some years ago now, when I lived near the east coast of England, I went to Filey, in Yorkshire, and saw a fleet of open boats running in with a strong wind behind them and a big sea. There is no harbor there and just before they hit the beach they swung round and faced the curling breakers and came in stern-first! It was a most stirring and spectacular sight. Tractors were waiting for them on the beach and as soon as the boats had backed in far enough two-wheeled axles were pushed underneath them and these towed up the beach. I decided, willynilly, I had to have one. So I went to Amble, in Northumberland, and ordered one to be built. I named her *Willynilly*. She was 20 feet long.

There being few harbors along the coble coast, cobles are designed so that they can fish straight off the beach. So they are launched bow first into the waves – their high sharp bows cutting the waves and their flat sterns sliding easily off the sand – and they are brought to land stern-first (if there is a big sea running at least) so that their deep fore keel cuts the sand and keeps them head-on to the breakers and their flat stern comes up easily on the sand. They are far and away the best beach boats in the world.

THE COBLE

The coble of the north-east coast of England is specially designed so that it can be launched and recovered from a beach. It is remarkable in being a keel boat forward and a flat-bottomed boat aft, the deep, pointed keel in the bow section of the boat giving way to a flat, shallow aft section. Steerage is maintained with a deep rudder that is hung from the transom, dropped into place once the boat is underway and removed just before the stern hits the beach. The peculiar shape of the boat makes it an ideal fishing boat for an area without many natural harbors. The scene below, at Whitby, in Yorkshire, shows two cobles, the one on the right being a 17-foot sailing version.

CORACLE MAKING

THE FIRST TIME I ENCOUNTERED those ancient, canvas-covered boats called coracles, I was cruising down the River Severn in a pleasure craft, and had reached Ironbridge. There I met Mr Harry Rodgers, who was the last working coracle builder and fisherman left on the Severn. He found time to show me how his coracle was made and when I later lived in Wales I learned about the *curachs*, as coracles are known in Welsh, in use on the River Teifi, and even rowed one.

A Teifi coracle is made with a framework of nine riven ash rods 6 feet 8 inches long, crossed by nine other rods 5 feet 3 inches long. Each rod is about an inch wide and a quarter of an inch thick. Once the rods have been soaked in the river for about a week to make them pliable, they are woven into a framework. This is done in two ways, either by sticking the rods into the ground and as the frame is built up bending them over with heavy weights to achieve the flat bottom of the craft, or by weaving the flat bottom first and then bending the rod ends up to make the sides. Either way the framework is then strengthened by weaving withies or hazel rods, basket-fashion, through the tops of the timbers, two of which are inserted through holes in a wooden cross piece that tensions the vessel and forms a seat. The framework is left to dry for a few days before being covered with calico or canvas which is then tarred. In days of old it would have been of ox or horse hide. The final touch is to fix a loop of hide, cord or canvas webbing so that the coracle can be carried on its owner's back.

The coracle is propelled by a small paddle worked over the bow of the vessel with a twisting motion that draws the boat forward. This only takes one hand, leaving the other free to work a fishing net. Coraclemen generally fish with the current, and get out and walk rather than row upstream.

In 1977 I helped organize an expedition by the coracle fishermen of the River Teifi to Westminster to lobby MPs about a bill proposing to outlaw coracle fishing. A fleet of four coracles paddled up the Thames and in our muddy Wellington boots we all fetched up in due course in the bar of the House of Lords where we were entertained in a most lordly manner. Nothing, unfortunately, came of our expedition, and I suspect that I will never again be invited to enter that noble establishment.

TYPES OF CORACLE
The size and design of the sturdy Ironbridge *or* Severn *coracle was governed by the ox or cow hide used to cover it. Welsh coracles like the* Llangollen *and* Teifi *coracles were more primitive in construction, their sides pulled in over the seat to allow clearance for a paddle. Wicker boats were made like baskets, a central seat strengthening the framework.*

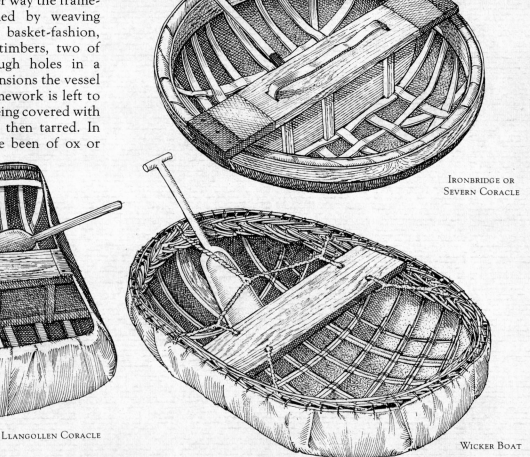

IRONBRIDGE OR
SEVERN CORACLE

LLANGOLLEN CORACLE

WICKER BOAT

SAIL MAKING

Y BOAT DREOILIN SETS A BASIC *gaff* rig, that is one small sail in front of the mast and a larger one behind, hung from an angled spar called the gaff. To equip her wardrobe properly, I required a basic suit of sails consisting of a *mainsail* (the larger sail), *foresail* or *staysail* (the smaller), a *working jib* and a *storm jib* (varieties of foresail).

Searching for a sail maker near to where I live in Ireland, I discovered Mr. Gerard Downer of Dunlaoire. I soon decided that he must know something about sail making because his great-grandfather was a sail maker on the Isle of Wight, his grandfather had migrated to King's Town (as Dunlaoire was then called) and set up his business there, his father carried it on, he took over from his father, and his son now works with him. He is the sort of sail maker who sails aboard the vessels which set his sails so that he can watch and evaluate their performance in action.

Mr. Downer showed great patience and considerable wisdom in the somewhat protracted talks about what sort of sails he was going to make for me. I tried hard to persuade him to make my sails of linen, which modern sailors now damn, even though their forebears, including Nelson, managed perfectly well with it for hundreds of years. But linen does stretch a little when it's new, and unless stowed away completely dry it will rot. Synthetics, on the other hand, all eventually degrade in sunlight, which flax does not.

Anyway, after some correspondence, linen proved too hard to get, so we had to compromise with a cloth that mixes flax with some synthetic substance, but woven in such a way that it looks like and feels like genuine linen. Sailcloth rolls are called *bolts*.

Mr. Downer kindly let me watch him during the more crucial operations of making the mainsail. The time-honored names for parts of a sail are shown in the daigram of Dreoilin's sails, right. The mainsail was to have an 11-foot *head*, a 21-foot *leech*, a 10-foot *luff* and a 14-foot *foot*, a total of 168 square feet. First, he chalked out the shape of the sail on the lovely polished wooden floor of his sail loft. This was a job requiring not only experience but considerable mathematical skill, for it

is vital that the mainsail has an efficient aerodynamic shape when it is full of wind.

He then unrolled the cloth so as to cover the shape chalked on the floor. The sail was to be vertically cut, the panels of cloth running parallel to the leech. Starting from the leech itself, he rolled out his bolt of cloth, cut the length off quickly with a sharp knife, then rolled out the next strip, and so on until he came to the *tack* of the sail. All these strips overlapped the pattern at both ends and each other by a few inches.

Then came the job of *scribing* the sail, making chalk marks on it, much as a tailor might on a suit, as a guide to the two busy women who sat behind industrial sewing machines at the end of the loft. Now, working very quickly and entirely by eye, he chalked in *swellings*, or dart lines, up to two feet long at both head and foot of the sail. The object of these darts is to provide a slight belly to the sail, for a flat sail obtains less power from the wind.

The strips of sail were then machine-sewn together. The machinist overlapped the cloths by an inch or two and sewed both edges of the overlaps, and then put in a

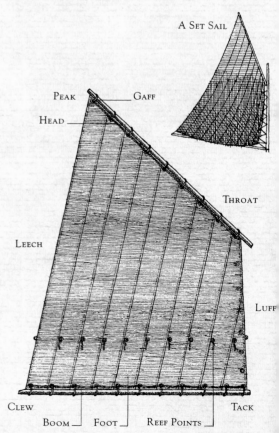

A SET SAIL

PEAK — GAFF

HEAD

THROAT

LEECH

LUFF

CLEW

BOOM — FOOT — REEF POINTS

TACK

Sail Shapes

There are many different sail plans. The lateen, Dutch boeier and gaff cutter are all *gaff rigged*, their mainsails hauled up on gaffs, while on board a Chesapeake skipjack you have to haul the mainsail straight up the mast.

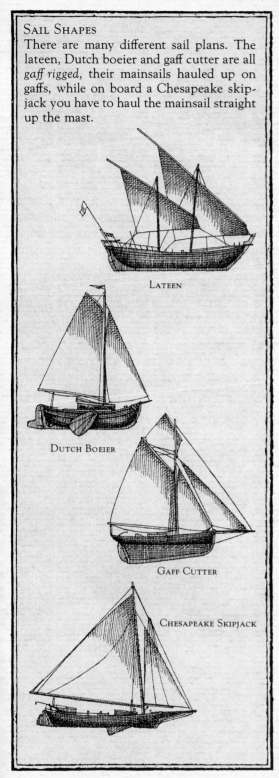

Lateen

Dutch Boeier

Gaff Cutter

Chesapeake Skipjack

ran a thin line of string around all four prickers and chalked along the line. He then cut the surplus cloth off, leaving about six inches all round. The final shape of the sail was now apparent.

Next he marked out and fitted the *reef points*. *Reefing*, for those who may not know, is reducing the area of a sail which you do in a strong wind or a gale. The reef points, small pieces of cord hanging down from each side of the sail, are sewn across the sail in rows, and are used to tie the sail securely along the boom. Some sails have up to three rows of reefing points, and if you ever need to use the highest row, you shouldn't be out sailing in a wind that strong!

Next, by eye, he marked out on the *clew*, *tack*, *throat* and *peak* – the points and corners of the sail (see the diagram opposite again), where the layers of sail cloth reinforcings were to be sewn and where holes should be pierced in them. He stamped a *delring*, or metal eyelet, into the four holes and re-inforced them further still with leather patches, for these important places take an enormous amount of strain. Lastly, he marked out where the lacing eyes were to be fitted along the foot, luff and head, through which passes the rope that attaches the sail to the spars, and turned his attention to the *bolt ropes* around the sail. A bolt rope is sewn along the foot and luff of the sail, giving it strength and protection from chaffing. The leech and head of the sail have doubled webbing tape sewn into them for additional reinforcement.

And that was how my mainsail was made. Made to last, by the look of it, for my life-time and for many winter gales to come.

Tools of the Trade

Once sails were stitched and finished entirely by hand, the sail maker using a needle and sealing palm wrapped around his hand. The serrated metal pad of the palm helped him push the needle through the tough sail cloth. Today all the sewing is done by machine, and almost the only work done by hand is the fitting of the eyelets, or thimbles. A spike is used to pierce the cloth, which is then shaped to size with a cutting knife. The two parts of the eyelet are placed either side of the sail on top of an eyelet block and jammed hard together using a fid and mallet.

third row of stitching right down the middle. The sail was then laid out again on the floor, and Mr. Downer began the task of scribing the edges of the sail. Starting with the leech, he measured each of the four sides of the sail in turn, pulling the cloth tight as he did so by driving a *pricker*, a steel pin set in a handle, through each corner, spread-eagling the sail on the floor. Then he

ROPE MAKING

WHEN I WAS A BOY I WORKED ON A farm in Essex for a summer. Old Bill Keeble, the foreman, called me to help him one day. He had with him a small instrument rather like a carpenter's brace that turned a hook – I later learned it was a *whimbel* (see p. 46). Bill led the way to a straw stack, caught up a hank of straw in the hook and told me to start cranking and walking backwards. As I turned he kept catching more straw into the straw that was already twisted. In not many seconds we had quite a long rope; not very durable, but as long as it was not allowed to untwist, it was quite strong. Bill used it for tying down the thatch on hay ricks. The simple twisting of fibers in this way is the basis of all rope making. For a useful, long-lasting rope, however, you need to use a stronger fiber than straw.

The best rope-making material in the world is hemp. The rigging for Nelson's ships, and those of almost every other navy in the world, was made of hemp. It is very strong, long-lasting and does not chafe that easily. However, most governments forbid us from growing hemp.

HOW TO SPIN YARNS

Ropes are made by twisting hemp *yarns* together. Hemp has to be *retted*, or rotted in water, and then *shived*, that is stripped of all its short fibers. A *spinster* (not necessarily an unmarried lady) then ties great bunches of the fiber to his waist, catches the ends on a turning hook, and walks backwards, paying out the fibers as he goes. The yarn produced is then hardened by twisting, *sized* by rubbing with a horsehair rubber, and then *laid*, or doubled back on itself.

OTHER ROPE-MAKING MATERIALS

Cotton is not as strong as hemp, nor as long-lasting or water resistant, but since it is far nicer to handle it is often used for sheets in dinghies and small boats. Other materials used for making rope include sisal, which was used for binder and bailer

ROPE FROM STRAW
Ropes are made by twisting fibers together and the principle of this is no better shown than by watching a straw rope being made. This rope maker is twisting straw into the rope by hand as he walks away from a fixing point, which in this case is an improvised device using an old bicycle wheel.

twine until artificial fibers came in; jute, a hemp-like plant grown in Bengal, but much inferior to hemp; and manilla, which is grown in the Philippines and makes a fine rope. But unfortunately all of these are being superseded by artificial fibers, which, incidentally, do not last for ever either.

FROM YARN TO ROPE

Many English seaports once had their rope-walks – long areas of open ground used for laying out the individual yarns of a rope prior to twisting them together. Such walks would be at least 80 yards long and some up to 240 yards. Every 20 yards or so there would be a T-shaped post called a *beaver* or *skirder*, which had a row of upward-pointing pegs that kept the yarns from tangling.

At one end of the walk was the *jack* (below), with at least three revolving hooks all turned independently by one handle. At the other end was a swiveling hook fixed to a post on a trolley or a sled – the *traveler*. The yarn was looped from end to end of the walk round the single hook and each of the three hooks in turn, the maker walking miles in his effort to make a thick rope.

When the yarns were all in place, the rope maker's assistant cranked the hooks on the jack while he kept the groups of yarn separate using the *top* held close to the traveler. As the yarns twisted into *strands* they pulled the traveler towards the jack.

When the yarns were twisted so they were almost kinking, the rope maker fixed the traveler in place and the real magic started. He pushed the top towards the jack and the tension in the strands twisted them together behind the top in the opposite direction to the twist of the yarns. That is why rope does not unravel itself. A good maker knows how much tension to use.

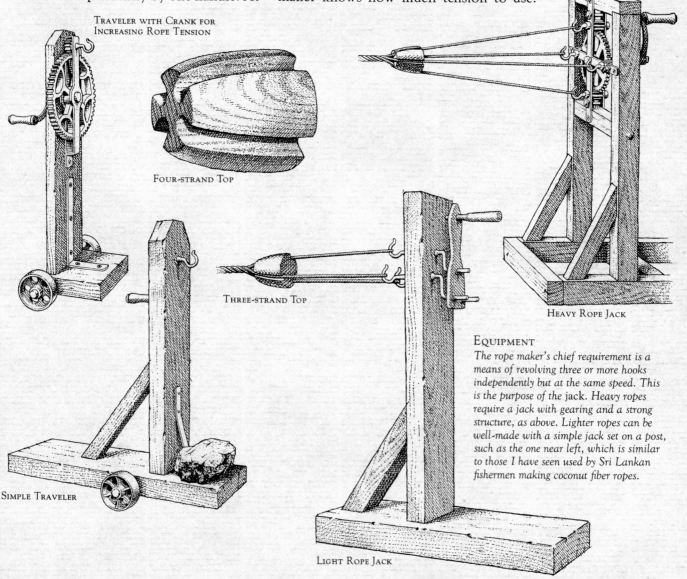

TRAVELER WITH CRANK FOR
INCREASING ROPE TENSION

FOUR-STRAND TOP

THREE-STRAND TOP

SIMPLE TRAVELER

HEAVY ROPE JACK

LIGHT ROPE JACK

EQUIPMENT

The rope maker's chief requirement is a means of revolving three or more hooks independently but at the same speed. This is the purpose of the jack. Heavy ropes require a jack with gearing and a strong structure, as above. Lighter ropes can be well-made with a simple jack set on a post, such as the one near left, which is similar to those I have seen used by Sri Lankan fishermen making coconut fiber ropes.

NET MAKING

ETS ARE MADE FOR A THOUSAND different purposes to a thousand different designs. Yet all hand-made nets are made in much the same way, and the process itself, although very time consuming, is very simple. All you need is a head rope, tied up at a convenient working height and running the intended width of the net, plenty of twine and mastery of two knots – the *clove-hitch* and the *sheet bend*. Of course, there are refinements to learn, such as using a piece of wood to space the mesh consistently and making sure that every knot is tied to a similar tension, but the principle is easy.

The Netting Needle
To haul the whole length of twine through each loop of the mesh would be very cumbersome and would, I should imagine, drive the net maker mad. So the netting needle was invented. It is a small piece of wood or bone with a groove at one end and a tongue carved out in the middle of it. The needle is loaded by winding the twine around the groove and the tongue, and is quite easily passed through the mesh, making the knots as it goes, without tangling.

Nets for Trapping
Most common of the countryside trapping nets are ferreting or *purse nets*, which are small bags of netting placed over the mouths of rabbit holes before a ferret is sent down the burrow. The rabbit bolts and finds itself caught in the net. *Long nets* are set up on small stakes and then dropped on the rabbits as they move between their feeding ground and their burrows.

Fishing Nets
Most of the nets made in the world are made for catching fish. Needless to say, the variety of designs and uses are legion.

Nimble Fingers
I suspect that large nets are now made on sophisticated machines but it is comforting to recall that very large fishing nets can be made by hand. And where there is any need for subtle shaping or mending, the practised fingers of ladies, such as those below, are best.

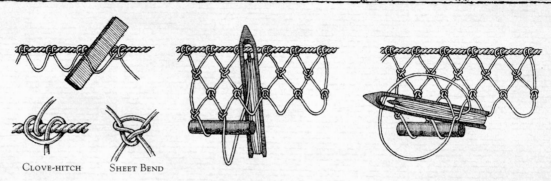

FISHERMAN'S METHOD
The twine is clove-hitched to the head rope using a spacer that gives half-size mesh. For the second and subsequent rows, you use a spacer twice the size and use sheet bends to join each loop of mesh. Once the net is underway, each sheet bend is made with swift loops of the needle.

CLOVE-HITCH   SHEET BEND

Gill or *tangle nets* are either fixed to a drifter, or float free in the sea, in which case they are better known as *drift nets*. They have been used for thousands of years to catch pelagic fish, those such as mackerel, herring and sea trout that swim close to the surface, ensnaring them by the gills as they try to swim through the mesh.

The salmon fishermen who fish the river in front of my house in Ireland, completely illegally I might add, use what they call *stake nets*. These are gill nets that have an anchor off-shore to hold them against the current, and a stake driven into the shore to hold them firm. Very light, almost invisible, synthetic twine, has revolutionized this sort of fishing, for the fish cannot see the net and can thus be caught in the day as well as at night.

A variation of this long, floating type of net is the *set net*, which is weighted at the bottom causing it to sink to the sea bed, and catch the deeper-swimming fish. Many small fishing boats work up to 10 miles of these nets, and the destruction to fishing grounds can be easily imagined.

TRAWL NETS
The next big group of nets are the *trawl nets*, which are bags of netting dragged through the sea, their mouths kept open by devices called *trawl heads* or *otter boards*, which act like kites in the water.

A variation on the trawl net is the ancient fine mesh *stow net*. It is fastened to a stationary boat in a tideway, and the fish are driven in by the incoming tide. Smaller versions are used in creeks and small rivers where they are fastened to each bank to catch whatever the tide can offer.

SEINE NETS
Seine nets are particularly effective if used in the right conditions. One end is fixed to the bank, the other is attached to a boat. The boat pulls the net in a semi-circle from the fixed end and then both ends are hauled in

up the beach with the fish enclosed. Recently, the seine net has been adapted for use by trawlers at sea, one end being *shot* (that is, thrown into the sea) and marked with a buoy, or even the ship's boy, who is left bobbing in a small boat attached to the end of the net. The trawler sails in a large circle and returns to the buoyed, or boyed, end, ringing the water and its fish with net. Then the foot rope, which runs freely through rings in the bottom of the net, is hauled in and the whole package is slowly hauled aboard the boat.

FISHING ENGINES
A fascinating kind of net is the *dip net*, or fishing engine, which is a square net hung from its corners on lines which connect it to a pole above. The net is lowered to the bottom of the water, where it lies flat on the bed, and is then raised after an appropriate interval. Any fish swimming around as the net is raised thus get scooped up. I have seen such nets in use in Cochin, in India, and am told that they are commonplace in China. Recently I saw one in action in the Venice lagoon so big that it covered nearly a quarter of an acre.

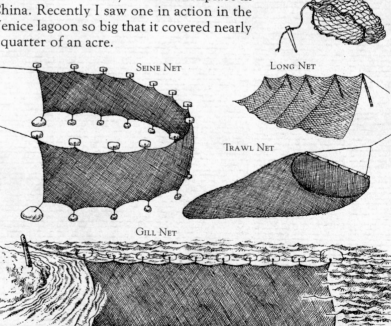

PURSE NET

LONG NET

SEINE NET

TRAWL NET

GILL NET

TANNING & CURING

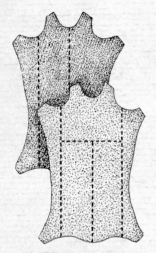

CUTTING HIDES
Large hides are divided according to the use to which they are to be put. A single cut down the middle of the back gives two half-hides, or the heavy shoulder leather can be divided off for use in such things as making horse halters.

HAND TOOLS
The tanner's and currier's hand tools consist of sharp blades for cutting and shaving the hides, and blunt blades, including the sleaker, for making them clean, smooth and supple. For much of the work, curved, two-handled knives (with a sharp edge and a dull, scraping edge) are used, but for fine shaving of the flesh side, the currier has a double-edged knife which has two opposite-facing handles to control the pitch of the blade exactly.

F YOU SKIN AN ANIMAL AND JUST leave the skin alone it will become as hard as a board and you will be unable to bend it or use it for any purpose at all. If you keep it wet it will simply rot. There are two ways to avoid these results: one is to steep the hide in a chemical which will convert the proteins in the hide to a stable non-putrefying material and will prevent the crystallization which causes the skin to harden. The other method, used by Eskimos, American Indians and Kalahari bushmen, is to *work* the skin. Eskimo ladies, we are told, chew their husbands' boots. Whether this is so I have no means of knowing, but I have seen Kalahari people working rawhide rope.

KALAHARI CORKSCREW

A cowhide, or the hide of a large antelope such as a *kudu* or a *gemsbok*, would be laid out on the ground and cut in a spiral to make a long continuous strip, about as wide as it was thick – in each case perhaps an inch. This strip, many yards long, was then threaded over and over the branch of a tree and through a loop of heavy wire which had been twisted round a rock. A pole was thrust through the wire loop and the coils of hide were twisted up into knots by a tribesman pushing the pole round and round, turning the rock. When the man could twist no further he would withdraw the pole with a jerk and the rock would spin violently as it straightened out the tortured hide and headed towards the

ground again. When this momentum-spinning stopped the tribesman thrust his pole into the wire loop again and started turning again, but in the opposite direction.

At the end of not just a day, but a week of repeating this process, interspersed with daily applications of ostrich fat to the hide and re-arrangement of the loops, the tribesman would be left with a long rope which would remain permanently supple. It would defy the weather, and would easily pull an eight-ton ox wagon out of rough ground.

MINERAL AND VEGETABLE TANNING

Nowadays tanning is almost invariably done by soaking the hide in *chrome alum* (chromium potassium sulphate), preceded by a pickling process in an acid solution. This is termed mineral tanning and it is the way I prepare the odd sheep skin to lay on the floor. Only in cases where very high-quality leather is required (as in surgical uses) is vegetable tanning still employed.

Oak bark was used for this and it was once gathered for the purpose in large quantities and sent to local tanneries. My dear old friend, Mr. Penpraise of Morwelham in Devon, still owns his oak bark *stripper* which was made from the leg bone of an ox. With this he used to strip the bark off oak trees in the spring time, first taking a cylinder of bark off the standing tree as high as he could reach, then felling the tree to strip the rest.

The chemical process of vegetable tanning is understood now, how the *tannin*

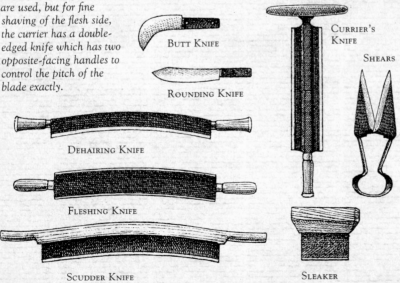

BUTT KNIFE

ROUNDING KNIFE

DEHAIRING KNIFE

FLESHING KNIFE

SCUDDER KNIFE

CURRIER'S KNIFE

SHEARS

SLEAKER

STANDING TOOLS
The fleshing beam is a shaped board or, for large hides, a riven half tree trunk with the curved side debarked and smoothed. You throw the hide over the beam and work from the top of the slope. The stake beam holds a blunt, half moon-shaped blade, over which the leather is pulled from side to side.

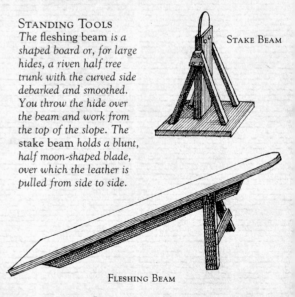

STAKE BEAM

FLESHING BEAM

TANNING
The tanning process involves messy, hard work. The soaked hide of a large animal is very heavy to haul in and out of the tanning pit, while fleshing, above, means removing waste flesh with the sharp convex blade of the fleshing knife – not a job for the squeamish.

(tannic acid) from oak bark seeps, very slowly, through the pores of the hide and drives out the water, coating each fiber with preservative, but it amazes me that early man discovered that such a thing as oak bark could achieve this.

THE TANNER AND THE CURRIER

At one time the crafts of tanning and curing, or currying, were separate (by law in the United Kingdom). The tanner produced hide that was stiff and of poor colour; the currier then turned it into supple, highly polished leather fit for the saddler, and other leather workers, by further soaking and then working and scraping and cutting or splitting the hide. More recently, the two crafts have been brought together under one roof and this was the case when I visited the tannery at Llangollen in Wales just before it closed down.

The manager told me that the first job had been to soak the hides in a lime pit for two weeks (to loosen the hair), then in *bait* for a week. The latter rather unsavory stuff was made from the excreta of dogs. In other tanneries hen manure was used, and pigeon droppings too were considered efficacious. The Llangollen Tannery got its dog manure from hunt kennels.

After this the hides were washed (thoroughly one hopes) and *fleshed* in the beam house. Each hide was laid over a *fleshing beam*, and all fat, flesh and membrane removed by careful scraping.

The *tan* was made by steeping finely ground oak bark for a few days. The liquor was then pumped, several times, on to fresh bark and allowed to stand. The hides were then soaked in this liquor in pits. At first the hides were said to be *hungry* and *thirsty* for the tan, so for the first three months the hides were continually moved from the solution they were in into freshly steeped solution.

The hides were then *laid away* in strong tan for six months, before being hung up to drip, and then dried, or *sammied*, by heavy rolling.

Currying involved cutting the hides into sections, and scraping them with *sleakers* before soaking them in a solution made from the dried and chopped leaves and shoots of the sumach tree. When half dry after this the sections were *flatted*, which means shaved on the flesh side using the double-sided currier's knife (see opposite), which is sharpened and then the edges turned, as a cabinet-maker turns the edges of his scrapers. The hides were then stretched over a table and *glassed* (with steel blades), rubbed with cod-liver oil and tallow on the flesh side, dried, the grease cleaned off, and were then ready for sale.

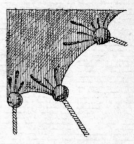

STRETCHING HIDES
An Australian who came to my farm cured sheep skins with the wool on. After soaking and scouring, he stretched the skins, wool side downwards, over a wooden frame. He folded pebbles into the edges of the skin and tied binding lanyards to them, so as to avoid cutting slots into the precious leather. He could then easily work at the skin and apply the mineral tan, chrome alum, as a paste.

HARNESS MAKING

WE ARE TOLD, BY PEOPLE WHO I should imagine know very little about it, that the first men to drive horses did so by tying their plough or some other device on to the horse's tail. No horse that I ever met would put up with this for more than five seconds. It is obvious to me that the first person who had the idea of making some creature, other than his wife, pull a cart, would have devised something very much like our modern *breast plate* harness. The animal pulls with his chest against a broad, padded band of leather and, provided the breast plate is not too high and not too low, pulls quite well. But when it came to heavy loads, or heavy ploughs in heavy ground, it was found that the breast plate hampered the animal's breathing and the *collar* came into use (see p. 128).

Now a horse cannot control a wheeled vehicle which is just dragging behind him, even if it has brakes. There must be rigid *shafts* to hold the vehicle at a decent distance from the horse.

HARNESS FOR COLLAR AND SHAFTS

You need a wide, padded saddle to take the weight of shafts (and maybe part of the load if the vehicle is a cart, which has only two wheels, and it is front heavy) and you also need a *girth*, or strap round the belly, to hold the shafts down if the vehicle is back heavy. Then again, to prevent the vehicle from overrunning the horse, you have to have a *breechin* (generally pronounced "britchin"), which is a wide strap that goes round the horse's buttocks. There are *tugs* (small chains or straps) on all of these that connect with fittings on the shaft. And further, to hold the whole system of harness from slipping forward on the horse's back, you have a *crupper*. This is a strap with an eye in it which is put over the horse's tail. It is most important that all harness should be adjusted perfectly, otherwise you have an unhappy and inefficient horse.

PRINCIPLES OF THE CRAFT

I have made breast plate harness from old car tire inner tubes before now but, although effective, it was a far cry from the beautiful leather harness produced by a skilled harness maker.

For the real thing, leather is cut into strap widths with an instrument called the *plough*. This is like a carpenter's depth gauge, but instead of scribing a line, it cuts. To make strips thinner, the harness maker uses a *splitter*, which is a very sharp blade, screwed to the bench horizontally. Edge tools are used to remove any sharp edges from the strips and most edges are *creased* with little sharp-edged tools that are heated over a flame (but not made so hot as to scorch the leather). Creasing is a decorative line impressed close to the edge of the strap.

The crux of the art of harness making is stitching the leather. Flax thread is used because it is extremely strong and long-lasting, but is flexible and does not cut the leather. You need eight times as much thread as the length to be stitched and all thread must be waxed by dragging it across beeswax. All stitching holes are marked out with *pricking irons* before they are finally pierced with an awl. If you want to join two ends of a strap, the ends are *skived*. This is done with the *half-moon* or *round knife*, and the idea is to remove some of the flesh side of the leather until both ends are wedge-shaped and can be joined without a bulge in the thickness of the harness, so creating a much neater finish.

HEAVY HARNESS
The harness below is suitable for pulling a heavy, wheeled vehicle, such as a farm wagon. You have to imagine the shafts of the vehicle running up along the side of the horse and joined to the tug chains on the breechin, saddle, belly band and the collar.

SADDLE
RIDGE CHAIN
CRUPPER
HIP STRAP
LOIN STRAP
BREECHIN
COLLAR
GIRTH
BELLY BAND

SADDLERY TOOLS AND THEIR USE

TOOLS FOR LEATHERWORK HAVE A VERY individual feel. Those shown here are a selection from tools used for harness making, saddle making and collar making – the three crafts collectively referred to as saddlery. The *clam* is placed butt end on the floor, with the opening jaws between the knees. By squeezing with the knees, you can grip the work for sewing while leaving both hands free to pierce the leather with the awl and stitch with the needles. I have used laundryman's pincers as a clam but they are very makeshift. With the work clamped, stitching proceeds, usually with two needles at once. You pull the entire length of thread through the first hole of the run of stitching, then, with a needle threaded on to both ends of thread, you take thread through each hole from opposite sides, tying a half-hitch

or half reef-knot in each hole. The stitching must not come undone even if cut or broken.

Most of the other tools can be divided into those used for cutting the leather (the *punches* and knives) and those for marking it (the *creases* and *prickers*). The creases are usually heated before use – the large *shoulder crease* being used on heavy leather with the weight of your shoulder behind it. The *palm iron* is a species of thimble. It sits in the palm of the hand, its indented surface stopping the needle slipping.

The *masher* is gripped with the fist and used to compress the stuffing in the padded parts of the saddle. The *bulldogs* are special pliers used for pulling materials tight over an edge. You use the side projection, near the jaws, as a fulcrum to lever against as you pull webbing and the like tight for tacking to the saddle tree.

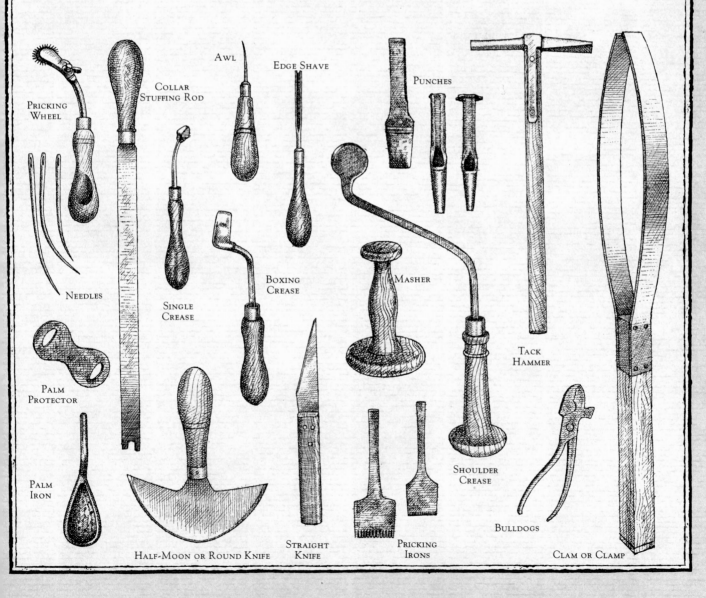

PRICKING WHEEL

COLLAR STUFFING ROD

AWL

EDGE SHAVE

PUNCHES

NEEDLES

SINGLE CREASE

BOXING CREASE

MASHER

TACK HAMMER

PALM PROTECTOR

PALM IRON

HALF-MOON OR ROUND KNIFE

STRAIGHT KNIFE

PRICKING IRONS

SHOULDER CREASE

BULLDOGS

CLAM OR CLAMP

SADDLE MAKING

STRUCTURE OF A SADDLE
The cutaway diagram, below, shows how the tree *– the rigid frame of laminated beech (here with additional steel springing) – is sandwiched between an upper saddle and a well-padded lower saddle called the* panel. *The* points *of the tree slip into the* point pockets *(sewn on to the panel) when the panel is finally laced to the upper saddle.*

I ONCE CAME INTO VERY INTIMATE contact with a saddle while working on a sheep farm in the Karoo area of South Africa way back in the 1930s. For six months I sat on a saddle for 10 or 12 hours every day, except Sundays, and after a few weeks of this, a boil grew up on a certain part of my anatomy. This boil seemed to me, though I was unable to inspect it visually owing to its peculiar location, to be as big as an ostrich egg. The memory is painful indeed, but not so painful as it would have been if I had had a poor saddle, or worse still, no saddle at all. And not just painful to me but painful to my horse too, for a good saddle is a necessity for an efficient horse/rider combination. I believe that the horse should be an important means of transport and power in the future and I rate the noble craft of saddle making highly.

The saddles I used to ride in Africa were known as *semi-military*, and were made in far-away Walsall, in the West Midlands of England. They had fairly high *pommels* (the front part of the saddle), fairly high *cantles* (the hind part), and large knee-rolls on the flaps in front of the knees. They also had several D-shaped buckles of brass in various places to hang things on, like a waterbottle or a pair of *hobbles*, which were like handcuffs to chain the horse's fetlocks together so he could graze but not run away. A pair of leather saddlebags held rusks and *biltong* (strips of sun-dried lean meat) and, if I was to be away for a few nights, I strapped down a tightly rolled blanket over the pommel. This reinforced the knee-rolls to give a feeling of security.

What all we young back-velders really wanted was an *Australian stock saddle*. This was enormously heavy, with a very high cantle and a deep seat, and it looked pretty flashy. It was also very expensive – far out of the range of most of us, certainly of me.

HISTORY OF THE SADDLE

There were two major technical discoveries connected with saddles. The first was probably adopted by the Romans from the Mongolian nomads. It was found that a horse would go further, faster, and certainly more happily if there was no direct weight pressing down on its backbone. Therefore raised pads on each side of the backbone were introduced.

The second great innovation which really made the horse an effective vehicle and certainly an effective war machine, was stirrups. With stirrups a man can really stay on a horse, maneuver, use a lance or a sword, or jump fences. Quite who did invent this simple yet effective device is not known, but it is certain that stirrups were in use in Asia by AD500, spreading across to Europe during the next few centuries.

In the little museum in the cloisters of Westminster Abbey is what is claimed to be the oldest complete saddle in the world. It was used by Henry V, and was carried in his funeral procession in 1422. What interests me about it is that it is almost exactly the same as the saddles I have seen Ethiopians riding about on, mounted on mules. Henry's saddle was made chiefly of wood, with high vertical pommel and cantle without much dip or shape to the seat. It looks the sort of saddle you would not be knocked out of easily by a lance.

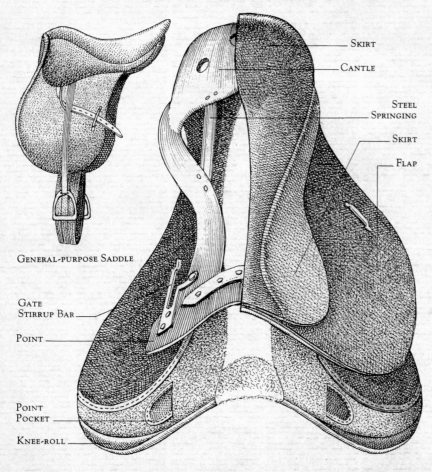

GENERAL-PURPOSE SADDLE

GATE
STIRRUP BAR

POINT

POINT
POCKET

KNEE-ROLL

SKIRT

CANTLE

STEEL
SPRINGING

SKIRT

FLAP

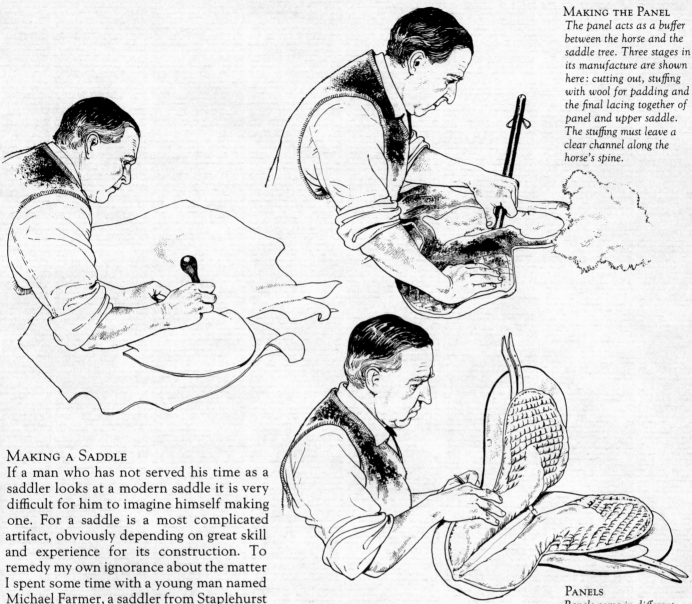

MAKING A SADDLE

If a man who has not served his time as a saddler looks at a modern saddle it is very difficult for him to imagine himself making one. For a saddle is a most complicated artifact, obviously depending on great skill and experience for its construction. To remedy my own ignorance about the matter I spent some time with a young man named Michael Farmer, a saddler from Staplehurst in Kent, England.

If Mr. Farmer is to make a saddle in order to fit a particular horse, he goes and visits the horse with a piece of equipment which I am certain the Romans did not have, nor the Mongols, and that is a piece of lead-covered electric cable. He lays this over the horse's back and bends it (and it bends quite easily) to the shape of the horse. Then, being careful to preserve its shape, he draws the outline of the lead cable on a piece of paper.

THE TREE

Back at the workshop he chooses a *tree*, a U-shaped framework, mostly of wood, which fits exactly the shape of the horse. English saddlers get their trees from specialist manufacturers in Staffordshire. There is no reason why a good carpenter should not

make trees but, so far as I know, all saddlers actually buy them from specialist producers. Nowadays they tend to be made from laminated beechwood, reinforced by steel straps.

There are two edges to the piece of laminated wood that forms the *head*, or front end of the saddle tree, and these must be extended by rivetting flaps of leather to them. These flaps will ultimately be pushed down into two leather pockets in the *panel*, which is the under section of the saddle.

WEBBING AND BELLIES

The next operation is to fit the *webbing*, a system of very strong canvas bands, some longitudinal and some lateral. The longitudinal pieces are tacked to both head and cantle, the lateral pieces tacked over the front part of the tree only. These lateral pieces are enormously important, for the *girth straps* (the straps that hold the saddle on the horse) will be stitched to them. Before putting on the webbing all the steel parts of the tree must be covered with leather. The edges of the lateral webbings are stitched together and then the whole of the rear part of the saddle covered with a tightly-stretched piece of waxed canvas.

Now the *bellies* have to be fastened to each side of the rear part of the saddle. These are leather pockets of shoulder hide (the saddler has to select exactly the right leather for every part of the saddle, see tanning and curing, p. 120) and in days of old they used to be stuffed with wool to make soft pads under the rider's buttocks.

Adding the Seat

The *seat* now has to be added. These days this tends to be of rubber rather than canvas stuffed with wool as it used to be. Probably rubber is better because it cannot lose its shape. The seat is glued to the webbing and the bellies, and is stuck down by rolling it with a rolling-pin.

A piece of serge cloth is stretched tightly over the seat and tacked down very tautly where it overlaps underneath the wood of the tree. This I might say, after watching the process, is much easier said than done. It must be dead tight and have no creases.

Next comes the *blocking* of the seat, which means shaping the piece of leather that we actually sit on. This should be of pigskin and it is a sign of the poverty of our times that there are actually machines for impressing a pattern on cowhide to make it look like pigskin. It is sad that the Western manner of dealing with a pig causes the skin – one of the finest materials that there is – to be turned into pork crackling, to break people's teeth, or to bacon rind which is mostly thrown away. The Chinese fortunately are no such fools and carefully skin their pigs, and it is from China that our pigskin comes.

The pigskin is soaked and then tacked into position, but not too tightly for the tacks will have to be withdrawn. The pigskin is then boned out to smooth it and left to dry. But we have not finished with the seat just yet.

Skirts, Girths and Flaps

Next come the *skirts*. These are the two stiff and thick components that extend the seat laterally up near the pommel of the saddle. They are built up with pigskin, other pieces of leather, and canvas, and are stitched to the seat with a *welt* between the two components. The welt is a piece of cord with very thin (*skived*) leather sewn round it like a piece of sausage skin. The seat is removed from the saddle while this operation is done and it is an operation demanding great skill, for the correct marrying of these two skirts with the seat can make or mar the whole saddle. The seat is then wetted again and *set*, that is pulled on to the tree, very tightly, and this time tacked for good.

The girth straps are stitched on next. This process is very important because if the stitching goes the rider goes too and may break his or her neck. Saddlers, incidentally, roll up their own threads, twisting and waxing several strands of best hemp twine together.

Then the *flaps* have to be prepared. These are the very big pieces of leather that hang down each side of the saddle and take the pressure from the rider's knees. The leading edges of both flaps have to be blocked, wetted and tacked down on a board on which is nailed a block shaped exactly like the knee-roll, the raised ridge that restrains the rider's knee. When in position the flap must be allowed to dry naturally. A folded strip of panel hide is stitched round the front of the flap to reinforce it and the flap is

Saddler's Clamp
The traditional harness maker's clamp (see p. 123) is a free-standing affair grasped between the knees while you sit on a suitable stool. Some saddle makers have a heavier duty clamp combined with a stool and operated by foot pressure on a treadle.

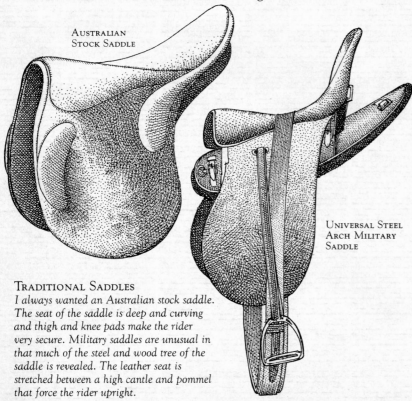

AUSTRALIAN STOCK SADDLE

UNIVERSAL STEEL ARCH MILITARY SADDLE

Traditional Saddles
I always wanted an Australian stock saddle. The seat of the saddle is deep and curving and thigh and knee pads make the rider very secure. Military saddles are unusual in that much of the steel and wood tree of the saddle is revealed. The leather seat is stretched between a high cantle and pommel that force the rider upright.

GREEK PACK SADDLE

MOROCCAN SADDLE

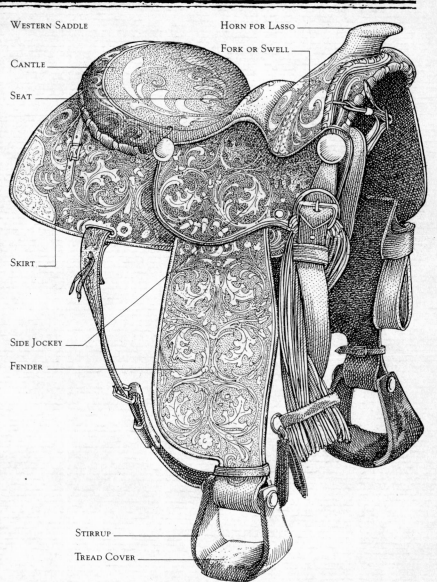

WESTERN SADDLE

HORN FOR LASSO

FORK OR SWELL

CANTLE

SEAT

SKIRT

SIDE JOCKEY

FENDER

STIRRUP

TREAD COVER

tacked and nailed with saddle nails to the tree and stitched to webs. This, of course, is done on both sides of the saddle.

MAKING THE PANEL

Now the saddler has completed what I would call the top saddle, he has to make the *panel*, or under saddle, which comes in contact with the horse. The panel is, if anything, more complicated than the top part of the saddle, with 11 leather and canvas components of strange shapes and various sizes. Basically it is two sheets of leather sewn together and stuffed with wool, which fits underneath the tree, to act as a cushion between the tree and the horse, just as the top part of the saddle acts as a cushion between the tree and the rider. When the panel is made, the *points* (the ends of the head or pommel, extended by flaps of leather) are pushed into little leather

pockets which have been stitched on to the panel, and the panel laced to the seat.

It is inconceivable that anyone could design the modern saddle from scratch without the thousands of years of experience that have moulded it. And then there are so many different sorts of saddle, from donkey pack saddles, which are still a part of day-to-day life in the less industrialized parts of the world, to ornately tooled Western saddles made for sitting in all day that remind me of the long hours I have spent on horseback. If anyone is interested in what happened to the ostrich-egg-sized boil that I introduced at the start of this article, well, I had to stand in the stirrups until, suddenly, my horse put his hoof in a meercat hole and – bang – down I went, experiencing a feeling that seemed like sitting on a red-hot poker. But it did the trick for, blessed relief, the boil was burst.

EXOTIC SADDLES

The saddle maker's art has developed along sharply contrasting lines in different parts of the world. In northern Africa and southern Europe, saddles are still made using a heavy wooden frame which remains evident even when the saddle is padded and decorated. The heavy Western saddle is often highly decorated with tooling of the leather parts (gouging and cutting the leather surface). The maker also adds a deal of ornamental metal work that increases the weight of the saddle further. It amazes me how comfortable Western trail horses appear – I am sure the length and width of such saddles help to spread the load.

MAKING HORSE COLLARS

ATCH A HEAVY HORSE PULLING A plough, if you are lucky enough to find a farm that still uses horses, or a dray horse delivering beer barrels, and the first thing you notice is how well suited the horse is to pull a heavy load. But look closely, and you will notice that it is the rigid collar that is taking the strain, putting the load evenly across the horse's shoulders rather than on its neck and windpipe. It all looks so simple, yet the horse collar is a comparatively recent invention.

CAMELS, OXEN AND HORSES

It was not until around AD500 that a camel-driver in China first harnessed his beast of burden with a fixed, rigid collar, and the invention, adapted by the Mongols for the horse, did not arrive in Europe for quite some centuries. Previously, horses had been put in *breast plate* harness (see p. 122), or had been yoked to their loads, rather like oxen, the throat-straps of the yoke cutting into their windpipes, or had been harnessed with a soft collar around the neck that tightened with use. Such arrangements severely restricted the work the horse could do, and prevented it replacing the ox as the main draught animal used in farming. The Romans even had a law to protect their horses, which prevented a pair from pulling a load in excess of about half a ton, which a modern dray horse can do by itself with ease. But once equipped with a rigid collar, the horse came into its own, and it was this that allowed the agricultural revolution of the Middle Ages to take place, and encouraged the industrial one of the eighteenth and nineteenth centuries by releasing manpower from the land to run the ever-expanding factories.

MAKING THE FOREWALE

Horse collars are made by saddlers, usually those who specialize in making *black saddlery*, the saddler's term for harnesses and the like. The collar is made of the *forewale* and the *body*, which are then joined together.

The forewale is simply a long strip of leather sewn into a tube, with one edge of the seam extending well beyond the other to make a flap, known as the *barge*. This tube is then stuffed tight with rye straw, wool flock or even horsehair. Whatever the material, the stuffing is rammed hard into the wale with an iron rod, and when tightly packed in, the wale is placed over a wooden model of the horse's withers, on which the collar is eventually to sit. There it is beaten into shape with a mallet. If the collar is closed at its ends, as is usual, the two ends of the wale are sewn together, otherwise they are left apart. Open collars are only used for those horses, like heavy horses or donkeys, that have exceptionally large heads and do not take kindly to having collars put on. These collars are simply pried apart, slipped over the head of the horse, and then clamped shut with straps and buckles. Closed collars are put on upside down, so that the widest part of the collar passes over the broadest part of the head, and are then turned the right way up and pushed down the neck into position.

PARTS OF THE COLLAR

A horse collar is in three parts, the leather wale and the body, both stuffed tight with either rye straw or wool flock, and the metal hames, fitting snugly into a groove on either side of the collar. The largest collars have a raised leather shield behind the tops of the hames called the housen. Folded back, it stops rain trickling down a horse's withers.

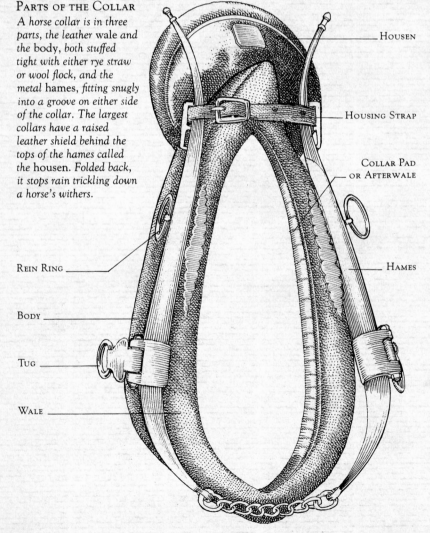

HOUSEN

HOUSING STRAP

COLLAR PAD OR AFTERWALE

HAMES

REIN RING

BODY

TUG

WALE

MAKING THE BODY

The next stage is to make the body. For this the saddler cuts out a broad strip of leather and stitches it to the barge, together with one edge of a strip of heavy woolen cloth. Then taking straw or whatever padding is being used, he encloses it in the leather and cloth at the throat of the collar, stitching around from the throat to the neck, stuffing and shaping as he goes. After all the stuffing, stitching and shaping necessary to produce exactly the right collar for the breed of horse in hand, the maker sews on a piece of soft leather called the *afterwale* to stop the collar rubbing on the neck of the horse.

THE HAMES

The final job is to attach the *hames*. These are the tubular arms that fit either side of the collar in the groove between wale and body to which the traces and reins are attached. Once the hames were made of hardwood, but now they are of brass-plated steel. At their top is a pair of rings which takes the housing strap that clamps the collar together. Below them are the rein rings through which the reins pass on their way from the harness to the driver's hands, and below them are the two *tugs*, one each side. These are rings that take the chains that lead to the *traces*, the leather straps by which the horse pulls its load.

Much of this work is detailed and precise, for the collar must fit its intended horse perfectly. There should be just enough room to place a hand between the bottom of the collar and the horse's wind-pipe. If it is too tight, the horse cannot breathe, too loose, and it will rub its neck raw. Yet few measurements are made by the saddler – he prefers to work by eye.

THE RUSH COLLAR

One unusual collar I have come across is the rush collar. These are rarely made today, and I have never yet met a man who can make one. They are made of plaited rush weave, the ends of rush bound together and the centres frayed with a metal comb so that further lengths of rush can be worked into the fibres to pad the collar out. The whole length is then bound tight with a three-inch wide plait, and the ends joined together. A rough cover made of burlap, or some such material, is sewn round the whole structure, and the collar is then ready for use – as a strong but light collar used for young colts unwilling to accept the heavier affair.

SHAPING THE WALE

STUFFING THE COLLAR
Long straw fillers were harness makers who specialized in nothing else but putting the stuffing in horse collars. They preferred to use long rye straw, although wheat straw would do, wetting the straw and leather to make them supple enough to work with. A filler would complete three collars a day.

THE WALE AND THE BODY
Once the wale has been sewn and stuffed, it is beaten into shape over a wooden mould. The saddler then stitches on the body, sewing the leather to the barge, the loose flap of leather that forms part of the wale. All this is done by hand and eye, and few measurements are taken.

BOOT & SHOEMAKING

N africa in the 1930s, i had to make my own shoes, because if I didn't, I didn't have any. The shoes were called *veldschoenen*, which is Afrikaans for field shoes. They were fashioned out of the leather made by soaking hides in copper sulphate solution.

They were the simplest things in the world to make. You got a fairly tough piece of leather, placed your foot on it and drew the outline. You then drew another line half an inch outside the first one, cut the shape out with a knife, and you had your sole. A more flexible leather was used for the uppers, which were sewn to the sole.

North American Indians have a far more sensible way of making shoes or *moccasins*. They simply bend a piece of rawhide into the complete shape of a foot, sides and all, stitch it through to one or more sole pieces, and then add a top piece that encloses the toes and outstep. I have worn Indian moccasins. They are marvelously comfortable and, as the piece of hide that goes round your foot is all one piece, watertight.

SACRED BOOTS

To meet a real boot maker I went to Crete. Boots are almost sacred objects to a Cretan man, like the dagger he wears on festive occasions. These boots are of black leather, made carefully to measure, and come nearly to the knee. They last 20 years and are worn every day. A pair costs about $60.

High up on a Cretan mountain is the village of Angia and here at least two boot makers ply their craft. One of these, Mihalis Roditis, who has been a boot maker for 40 years, told me that he fails to make a sufficient living these days, not because of competition from factory-made boots but because of better roads. The mountain men are now more apt to travel in cars and their boots last longer!

It would take Mihalis two days to make a pair of boots if he did nothing else. He went to endless trouble to show me how to make a pair. When a customer came he would draw the outline of his feet on a piece of leather. He measured the height the boot should be, the circumference of the ankle and leg in various places – six measurements in all. He then made paper patterns and cut out the different pieces of

THE SHOEMAKER'S TOOLS

Shoemakers require a considerable number of hand tools for their trade, for a shoe is a very complicated item to make. The only nails are in the heel, the rest of the shoe being stitched together through holes already prepared by an awl. The leather is cut to shape with a variety of different knives depending on its quality and use, and is glazed and burnished with special irons. The pieces of leather that make up the heel are finally trimmed with a heel shave. Seat and fudge wheels are used to score the leather, which is moulded to the sole with a waist iron.

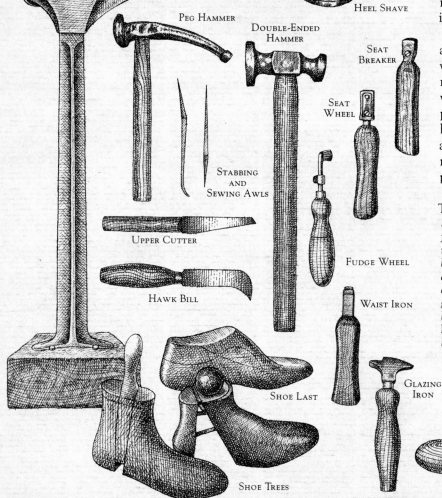

COBBLER'S LAST

PEG HAMMER

DOUBLE-ENDED HAMMER

HEEL SHAVE

SEAT BREAKER

SEAT WHEEL

STABBING AND SEWING AWLS

UPPER CUTTER

FUDGE WHEEL

HAWK BILL

WAIST IRON

SHOE LAST

GLAZING IRON

SHOE TREES

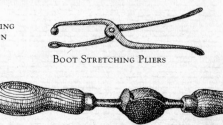

BOOT STRETCHING PLIERS

BURNISHING IRON

leather. There are five patterns for the uppers of the boot: *psidi* (toe-cap), *kalami* (vamp or front), *fittet* (the two lacing panels) and *fterna* (quarters or heel).

The uppers were sewn together, three times by sewing machine then once more by hand, then a canvas lining was made to match. Mihalis had dozens of *lasts* and he chose the right pair to suit his customers' patterns. Now the last is a wooden foot to which the maker tacks the *insole* (leather cut to the shape of the outline of the foot). Last and insole are then pushed down into the embryo boot, the boot turned upside down, and the sole of the last becoming the maker's working platform as he makes the boot. Both the lining and the leather of the uppers have to be pulled hard to overlap the insole – "as tight as glass" were Mihalis's words. When satisfied he tacked the uppers and lining to the last through the insole – all the steel tacks used were removed once they were replaced by stitching.

The thing about stitching the sole of a boot to the uppers is that you cannot get your hand inside the boot to sew, and stitches inside the boot would be very uncomfortable anyway. The solution, as Mihalis showed me, is to use a curved needle, to stitch the uppers only part way into the insole, then to join a strip of leather to the insole and uppers that can be stitched to the sole proper from the outsides of the boot only. This strip is called *vardoulo* in Greek, *welt* in English. Mihalis attached the welt and indeed the sole itself with wooden tacks called *sites*. These were permanent and were first hammered home then rasped flush. Before stitching sole to welt, Mihalis cut a slanting groove around the sole that he could stitch into and so protect the stitches. After stitching, he stuck back the leather cut from the groove to protect the stitches even more. The only place where steel tacks were used for permanent fixing was in the heel which was made with thick pieces of hard leather, called *lifts* in English.

WEST END BESPOKE TRADE

There is a street in London's Soho called Meard Street. It is not the sort of place you would let your unaccompanied daughter wander down. There I was introduced to the bespoke shoe trade by Mr. Bill Bird of the firm of H. Peen, tree and last makers. For just £600, you can have a pair of boots made to your exact measurements. This includes the wooden lasts on which the

boots are made. These are stored by the shoemakers so that in 30 years' time when your boots wear out (they should last this long) the maker can build another pair. The price also includes a pair of *trees*, which you put inside your boots every time you take them off. These are exactly the same size and shape as the lasts and prevent your boots from wrinkling. It is the wrinkles that form in neglected shoes which collect injurious dampness and acids that rot the leather. Bill Bird told me, "they were born on the last and they are reborn on the tree."

As well as the tree and last makers, there are *clickers*, the foremen shoemakers who cut out the leather (the noise of cutting gives them their name), and distribute the work; *closers*, who trim and sew the uppers; and *makers*, who add the soles and heels. It is highly skilled work and there are few people left now who can do it.

THE VILLAGE COBBLER
Sitting on his specially made low stool while he worked, the cobbler was once a familiar sight in every village. When I was a boy there were still boot makers in East Anglia, and they would make a pair of boots for two weeks' wages of a farm laborer. At that time a laborer received 30 shillings a week, so a pair of boots would cost him £3.

—131—

CLOG MAKING

PROTECTOR OF FEET
At one time the clog maker shod the working feet of most fellow villagers. He would keep paper patterns of his customers' foot sizes and provide long-lasting and comfortable footwear. Attaching an iron ferrule, as below, protected the edge of the wooden sole from wear and preserved the sole thickness almost indefinitely.

 S FAR AS I KNOW, CLOGS SUCH AS the Dutch, Belgians and northern French still wear, which are made out of one piece of wood, were never popular in the British Isles. If you go to a Dutch cattle market you will generally see a clog seller with some hundreds of new wooden clogs (known as *klompen* in Dutch) and a pile of worn-out clogs beside him. Farmers come up, shuffle off their worn-out clogs, which are added to the pile, buy a new pair and depart newly shod and well pleased. The clog maker presumably doesn't have to buy any firewood.

Dutch clogs are usually cut from willow, roughly to size with a cross-cut saw, froe and bench-knife, then hollowed out with a special machine that drills out the interior wood (see opposite) and hand-finished with specially shaped chisels. I wore a pair for years while working round the garden. Once your feet get used to them they are very comfortable – but you cannot run in them. Or at least I could not.

The British clog, found chiefly in the north of England and in Wales, is another kettle of fish. I have a pair that I have worn for 10 years and which still could be re-furbished to extend their life even further. They have wooden soles but leather uppers. They are excellent if you are on your feet a lot, as the well-shaped wooden sole gives great support. Furthermore, they are ideal for working in such places as dairies, mills, slaughterhouses or similar locations, where the floors are apt to be stone, hard, cold and often damp. They are warm to wear and healthy, and the next time I look into Carmarthen Cattle Mart I shall seek out Mr. Luther Edwards and buy another pair.

Mr. Edwards lives at Cynwyl Elfed, just north of Carmarthen town, and is one of the very few Welsh clog makers left. He is

ATTACHING THE UPPERS
After the uppers have been cut out and stitched, the clog maker grips the leather with lasting pincers and pulls it over the last (1). When shaping is complete, the uppers are placed over the sole (2) and secured in the rebate with tacks. A welt (leather strip) is then tacked around the rebate (3) and a brass toe plate added (4).

getting on in years now but still very active and productive, and he supplies clogs to quite a large clientele of discriminating farmers. He has no apprentice and says that boys do not want to work hard any more.

THEN AND NOW

Mr. Edwards served a four-and-a-half-year apprenticeship to an orthodox boot maker and another year and a half to a clog maker before he felt ready to start making clogs on his own. He cuts all his own wood, preferring maple, although many of the old clog makers used the less expensive alder – about the only thing alder was good for. In times of old, *cloggers* were men who made a living by going into the wild wet alder woods of west Wales, felling trees, cross-cutting them into clog lengths, riving the logs with the froe, and then rough-shaping the pieces right there in the woods. Each man had his own portable bench with a *stock* or *bench-knife* hooked to it. You can obtain great leverage with the bench-knife and it will cut through any piece of wood you can get under it. The step of the heel would be sawn with a hand saw then cut out to the sawmark with a drawknife. The steeply bent shape of the bottom of the sole would be cut with the bench-knife. The rebate that runs right round the sole to take the upper would next be cut by hand using a *gripping knife*, which works like the bench-knife but has a gouge-like blade. The soles would then be stacked in neat piles to season. *Clogging*, however, is a distinctly different craft from clog making (see p. 32).

Nowadays, Mr. Edwards fells trees on his neighbors' lands, cross-cuts the trunks on the spot and takes them back to his workshop to shape. He does the job in exactly the same way as the cloggers of old. The next stage of clog making is attaching the leather uppers to the shaped wooden sole.

Depending on the design of the clog, the upper can be made from either one, two or three pieces of leather. Clogs for women or children often have a one-piece upper fastened with a single button. A more usual arrangement consists of two pieces of leather and a clasp fastener. One piece of leather is used to form the front and tongue while the second piece is for the back and sides. The first step is to mark out on the leather the size and design for the particular clog. A village clog maker would once have had paper patterns for most of his customers' feet. The leather is then cut out with a *clicking knife* (see p. 130) and, for extra comfort, the inside edge round the ankle area may be thinned before the pieces are stitched together. Next the uppers are fitted over a wooden last, a wooden replica of the human foot, pulled into position with *lasting pincers* and tacked securely to the last itself. A hot *burnishing iron* may be rubbed over the leather to help shape it permanently. Shaping complete, the uppers are removed from the last and placed on the clog, with the leather fitting into the sole rebate. The maker then tacks the uppers to the sole before adding a *welt* or strip of leather right round the rebate secured with brass and steel tacks.

WOODEN CLOGS

The clogs worn for centuries in countries like Holland, where they are called *klompen*, and France, where they are known as *sabots*, differ from the common British clog in that they are made entirely from one piece of wood, without leather uppers. The French *sabot* is, in fact, where our English word "sabotage" comes from. The connection isn't really that obscure when you realize that the French workers, during the late nineteenth century, used their *sabots* to damage machinery as a form of industrial protest. Modern clogs are shaped using traditional tools, such as the special gouge you can see being used on the left. The finished clogs are then stacked and left to season, right. In Holland you might easily see wonderfully colorful, hand-painted and decorated clogs used on special occasions.

FINISHED CLOGS
STACKED AND SEASONING

KNIFE MAKING

IT IS HARD TO SEE HOW MEN COULD survive without knives, and when I was a boy I was always told by countrymen older and wiser than I was that I should never be without "a shilling, a shut-knife and a piece of string". But when it came to finding a knife maker, outside the huge factories of, for example, Sheffield, I had to go to some strange places. I went, for instance, to the slopes of Mount Idi, in Crete. To a little village very high up, called Zoniana. Zoniana means "the god of the gods' village". Zeus was born in a cave nearby you see.

The true Cretan man must have his dagger, which he sticks into the front of his cummerbund on all festive occasions and carries in its scabbard at his side while working or up in the mountains. He is not content with a factory-made product.

Anastasios Parasiris is the last knife-maker in Zoniana and he is over 80 now. He told me, quite simply, that he would not be making knives for much longer because soon he would die – something he did not seem at all worried by. He still made me a knife and I learned that all is not lost for the knife-users of Crete, however, for his 12-year-old grandson is already learning the craft from him.

THE FRENCH TECHNIQUE
The knife makers of Thiers in France, lie on wide planks over their water-powered and water-lubricated grindstones. In this way they can get more purchase against the wheel, and the planks protect them from the heavy spray of water that shoots off the spinning wheels.

KNIFE MAKERS NEED SMITHS

Besides being a knife maker, Anastasios has always been a shepherd and still owns a flock of sheep. He took to knife making to augment his income. His workshop is a small dark dusty room, with an electric grinder in it, an electric pillar drill, and a bench with some simple tools. He works in league with the village blacksmith who roughly forges and tempers the blade.

I watched the blacksmith forging a knife blank from an old truck spring. He heated it red hot, cut it roughly to shape on the *hardie*, a chisel head fixed in the anvil (see p. 70), took a heat again, then rough-shaped the blade on the anvil with the hammer. He did not take much trouble with tempering the blade at this stage, putting in the final temper after Anastasios had fashioned it.

Anastasios did most of the blade shaping on the electric grinder. As he ground he continually dipped the blade in water to stop it getting too hot. He made the blade with a *tang*, or handle, and he shaped the metal in the manner preferred by Cretan villagers. After this he drilled three holes in the tang with the electric drill. I asked him what he had done before he had got electricity and he showed me a hand-turned grinder and said his son used to turn the handle, before he grew into the village schoolmaster. He also showed me a drill which you pushed against the work with your chest and caused to rotate by means of a bow, the string of which made several turns round the rotating part of the drill.

FINAL TEMPERING

The blade went back to the blacksmith for its final tempering. He moulded a pad of clay into exactly the same profile as the curved edge of the blade, took a heat with the latter, then plunged the edge only into the damp clay. Thus the cutting edge only was tempered hard while the spine of the knife was left with a softer temper. With this treatment the blade would take a good edge and keep it, while the knife itself flexible enough not to snap with heavy use.

Anastasios then took the blade back and buffed it well with cloth discs spinning on the grinder, the edges of the discs dressed with emery powder, and then what looked to me like knife polish, and then he fitted

the handle. This, in the case of my knife, is two pieces of olive wood, carefully and elegantly shaped, and riveted through the tang of the blade with three rivets. He then put a final edge on the blade, gave it a final buffing and the knife was complete.

THE SCABBARD

The scabbard couldn't be simpler. It is made of two pieces of willow cut into such shapes that, if put together, enclosed the knife blade comfortably. He then glued them together, wrapped a strip of thin steel around the open end and soldered the two ends together. He banged three small nail-holes in each side of the strip so that the resulting burrs in the metal penetrated the wood a fraction to prevent the strip sliding off, cut a groove round the scabbard at the pointed end and twisted a piece of copper wire round this. It is by far the best knife I have ever had, and when I took it to a black-smith friend of mine in Ireland, he tested it and pronounced it an excellent blade.

Anastasios showed me a whole collection of antique knives he has, all of them made in the time when the Turks occupied the island. Many had flamboyant handles made from ivory, or bone, or rams' horn. These knives, he said, belonged to Crete.

FRENCH KNIFE MAKING

To see a more organized, but still small-scale knife-making industry, you can go, as

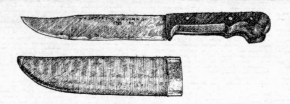

I did, to Thiers, in France. The blades are forged first from strip steel with a trip-hammer, which is driven by a waterwheel, and then by hand. The blades are tempered simply by plunging the blade into hot oil.

Grinding is done on water-driven sand-stone wheels. The grinder lies on a cushion on a plank set above the wheel, lying on his stomach and looking down over the spinning wheel below him. I noticed in old photographs that the workman's dog would often appear lying on the grinder's back. And lo and behold, on my visit, there was the grinder on his belly, and the dog on his back: a matey arrangement!

KNIFE FROM ZONIANA
This is a drawing of the knife and scabbard made for me on Crete, by a knife maker from the village of Zoniana. The blade is nearly seven inches long and holds a good edge. The handle, fitted either side of the same steel as the blade (the tang), is of beautiful dark olive wood, while the scabbard is made of willow.

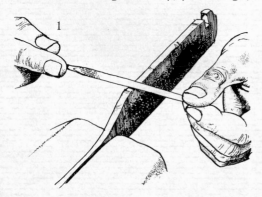

FITTING THE HANDLE TO A HUNTING KNIFE
Knives like my Cretan knife and those from Thiers, like the one made here, are particularly strong because blade and handle are fashioned from the same piece of steel. Once the blade has been roughly tempered and ground to shape, the knife maker shapes the tang (1), the section of steel that forms the core of the handle. He then drills the tang (with an ancient hand drill if he is a knife maker from Thiers, 2) so that the hand pieces can be riveted in place (3).

MILLSTONE DRESSING

ILLSTONES, WHETHER TURNED BY water or by wind, wear as they grind and their grinding surfaces have to be *dressed* periodically, that is recut so that they grind efficiently again. A pair of stones working full time (10 hours a day) grinding corn probably have to be dressed about once every 10 days, if made of Derbyshire Millstone Grit, but at longer intervals, perhaps three weeks or a month, if of the quartz-like stone that French millstones, or *burrs*, were hewn from. British stones tend to be monolithic, cut from a single piece of material, while the French stones were more usually constructed from shaped and faced segments bound with iron. Towards the end of the nineteenth century *composition stones* came into use, which were harder still and made from a bond of cement and stone chips. Obviously, for a working miller dependent on the turning of his stones to make a living, the less he had to dress his stones the better. For while they were being dressed they were out of action and – unless he employed a man to do his dressing for him – so was he. A big mill with four pairs of stones would seldom have had more than three of them working at any time.

KNOWING THE STONE

Mr. Sid Ashdown, who now lives in retirement (or semi-retirement) at Cross-in-hand in the Weald of Sussex, was a windmiller all his working life, and he is still called on frequently to go and dress the stones of the few stone mills that are still working. The number of working mills is growing in the British Isles, as it happens, as more and more people are rebelling against the wrapped-sliced-pap that modern milling and bread factory techniques turn out and are insisting, again, on bread. In this country, campaigners for real bread are marching alongside those for real ale.

The dressing of millstones is a very difficult art. It is not simply a matter of picking out the grooves so as to deepen them. For one thing, the wear on a pair of stones is not even – it is greater near the circumference than at the center. This problem is corrected by marking the stone with *staff*, *jack-stick* and red ocher. The jack-stick is a wooden gauge, part of which fits through the hole in the *bed stone* (the lower one), while the other part sweeps the face of the stone and shows the dresser how much he has to remove from the stone nearer the center to make up for the greater wear nearer the outer edge. Most millstone dressers would lay a penny coin on the stone near the center after they had worked on the stone. They would run the jack-stick around again and make sure that it cleared

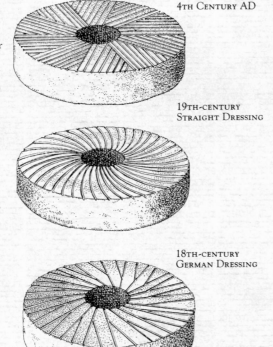

DRESSING PATTERNS
The science of grinding corn is as old as the hills. Through its history millers have altered the patterns of furrows and lands (the channels and raised grinding edges respectively) for more efficient grinding. But it is marvelous to think that the pattern of dressing that you are likely to see now is almost identical to the dressing found on Roman millstones. The breast, or milling surface of the stone is divided into sectors of furrows called quarters *or* harps, *because they are shaped like harps.*

ROMAN DRESSING
4TH CENTURY AD

19TH-CENTURY
STRAIGHT DRESSING

18TH-CENTURY
GERMAN DRESSING

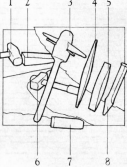

DRESSING TOOLS
1 Sledge hammer 2 Wedge
for supporting upturned
runner stone 3 Thrifts –
wooden handle that holds
interchangeable mill bills
and picks 4 Mill pick
5 Mill bill 6 Hand
hammer 7 Sharpening file
8 Chisel.

the penny, showing that their dressing compensated for the extra wear that would occur toward the outer edge.

The staff is merely a straight-edge. It is smeared with red ocher and then passed over the stone. Any areas of the stone that are standing proud show up as red and can then be taken down level. This process is called *proving the stone*.

Next comes *knocking it down*. This is achieved either with the *flat bill* or *mill bill*, which looks very similar to a miniature adze or, if only a little stone has to be taken off, by rubbing it with a *rub stone*, which is an old piece of French burr stone. The tools used by the millstone dresser may look clumsy and crude, but in the hands of a skilled craftsman they are capable of producing very delicate work.

Then, if necessary, the furrows in the stone have to be deepened with a tool called the *pick*. In the case of Peak Stone (with the apt geological name of Millstone Grit), which is softer than French burr, you would probably have to do this every time the stone was dressed. The depth of these furrows is important as it is the device by which the meal is expelled around the circumference of the stone.

DRESSING THE LANDS
Now the *lands* have to be dressed. These are the pieces of high ground between the furrows or grooves. In the case of French burrs this operation is called *cracking*, and consists of cutting out tiny furrows in the face of the stone as close together as you can get them without actually breaking in to each other. In the case of Peak stone the operation is known as *stitching* and in this, tiny peck-marks are made all over the face of the stone. If this cracking or stitching is not done, the stones do not cut the *bran* away cleanly from the wheat. The outer skin of the grain kernel is called the bran and it is the roughest, most fibrous part. It makes extremely good and healthy food for all stock, from guinea pigs to horses, if you can obtain it nowadays. It is sieved out of the *meal* – the term for what comes out from the millstones.

Recently, of course, the importance of bran in our own diet has been rediscovered, after years of eating over processed, fiber-free foods, and lots of people are experimenting with bran-full diets. A finer sieve removes the next coarsest extraction, called *middlings* or *sharps*. If the flour that is left is 80 per cent of the original weight of the

AMERICAN
POST MILL

ENGLISH
TOWER MILL

GERMAN
STOCK MILL

wheat it is called *standard flour. White flour* is only 75 per cent of the total original weight. But this is by the way.

THE WORKING LIFE OF A STONE

A Peak stone, working full time, would last anywhere from 20 to 25 years. When new, the *runner stone* (the top stone that revolves) would be perhaps a foot thick. The stationary bed stone would be 15 inches thick. The bed stones would wear out first, and these would be replaced by the runner stones, so the miller only had the expense of replacing the runner stones each time. Fifty years ago one stone, unbound and undressed, would cost about £8 delivered to the mill. Bound, that is with an iron hoop right round it, and also with *the work put in* (meaning with the initial furrows of the milling surface cut), a pair of stones would cost about £20. Normally the stones would come in the raw state from the quarry (just cut into the round) to a firm like the Silex Works, on the Isle of Dogs in London, where they would dress them or *set them out*.

The hole in the middle of a stone, where the grain enters, is called the *eye*. A heavy hooped iron bar goes across the eye of the runner stone and this is engaged by the *driver* or *mace*, which is the piece of the mechanism that turns it. A new runner stone alone probably weighs the best part of a ton so you can imagine that the supporting structure has to be massive. It is also important that the stones do not *run dry*, that is turn without grain between them.

WORKING ON A BEDSTONE
Millstones are pretty uncomfortable things to work on. The classic working pose involves kneeling over a softening sack with one hand controlling the fall of the bill very precisely. The projection in the middle of the stone is called the mace *(see diagram below).*

Damage is done to the stone faces if the supply of grain stops while the runner stone is in motion, for the grain acts as a lubricant to the stone.

It takes an experienced dresser two days to dress a pair of stones, so in a mill with four pairs of stones, dressing was pretty much a full time occupation, and many dressers were needed in the heyday of traditional milling. Harder modern composition stones need less regular dressing but even so, the increasing popularity of traditional milling must swell the numbers of dressers again, many of whom will have to learn the craft from scratch.

POWER SOURCES
Milling on a local scale could be totally self-sufficient again, the mills being powered by wind or water. Examples of windmills are shown above and the beautifully simple mechanism of a watermill is shown right. Although the stones weigh several tons, they are a small part of the workings of a mill. More than one pair of stones is necessary, each with its own gearing that can be engaged or disengaged into the great spur wheel.

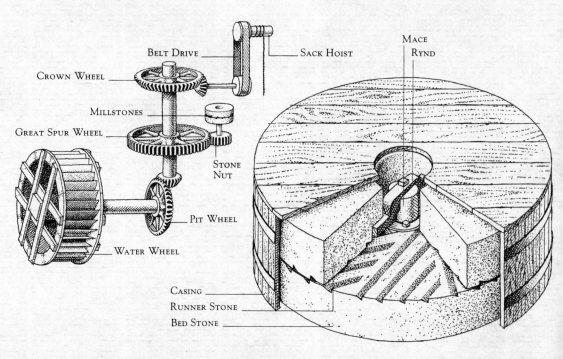

BELT DRIVE

CROWN WHEEL

MILLSTONES

GREAT SPUR WHEEL

STONE NUT

PIT WHEEL

WATER WHEEL

SACK HOIST

MACE
RYND

CASING
RUNNER STONE
BED STONE

STICKS & CROOKS

DIFFERENCE BETWEEN YOUNG MEN of today and those of the time when I was one, is that we used to carry walking sticks. We didn't use them to help us to walk: we could walk quite well in those days. We carried them jauntily and, if they were the type with crooked handles, spun them round like the sail of a windmill.

I used to scorn sticks bought in shops and cut my own. I would search the hedges for ash plants, which had to be dead straight, the right thickness (they were never peeled), and have a nice knob on the end. The knob was nice to grasp and I had a belief that I could use it on the head of a transgressor if necessary. But although I used to effect a distain for the shop-bought stick with that bent-over handle, I used to wonder how they were made.

I found out one day in a strange wood in Sussex. It contained thousands of young ash saplings all twisted in an extraordinary manner into the shape of walking sticks. Many had templates of iron strapped to them to ensure that they grew straight and that the crooks were in the right place. I had come across a walking stick farm.

SHEPHERDS' CROOKS

I was introduced to shepherds' crooks on the Romney Marsh when I worked as an assistant to a *looker*, the local word for a shepherd. My looker had a fine white beard, a gentle and faithful dog, and a large *crozier* or crook. The crook had a long pole and was wide enough in the *bite* for it to go round a sheep's chest. The crook itself was made of wrought iron. My looker told me that Marsh crooks were made big like this so that you caught a sheep by the chest and not its hind leg because small wounds caused by nicking the leg would fester.

In Wales, where I next saw crooks, I found they were small things made to fit the hind leg of a sheep. The best of them are carved out of a single piece of wood – again an ash or thorn plant with a good stool to its base. In Wales, too, there are fancy crooks, highly decorated, with running dogs carved in the handle or very often leaping salmon. The one-piece models can be used for sheep, but those with stuck-on handles are ceremonial or for the tourists.

TYPES OF CROOKS AND STICKS
Most country folk use walking sticks more as ornamentation than as an aid to mobility. The group of four below gives some idea of the variety available. Crooks, on the other hand, are working tools, invaluable to the shepherd. The two on the right are made of ram's horn and their wide mouths are designed to catch sheep round the chest. The metal crook, far right, is known as a leg crook.

BLOCK

STICKS

SHANK

1   2   3   4

ONE-PIECE CROOKS
The strongest crook is made from one piece of wood – the shank growing from a thicker branch (1). Saw the sides of the block in line with the shank (2). Starting on the inside of the curve, use a bow-saw to remove surplus wood (3) and a file for the final shaping (4).

SHAPING THE HANDLE
Simple, elegant walking sticks can be fashioned from wood taken from well-established hedges. A variety of different woods can be used, including oak, maple, ash or hazel. In the photograph, left, you can see one method of shaping the handle – over a source of heat. This is a tricky process, because too much heat will scorch the wood.

CROOKS

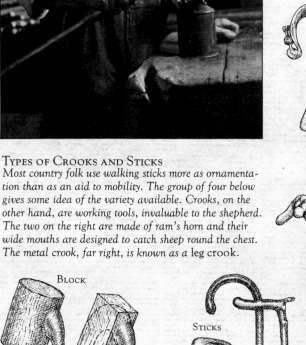

MAKING FIELD GATES

 NCE, THE VILLAGE CARPENTER was often hard at work making a wooden field gate for a local farmer. The carpenter's job was a skilled one, for sawn timber field gates were made to traditional local designs individual to various parts of the country. A good carpenter would add one or two details of construction that made the gate his own — an extra brace or decorative chamfers. Such gates were built to last, to withstand constant use as well as wind and weather.

Nowadays few gates are made in this way, for not only are there not many village carpenters left in business, but the coming of wide farm machinery such as combine harvesters has meant that many a beautiful wooden gate has been replaced by a wider, cheaper metal one. True, there are many machine-cut softwood gates made nowadays, pressure-treated with creosote to stop them rotting quite so quickly, but they are merely another sign of the deteriorating quality of our times.

HEREFORDSHIRE GATE
A few gate makers prefer to use cleft oak for parts of their gates. The craftsman, below, from Herefordshire, is such a one, and is seen here joining a slat, *or upright strap, to the top rail of a gate. The strong uprights at either end of the gate, the* heel *and the* head, *are of sawn wood so that the hinges and catch will align accurately.*

How Gates are Made

Good field gates should be constructed of heart of oak, or a wood which is similarly strong, such as chestnut. They measure up to 10 feet long and four feet high. The most important parts of a gate are the two uprights, one at the hinged end, called the *heel* or *harr*, to use its Scandinavian name, the other, thinner one, at the opening end, known as the *head*. Between these uprights are the top and bottom *rails*, with a number of *bars* in between. The total number of crossbars varies, according to the local design, from four to seven (a six-barred gate is the most common), but the lower bars are placed closer together to stop lambs slipping through. These crossbars are mortised into the uprights and made to fit tightly up and down, but not too tightly across for the carpenter might split the uprights at their most vulnerable point. Dowels are driven through the joints to ensure the bars stay firmly in place and there is a trick to this. The good carpenter deliberately drills the holes for the dowels so that the holes through the tenons are slightly off-line with the holes through the walls of the mortises. The effect is to draw the tenon even tighter into the mortise. When the crossbars are rammed home and the dowels driven in, considerable tension

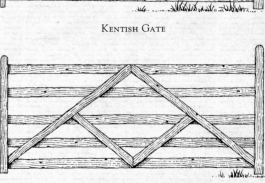

KENTISH GATE

DEVONSHIRE GATE

SOUTH EASTERN GATE

is created as the dowels have to find their way through the staggered holes.

Braces, or diagonal pieces, are used to prevent the gate sagging. Again, local custom determines the number and position of the diagonals, although the main brace always reaches from the bottom of the heel up to the top rail to counter the weight of the hanging gate. Upright straps can be fixed between the top and bottom rails of the gate in order to keep the crossbars firm and taut.

A very important part of the gate is the post it hangs from. Yew is the best wood for posts because it is the strongest, and if the post is tapered at the top it prevents water settling and rotting the wood. They are squared up by hewing with an axe, but only the visible part of the post above ground is so treated; that part below ground is left naturally rough. This makes for the securest possible fixing in the earth.

Riven Ash Gates

I have often made gates by nailing pieces of riven ash together, with no mortising and tenoning at all. The more important joints were bolted together. Of course, it was necessary to drill holes for the nails and bolts as otherwise the wood split. Ash gates made like this are very strong, but will only last for 20 years or so in the British climate and, obviously, they are primitive compared with the sawn oak gates made by the village carpenter of old.

Hardware

The iron furniture of the gate, such as hinges and hooks, is made by the blacksmith to be as strong as possible, for a gate weighs upwards of several hundred pounds. A gate is hung the same way as the rudder of a ship, with gudgeons or eyes driven into the *heel* of the gate that drop on to the *pintles* driven into the post. Latches come in many different designs, from a very simple hook and eye to complex wooden constructions and elaborate sprung devices easily opened from above by horseriders.

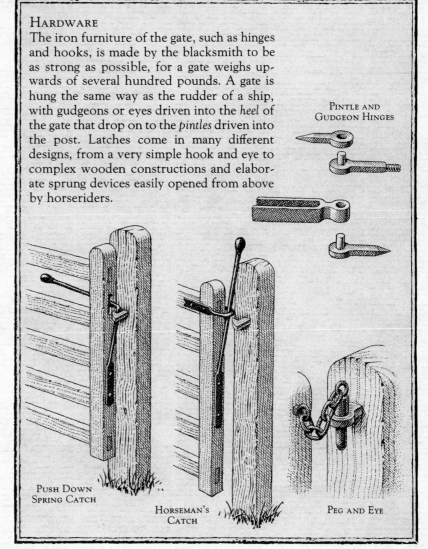

PINTLE AND GUDGEON HINGES

PUSH DOWN SPRING CATCH

HORSEMAN'S CATCH

PEG AND EYE

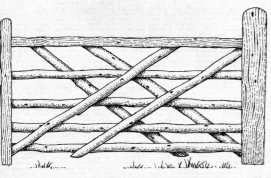

WELSH POLE GATE

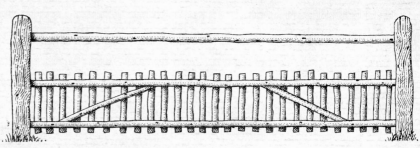

HINGELESS GATE FROM SUSSEX (HEAVED INTO PLACE)

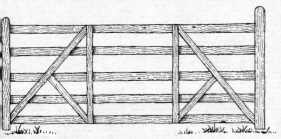

CAMBRIDGESHIRE GATE

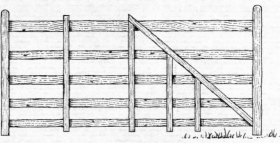

CAMBRIDGESHIRE GATE

POTTING

UST AFTER THE SECOND WORLD War I was cruising up the Yorkshire Ouse in my home, which happened to be a Dutch sailing barge at the time, when, near a village called Littlethorpe, I saw a sign by the riverside which read: "The Pottery". Following the sign I came to what I took to be one of the last surviving traditional potteries in England. Mr. Curtis, I am told, throws pots to this day in the traditional way and still fires them in two large old brick bottle kilns which, when I was there, he heated with coal. He dug his own clay from a pit behind his long brick shed.

Mr. Curtis tried to show me how to *throw* a pot – to turn a lump of clay into a vessel of sorts while it turned on a wheel. He took a big handful of clay and flung it hard down on his steel potter's wheel as near the center as he could. Splashing water over the clay he then cupped his hands over it and, exerting great pressure from both sides, let the clay spin between his palms until its eccentric motion ceased. This is *centering* the clay and is the most difficult thing about potting. If you cannot manage it you will never pot; if you can you have no problem. I might as well come out with it now: I cannot.

After the centering you can do any number of things with the clay. You can draw it up into a high cone; you can push it back down again; you can hollow it out with your fingers; in fact, you can turn it into any round shape that you like. After you stop spinning the wheel you can even pull it out of the round if you like. A good potter is

Pots for Everyday Use
Potting used to be a vital craft that provided earthenware vessels for everyday use. Many of the products, such as chimney- and flowerpots, were fired once only (biscuit ware). They were turned out in their thousands (above) to fixed sizes and shapes. Big, part-glazed storage crocks were similarly thrown on the potter's simple treadle wheel, as well as jugs and bowls of all sizes.

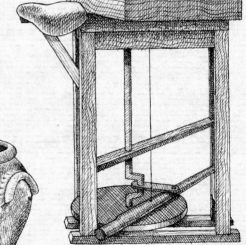

TREADLE KICK WHEEL

SIZE GAUGES

SHAPING TOOLS

TREADLE

STORAGE CROCKS

marvelous to watch, for potting is surely one of the most beautiful of the human skills still practiced.

Nowadays there is hardly a village in Northern Europe that does not have its *studio potter*. This person works inside a house or cottage, generally using an electric wheel (Mr. Curtis used an electric wheel too I recall), and firing (the vital hardening process of potting) in a small electric or gas-fired kiln. These kilns are so small (perhaps two or three cubic feet) that the pots studio potters fire must be small and worth a lot for their size. Both electricity and gas are expensive and to fire flower pots in such kilns (Mr. Curtis made most of his living from flower pots) would be quite un-economical. These potters, if they make a living at all, do it by the quality of their decoration. Nearly all of them buy their clay from centers like Stoke-on-Trent.

TRADITIONAL POTTERS TODAY

To find working potters nowadays who follow the old ways of one of the first and most basic of man's crafts, you must travel further afield. I found Mr. Yanis Atsonios at work in a very basic pottery in Marousi, a suburb of Athens. Yanis's father came from an island in the Cyclades (where *his* father had been a potter before him) in 1924

and set up in Marousi because the clay there was good and Athens was a ready market. Mr. Atsonios's work place is in a yard off a backstreet in what is now the ugly chaos of a modern suburb, but which was, only a couple of decades ago, an ancient and beautiful town on its own. There is a large open space in which stand huge piles of big unglazed pots – like most Greek potters Mr. Atsonios seldom uses glaze. The pots are of a beautiful light brick-red color and are of a dozen basic patterns and uses.

MIXING THE CLAY

In the middle of the yard is a *pug mill*, which in this case is a circular well, about six feet deep and five feet in diameter, with a steel paddle in it which is made to revolve by a small petrol engine. The paddle could easily have been powered by the once universal means of transport and power in the Mediterranean – the donkey – or indeed any draft beast. The clay, dug from a pit round the back, is thrown into the well, together with a lot of water, and worked with the paddle non-stop for about 24 hours. The local clay is red and Mr. Atsonios puts five wheelbarrow loads of this in his

FINISHING A JUG
After throwing, the jug is sliced off the wheel with a wire, and the rim pulled to make the pouring lip. A roll of clay is pulled to the correct length for a handle and attached to the body opposite the lip with plenty of slip (clay and water slurry). You then bend the other end round to join with the body.

THROWING A JUG
Once a lump of clay is centered on the wheel (that is, forced to spin symmetrically in the middle of the wheel), the skilled potter pushes down with the palm of his hand to open out the clay and create the thickness of the base (1). With the fingers of one hand controling the outside face, the fingers of the other hand start to form the rising wall of the embryo jug (2). It is magical to watch a potter using his knuckles and fingertips to pull the clay upwards and into the shape required (3 and 4).

pug mill together with five barrow loads of a white clay that he has to buy in to give the right consistency and color.

After the stirring is completed he pumps the liquid (for there is much more water than clay) through a screen, which removes any stones, and it runs into big open pans, some 20 feet square. These are just shallow depressions in the ground lined with brick. The water gradually drains away, leaving a layer of clay deposited about 10 inches thick. This is cut into cubes with a blade on a long handle. Mr. Atsonios says it is like cutting spinach pie.

WEDGING THE CLAY

The cubes are taken, when they're needed, into the long brick shed that serves as the wedging and throwing room. Here Mr. Atsonios and his assistant *wedge* the clay. This is a process known to all potters, traditional or otherwise, where the object is to expel any minute air bubbles which might be trapped in the clay. The smallest bubble will cause a damaging explosion in the kiln during firing. The potter simply takes the lump of clay to suit the work in hand, throws it down on to a firm, smooth surface and then repeatedly cuts through the clay with a wire to remove a section before banging it back into the main piece.

POTS FOR SMASHING

I saw Mr. Atsonios's assistant throwing pots about two feet high on an electric wheel. He worked with deftness and great speed, drawing the pot up until it was shaped rather like a huge egg with its rounded side down. To my surprise he closed the top

PUG MILLS
Potters do not simply dig clay and start throwing pots. The clay needs mixing with water and sieving. A pug mill has paddles that churn the clay and water in a well-like pit. The paddles are either driven by a draft beast, left, or they are powered through belts and pulleys.

DRYING BEDS
When the clay has been mixed thoroughly, it is pumped through sieves and into drying beds (outdoors in warm climates) to allow the water to drain. Then the clay can be divided up ready for wedging, shown opposite.

ATHENIAN POTS
The Athenian potter I visited made the big, unglazed pots, shown right. They were decorated by scratching into the clay before the pots were dried and fired.

completely, leaving no way into the pot nor any way out. "What," I asked, "is such a pot good for?" For answer the man took a knife and cut a tiny slot high up in the side of the pot, just large enough to take a coin.

"These are given to children," he explained. "Kind uncles put in money. When the child grows up he gets the money out."

"How?" I asked.

"By smashing the pot."

The newly thrown pots are dried indoors, for two days in the summer and 10 in the winter, and then put outside in the sun. After a few days they are put in the kiln.

A Strange Use of Nut Shells

The kiln is a brick, tunnel-shaped structure, four yards long, four yards wide and four yards high. The potters fire twice a week and they were taking fired pots out when I was there. The kiln is never allowed to go cold and it was still enormously hot inside.

In one end of the kiln is the mouth for loading and unloading it and beneath the opposite end is a grate. Both ends open into brick sheds and the shed at the grate end is full of almond shells. Mr. Atsonios buys the

Wedging the Clay

Wedging is the business of kneading and dividing the clay to check its consistency and for the presence of air-bubbles. The technique is to slam the clay down, knead, slice or pull it in two, then slam the divided sections together and knead again.

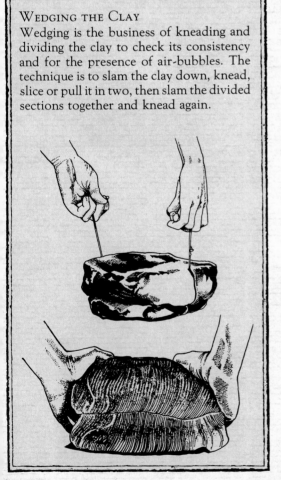

almond shells for one and a half drachmas a kilo from a nut factory in Pireus. The shells burn hot and clear and, as he said: "put a gleam into the pots." When he is firing he starts with gentle heat, warming the pots gradually, but then he goes on stoking hard for 12 hours to reach the required 1000 degrees centigrade.

Stepping Further into the Past

To find an even more basic potter I went to the village of Margerites in Crete. This is high up on the flank of a mountain and is a village of potters, for in that mountain, close by, good clay is found. There is an inexhaustible supply of it but, as the potter I found there said, somebody has to go and dig it out and return with it to the village using donkeys, which is very hard work.

Mr. Kalfakis Pantelis is a shortish man, with a mustache, like nearly all Cretans, and he wears the fine leather top boots that all real Cretan men wear. His pottery is a rough flat-roofed building with fine mountain views on both sides.

The potters of Crete found the way to make good pots back in Minoan times, and they have not found it necessary to change their methods or designs very much since.

Kick Wheels

Some traditional village potters still make beautiful pots working at primitive kick wheels. This French potter is seated at such a wheel, which has a large fly-wheel beneath the throwing wheel that is pushed around by foot. The throwing wheel is chocked while she attends to a finished vessel.

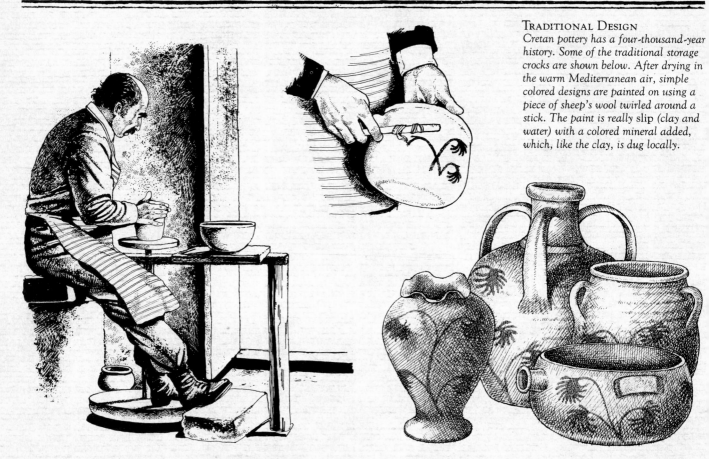

TRADITIONAL DESIGN
Cretan pottery has a four-thousand-year history. Some of the traditional storage crocks are shown below. After drying in the warm Mediterranean air, simple colored designs are painted on using a piece of sheep's wool twirled around a stick. The paint is really slip (clay and water) with a colored mineral added, which, like the clay, is dug locally.

CRETAN POTTER

When I traveled to Crete I found a potter working at a simple kick wheel. He sat on a ledge in his workshop, driving the heavy wooden underwheel around with one foot while he braced himself with the other foot. He was constantly dipping into a bowl for water to lubricate the spinning clay.

Preparation of the clay is as basic as the clay itself. The method is to mix two portions of the local red clay with one portion of a gray powder, which Mr. Pantelis calls *aluminum* (but in Greek) and is also dug on the mountain. The mixing entails first bashing the dry red clay on a brick floor with a large wooden mallet and then screening it to get any stones out. This reduces the clay to a coarse powder which is then put into a huge 10-gallon-or-so pot (made on the premises, of course), together with water. Mr. Pantelis then roughly mixes this with a plunger, and slops the mixture from one big pot to another, screening it between each transfer and finally dumping it on the floor. At this stage he mixes in the dry gray powder and then makes a heap from which he takes clay as needed for wedging and throwing.

SIMPLE TECHNIQUES IN AN ANCIENT TRADITION

The Cretan potter throws on a kick wheel, which looks very home-made, or ethnic as we must call it now. The small wooden throwing wheel is driven round when you push a heavy wooden underwheel with your foot. He throws with great dexterity and cuts the finished pot off with a piece of wire.

He makes designs on the pot with a small piece of metal curved at both ends which he calls a *xystri* and he also uses a wedge-shaped knife. The designs have not changed since Minoan times and you can see pots decorated just as he decorates them in the museum at Iraklion. Mr. Pantelis does not copy Minoan pots (he has never bothered to look at any), he is simply working in an unbroken tradition that goes back at least four thousand years.

Mr. Pantelis dries his pots on shelves in his shed, amongst bunches of onions and his farming gear – for like all true Cretan craftsmen, he is a farmer too. The pots are left there for a day or two. Then they are put out in the sun, upside down on planks without touching one another.

The kiln is a round, well-like structure of fire bricks, open at the top with a hole in the side at the bottom. It is packed very carefully, to cram as many pots as possible into its five foot height and four foot diameter, and then the pots are covered with old broken shards of pottery and then a layer of mud to seal off the kiln. Faggots of whatever light wood are available fuel the kiln, mostly prunings of olive trees. Firing starts slowly, then Mr. Pantelis speeds up the process and achieves the right temperature in 12 hours or so. He knows when he is up to temperature when the broken pots on top go black and then go white with the heat. Such mountain potteries serve the practical needs of local people. The produce is, technically speaking, *biscuit ware*, since it is only fired once, and includes bread-mixing bowls, little aladdin lamps for burning olive oil with wicks, pitchers for various liquids, often designed for tying round the necks of donkeys, pots for storing beans, olive and olive-oil crocks, bread crocks and crocks for storing some of the dough from the last baking. The yeast in the dough will stay alive for three months if kept in one of these vessels, with a little oil.

ELEFTHERNA AND VESSELS TO ENCOURAGE MODERATION

If you go to Knossos or any other of the many excavated palaces of the ancient Minoan civilization in Crete you will see plenty of enormous pots called *eleftherna*, rather like amphorae. They are enormous: two fat men could hide in one. Because one or two have been found with bones inside archeologists have been led to think that they were burial urns. I am perfectly sure that most of them were used just as their direct descendants are used today – for storing wine and oil. They are still made and are to be seen all over the island: there is hardly a peasant family without at least two of them.

Mr. Pantelis makes them but only in the summer, for they must be made out of doors. He makes them on the wheel but with the coiled pot technique. He first throws the base, up to about 18 inches high, allows this to dry, and then builds up a coil of clay on it. He stops building after about two feet and then turns the pot and smooths the inside and outside. He allows that stage to dry and then builds up another stage. He goes on like this until he has finished. After drying in the warm atmosphere, the pot is carried to the kiln, very carefully, by four men and fired.

Although their enormous size makes the coil pot technique the only way of making *eleftherna*, it is possible to throw pots of a size that would surprise most studio potters. I remember how Mr. Curtis of Yorkshire, whom I introduced at the beginning of this article, used to throw chimney pots four feet or more high. He had to stand over the spinning wheel rather than sit at it, and the operation was a wonderful demonstration of skill combined with great strength. He was keen to pass on the techniques but I fear they will die with Mr. Curtis.

Mr. Pantelis sometimes makes little pots he calls *mugs of justice*. These are so devised that if you pour wine into them to a moderate level you can drink out of them and very good luck to you. If, however, you are greedy, as I am, and fill them too high, the wine runs out on to the floor – or into your lap as luck may deal with you. These have also been found among the ruins of the ancient cities so they are no new thing.

GIANT COIL POTS
Potters of the old school had to throw some very large pots using lumps of clay that you or I would have difficulty carrying. But it is impossible to make the giant Cretan pots, called eleftherna, on a wheel. Only the base and the beginnings of the sides are thrown; the rest is gradually built up by adding coils of clay.

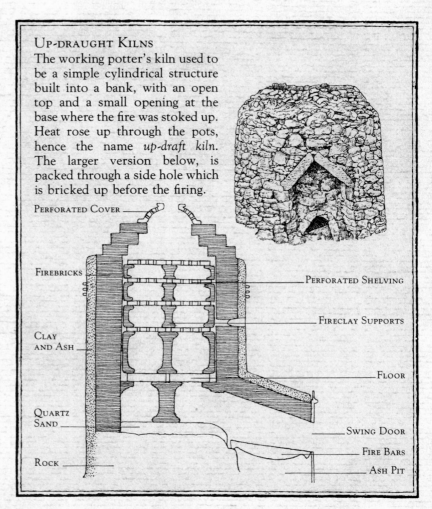

UP-DRAUGHT KILNS
The working potter's kiln used to be a simple cylindrical structure built into a bank, with an open top and a small opening at the base where the fire was stoked up. Heat rose up through the pots, hence the name *up-draft kiln*. The larger version below, is packed through a side hole which is bricked up before the firing.

PERFORATED COVER

FIREBRICKS

CLAY AND ASH

QUARTZ SAND

ROCK

PERFORATED SHELVING

FIRECLAY SUPPORTS

FLOOR

SWING DOOR

FIRE BARS

ASH PIT

BRICKMAKING

Y EXPERIENCE OF MAKING BRICKS was gained in Africa, many years ago, when the only way of obtaining most building materials was to make them yourself. Bricks were made, quite simply, by finding a suitable brick earth, moulding this into brick shapes and then air- and sun-drying them. Finally the bricks had to be fired, using either dry wood or charcoal.

Finding the right brick earth is not as simple as it sounds. Bricks are not made of pure clay but of a judicious mixture of clay and sand, and other grades of earth. The only way you can test a sample of earth is to mould it and fire it. Even a test in a very hot oven is better than nothing. Pure clay will crack in the firing, whereas a too sandy mixture will not hold together at all. Choosing the right earth is a matter of experience.

First, the earth has to be thoroughly *puddled*, which, in Africa, was an easy and even musical matter. I watched half a dozen Africans trample it with their bare feet singing heartily as they did so and took a leaf from their book. Once mixed to a smooth consistency the clay would then be forced into brick-sized moulds (slightly more than brick-sized actually because earth shrinks as it dries), placed on planks in the sun for a week or two (you can be sure there will be no rain in the dry season), and then built into a kiln and fired. In northern Europe the drying process is carried out under cover and takes a month.

ALTERNATIVE METHODS OF FIRING

There were two methods of firing the bricks. Both involved building a *clamp* of bricks, but in the first the brick piles crisscrossed so as to leave spaces in between them. Cavities (*fireplaces*) were also left at ground level along the windward side of the clamp. The whole thing then had to be plastered with mud, except for the fireplaces (which were no more than a yard apart) and some small vents on the leeward side where the smoke could escape during the burning. Next, the fireplaces were filled with well-dried wood and set alight. It was

ORNAMENTAL BRICKS
The main demand for ornamental and decorative bricks is from restorers of old buildings requiring replicas to replace damaged originals and from individuals and builders wishing to add a touch of originality to a new brick wall. The bricks are made individually in wooden moulds scaled up in size to allow for shrinkage as the bricks dry out. The design is raised in reverse in the base of the mould.

necessary to keep these fires burning for a week, which required a lot of firewood.

I gave this method up (although it produced perfectly good bricks) in favour of the charcoal method. In this layer after layer of bricks were built, with wide spaces between them, and the spaces filled with small pieces of charcoal. When the clamp was at least seven feet high – and as long and wide as you had bricks for – it was plastered all over with mud. As with the dry wood method, small holes were left high up on the leeward side to let the smoke out, and slightly larger holes at ground level on the windward side to act as fireplaces. We then lit the charcoal and just let it burn inwards, consuming all the small pieces of charcoal within the clamp. It would burn away quite happily for several days, and after about a week it would be cool enough to break open.

BRITISH BRICKS

Brickmaking in Britain goes back to Roman times. I have seen the hard and level sites they selected with an eye to drying their thin, wooden-moulded bricks.

The usual method of making bricks by hand today is *pallet moulding*. The brick

CLAY WINNING
While most clay for bricks today is extracted with excavators and dumper trucks, there are still a few individuals left making their own bricks who win, or dig, their clay by hand. This is a laborious and backbreaking job but it does allow the brickmaker to choose the best clay and reject the sub-standard.

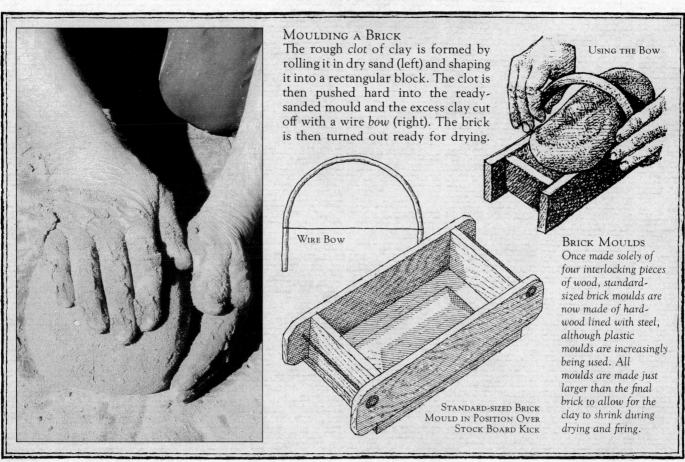

MOULDING A BRICK
The rough *clot* of clay is formed by rolling it in dry sand (left) and shaping it into a rectangular block. The clot is then pushed hard into the ready-sanded mould and the excess clay cut off with a wire *bow* (right). The brick is then turned out ready for drying.

USING THE BOW

WIRE BOW

STANDARD-SIZED BRICK
MOULD IN POSITION OVER
STOCK BOARD KICK

BRICK MOULDS
Once made solely of four interlocking pieces of wood, standard-sized brick moulds are now made of hard-wood lined with steel, although plastic moulds are increasingly being used. All moulds are made just larger than the final brick to allow for the clay to shrink during drying and firing.

maker prepares his work bench by nailing to it a *stock board* on which there is a raised *kick* which forms the *frog* or recess in the brick and over which the mould is placed. Dusting the board, and the mould, with sand, he rolls out a lump of clay to form a rectangular *clot* or *warp* of clay which is then pressed into the mould, ensuring that every crevice is filled. The surface of the clay is then leveled with a wire *bow* or a *strike*, which is just a damp stick and the mould is then turned out on to a *pallet board*. When sufficient bricks are made, a *bearer-off* transports them to a drying platform called a *hack*. Drying can take as long as six weeks, depending on the weather, although such refinements as underfloor heating do help.

The other process for making bricks, *slop moulding*, is not used so much now. In this process, the brickmaker wets the mould rather than sanding it, and the mould is placed directly on the bench without a stock. Since a slop-moulded brick is wetter, it requires more drying time before firing.

A Brick Kiln

The major requirement of a brick kiln is constant heat, produced by wood, charcoal, or I suspect anthracite would work. The bricks are piled up in a clamp, the fuel instaled and whole edifice plastered with mud and topped with fire bricks to seal it, with only a vent left to fuel the fire and some smaller vents on the leeward side to allow the smoke to escape. Once alight, the fire slowly burns itself out and after about a week the kiln can be dismantled and the fired bricks taken out.

The Hack Barrow

The traditional brickmaker's hack barrow is sideless, for easy loading, and carries as many bricks as the brickmaker himself can comfortably lift. It is much in use as the bricks have to be carried from the pallet board where they have been placed after moulding to the hack or drying platform, and from there to the ovens when dry.

TILE MAKING

RADITIONAL CLAY TILES ARE MADE from the same materials as hand-made bricks and made in much the same way. Tiles, though, are made in many different sizes and shapes, and different parts of the world have different patterns. Those beautiful pantile roofs of Italy and the South of France are curved to exactly the shape of the thigh of some Roman tile maker centuries ago. The tiles were made flat and to the right size, then folded over the thigh to form a curve.

Nowadays, tile clay is shaped and pressed in moulds and the tiles, after air-drying, are fired in the same way as bricks. Tiles can also be salt-glazed – with the kiln at a very high temperature salt is thrown in and the resulting gas hardens the surface of the tiles. Flooring tiles are often glazed on one side, as is pottery – *true glaze* as tile makers have it. Tiles are one of the artifacts though which, so easily made by machine, are practically never made by hand now.

ROOFING

There are many ways to fix tiles to form a roof. The Italian tile, thigh-formed or otherwise, is attached in tiers. The individual tiles are laid alternately convex and concave. In this way, rain water runs from the tile with its convex side uppermost into the troughs formed by its neighbors with their concave sides uppermost. This arrangement forms a series of troughs, kept watertight by successively overlapping tile edges, running right down the roof. The design makes it possible to have the comparatively flat roofs one sees in Mediterranean countries without fear of leaks.

Most northern European roofs are covered with small rectangular tiles, measuring $10\frac{1}{2}$ by $6\frac{1}{2}$ inches – time-honored dimensions. They are punched, for two roofing nails, and are moulded with two *nibs* (little projections) along one of the short sides. On the roof, the nibs hook over the tiling battens that are fixed parallel to the eaves and ridge. Plain tile roofs have a much steeper angle, or *pitch*, to help the overlapping tiles shed rain water.

PLAIN TILES
Plain tiles require peg, or nail holes and protruding nibs to hold them secure on steeply pitched roofs.

MAKING A TILE
You can make tiles by hand in a mould, the back of which is hinged to a square iron frame with the two prongs that punch out the nail holes in the tile. You shape the clay in the mould with a bow, using the flat wooden surface for smoothing the surface of the tile (1), and cutting away the superfluous clay with the wired end (2). The tile can then be removed for firing (3).

PAPER MAKING

HE FIRST PAPER MAKERS WERE wasps. They chew wood up, mix it with their saliva, and make those beautiful papery nests. Anyone can make paper. I know a lady who lives in Herefordshire and makes paper of the weirdest things – from nettles to rutabagas. She sent me once a little clip of samples of paper made from linen, bracken, rush, rush and linen, cotton straw, chamomile, spent hops, artichoke, cabbage and nettles. Some of these I had never considered suitable.

To see paper made by hand on anything like a sensible scale (small is beautiful but minute can be ridiculous) I had to go up the charming valley of the little River Dore, which flows into the Allier in the Auvergne, in central France. There I inspected the paper mill of the late Richard-de-Bas. The mill has been producing paper, with only one small interruption, since the seventeenth century with its present machinery, and before that there had been a paper mill on the site since the fourteenth century. The mill survives partly because visitors are allowed to inspect it (and pay for the privilege) and partly because it turns out fine paper used in limited edition books. Thankfully, there is still a demand for this type of product, albeit on a limited scale.

There is a fine overshot waterwheel, which has been turning continuously (except for halts for occasional repairs) for 300 years. The wheel turns an enormous horizontal beam, called the *chapabre*. This beam has pegs of apple wood sticking up from it in a pattern that resembles the workings of a musical box. As the beam revolves, the pegs catch the ends of huge wooden hammers, which cause the hammers to lift a few inches. As the pegs turn, the hammers drop. They drop into large stone mortars (called *creux de pile*), thus hammering whatever happens to be in the bottom of the mortars.

As the waterwheel revolves, these hammers thunder up and down in a strange

1 At the Richard-de-Bas *paper mill cotton rags are pounded for 36 hours by huge water-powered hammers.*

2 *The rag and water pulp is transferred to a vat. The ouvreur scoops out just the right thickness of pulp from the vat using a wire mesh tray.*

3 *The* coucheur *takes the tray and turns out now-consolidated pulp on to a sheet of felt. He builds up a pile – a layer of felt, a layer of pulp.*

rhythm of their own (determined in fact by the arrangement of the pegs on the great shaft). The material from which the paper is to be made is mixed with water (diverted by ancient wooden channels from the stream that drives the mill) and poured into the mortars under the hammers. The material used now in the mill is cotton rags, which make the best-quality paper. Wooden chips or shavings would do – practically anything, in fact, of vegetable origin. And for 36 hours these rags are mercilessly hammered to a fine pulp.

The pulp is then run off into the *cuve*, a simple vat. Here the liquid is heated by means of a charcoal fire and kept constantly stirred. Now for some team work: a man called the *ouvreur* takes up a shallow tray with a fine gauze bottom and with a deft motion he inserts this into the liquid, lifts it, to allow the surplus water to run through the gauze, and hands the tray to another man standing beside him who calls himself the *coucheur* – the "putter to bed". The *coucheur* has already laid a square of woollen felt beside him, and he turns the tray over and allows the sheet of pulp to fall on to the felt. He then immediately places another piece of felt on top of this. Thus he builds up a pile of alternating pieces of felt and layers of paper pulp.

Next he removes the pile to the *press*. This is a massive wooden press almost

exactly as can be found pressing apple pulp for cider or grape pulp for wine. Great pressure is applied to the pile and most of the moisture is squeezed out. The sheets – and now I suppose one can call it paper– are taken out and hung up from racks in a huge loft, which is warmed in winter, to dry. Now they are really paper.

Various Origins of Good Paper

I saw a paper mill in central India many years ago. The pulp was made by a heavy round stone being dragged around in a circular stone trough by a cow. The sheets were scooped from the pulp, then pressed

MOULD AND DECKLE
The paper maker's most important implements are the mould and deckle. The mould is a rigid framework covered in the fine wire mesh that strains the pulp and gives hand-made paper its characteristic pattern of laid lines. If you scooped out pulp using the mould only, the paper would end up thicker in the middle of the sheet than at the edges. The deckle is a detachable raised frame the maker uses to contain the pulp evenly across the sheet.

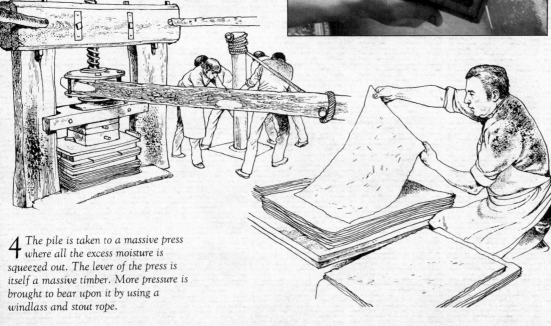

4 *The pile is taken to a massive press where all the excess moisture is squeezed out. The lever of the press is itself a massive timber. More pressure is brought to bear upon it by using a windlass and stout rope.*

5 *After pressing, the pile is dismantled, each sheet of paper being unpeeled and hung to dry.*

WEIGHING MINERAL
PIGMENT FOR
COLORING PULP

THE COCK BAG
*The cock bag, as paper
makers have it, is simply a
piece of felt or heavy linen,
set in a handled frame.
You put any pigment you
want to add to the pulp in
the bag, then dunk it into
the pulp, giving the soggy
bag a good squeeze to
filter out the color.*

and simply stuck to the wall of a shed where
they dried quickly in the warm atmosphere
of that region.

Less far afield, Mr. John Sweetman super-
vises the paper factory at Wookey Hole in
Somerset. Here anybody can be shown the
old mill where paper is made by ancient and
traditional methods. Old rags are first
boiled under pressure in caustic soda. In
days of old, the rags were thumped by hand
in a large pestle and mortar. Nowadays, a
machine called a Hollander is used, which
consists of a serrated roller turning in a
tank. The serrations just touch the bottom
of the tank and thus pummel the *half-stuff*,
as the mixture of pulp and water is known
in Britain.   The operator of the Hollander
is called the *beater* and, as probably every
batch of raw material he is given is different,
he must exercise good judgment. The
severity with which he beats the half-stuff
is all important to the quality of the final
paper, as is the amount of water he allows
to mix with the paper pulp.

Just before the end of the *beating* some
alum (aluminum sulphate) and sometimes
soap are added to *size* the paper. The *stuff*,
as it is now called, passes to the *stuff-chest*,

where it is mixed with enough water to
make it from one to two per cent by weight
of dry matter to water. It is then passed, as
required, to the *vat*.

The vat has an agitator in the bottom and
a warming device to keep the stuff at a
pleasant temperature. The *vatman* (the
English equivalent of the French *ouvreur*)
takes a *mould*, which is a shallow tray of fine
wire mesh. Around this he fits a *deckle*. This
is a frame that is laid over the mould to give
it more depth. He holds mould and deckle
together, dips them into the stuff, gives
them a shake to remove excess and even the
stuff out, lifts off the deckle and hands the
mould to the *croucher*. The croucher turns
it over on a piece of felt and the future paper
falls out. The two of them can make 10
sheets of paper a minute. The resulting pile
of felt and paper is called a *post*. This is then
pressed in a hydraulic press. After excess
water has been removed, the paper is sorted
out from the felts and put in a pile, which
is called a *pack*. This is, sometimes, pressed
again and the sheets laid out on burlap
trays in an airy room. The sheets may then
be sized by being dipped in a solution of
gelatine or starch, pressed again and dried.
If a very smooth finish is required, the sheets
are interleaved with shiny steel plates and
then rolled. High-quality paper made in
this way comes at a premium, and this
reflects the time and skill of craftsmen using
centuries-old techniques.

FOOLISH LAWS
In the eighteenth century, hemp (*Cannabis
sativa*) was the most favored material for
the making of paper. In fact, the hemp (or
marijuana) plants were grown for this
purpose alone. Old worn-out ropes made
of hemp were eminently suitable for this
purpose, too. The British navy of the time
must have been a plentiful supplier of old
ropes. Now, however, owing to foolish
laws in many countries, the cultivation of
this magnificent and useful plant is out-
lawed, and so we continue to use up the
world's forests, destroying the ecological
balance through vast areas.

It can be argued that, no matter how
good hand-made paper might be, it would
be impracticable to provide the paper for,
say, one of the mass-circulation daily news-
papers. This may well be so, but perhaps
the world would be a better and finer place
if there were more emphasis on quality and
less on quantity.

BASKETRY

CAN REMEMBER A TIME, not all that long ago, when most things that are now packed in cardboard or plastic came in a basket. All sorts of farm produce and seafoods were harvested and then traveled in baskets which now you would have to pay a deal of money for in their own right, supposing you could find someone who knew how to make them. Basketwork protected your bottles from breaking, your hats from squashing and your picnics from ants. Nor was packing and storage the end of the matter – basketwork was so much a part of everyday life that you might very well catch sparrows in a basket trap when you were young, and end up being pushed in a wicker bath-chair when you were old.

THE SUPREMACY OF WILLOW
When I lived in Wales I had a very good friend named John Jones, who was a Gypsy man and proud of it. He used to sit at my fireside many a night and, among the things he taught me, was basket making. He would often say that a man can walk out into the country with nothing on him but a knife and make any kind of a basket. He opened my eyes to using split hazel, blackberry briars with the thorns scraped off, dog rose briars and even honeysuckle and other creepers for basket making. (Elsewhere you can read about making baskets with oak, see p. 39, and rush, see p. 164.) But he always insisted on the supremacy of the thin pliable wands of various kinds of willow tree as basket-making material.

Willow basket making is what we refer to when speaking of *wickerwork*. It is the flexibility of willow that allows the most ingenious work and it is the ease with which willow can be grown and harvested that allows basket making on a large scale. What you call the young willow fronds used for

BLACKBIRD CAGE

HOP PICKING BASKET

STILTON CHEESEBASKET

EGG BASKET

SOUTHPORT BOAT BASKET for DAIRY PRODUCE

HARVESTING BASKET

BUSHEL

POULTRY BASKET

MULTIFARIOUS PRODUCTS OF WILLOW
We tend to forget just how versatile basketry is. If you look at the range of collecting, carrying and storage baskets here, it will give you some idea of what you can make from willow. Wickerwork has always been used for storing such perishables as dairy produce, because it breathes. Another attribute of weave is that you can make it tight or open. Make it open enough and you have a cage.

CUTTING THE WITHIES

WITHY BEDS ARE ESTABLISHED BY PUSHING willow branches into damp ground in rows – they grow with no trouble at all. They are left to grow for the first three years and then cut down to the *stools* (cut down to ground level) every year thereafter. The cutting itself is back-breaking work and, like the harvesting of reed and rush, is a wintertime activity. You need a trusty curved blade, such as the sickle used by the venerable gentleman above, and you have to bend double to cut the withy branches off flush.

The withy cutters that used to work near my home in Ireland were salmon fishermen making the most of the winter when they could not fish. The withies were poled down the river in barges with the tide and off-loaded near the basket works. Here the withies were seized on by an army of workers ready to strip them. Each worker would have a post, driven into the ground with a brake bolted to the top of it. The withies were pulled through the V of the brake, to bruise the bark. When the children were let out of school they would all come running down to the basket works and strip the loosened bark off with their fingers.

THE BRAKE
The brake consists of two pieces of round iron bar welded to each other at the bottom to form a narrow V shape. You simply pull the withy down into the V to split the bark ready for stripping.

basket making depends on where you come from. *Withy* is the term I use although it has West Country origins, whereas *osier*, or simply *rod*, are more widespread. In Ireland, from where my most recent experience of basket making has come, they talk of *sallies*, from *sallow*, the old word for a willow.

The World's Best Basket Maker

Thinking of the old time baskets that were once so common set me to finding a basket maker of the old breed. I began to inquire around. Simple, said everyone. The best basket maker in Ireland – nay in the British Isles – probably in the world – lives in the next town, 40 miles from you. This sort of advice is difficult to ignore. So is the fact that the first person I happened to meet when I went to the next town had worked at Shanahan Willow Craft for 26 years. He went on to say that Joe Shanahan, the great man himself, was the most famous man with baskets in the whole world and that I was the luckiest man alive to have found him so easily.

It was, however, some days later that I followed Joe Shanahan through the door of his workshop. Inside was a large room absolutely littered with basketry of various sorts, and basket materials. A very pretty girl sat on a low stool at one side of the room making, very deftly, a small rectangular basket with a lid. On the other side of the room sat a young man, similarly engaged.

The Basket Maker's Plank

Both workers had a big old door flung on the floor near the wall – the basket maker's *plank*. On top of this was a board like a table-top, about five feet by three feet, on the slant. This is the *lap-board* and the bottom end of it was caught against a piece of wood nailed to the bottom of the plank so that it would not slip. The top of it was propped up on wooden blocks. The basket maker sat with his back against the wall, on a low stool, facing the raised end of the lap-board. If he wanted the lap-board higher he simply put another block or two under it. If he wanted it lower he took a block or more out.

Soaking the Willow

An open door led into a yard in which willow bundles were soaking. Beyond this again was an enclosed garden. In it stood a shaving horse (see p. 25). Like many old town gardens, surrounded by ancient stone

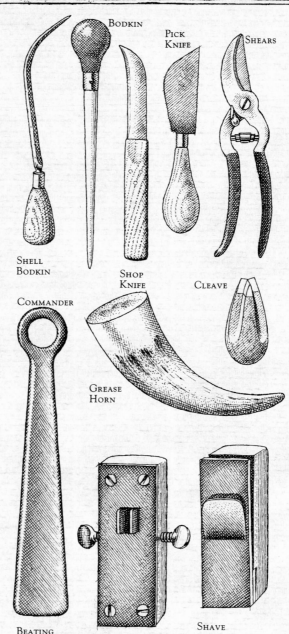

SHELL BODKIN

BODKIN

PICK KNIFE

SHEARS

SHOP KNIFE

COMMANDER

GREASE HORN

CLEAVE

BEATING IRON

UPRIGHT

SHAVE

shaving horse (see p. 25).

The Tools

The basket maker's toolkit is small, comprising of clever little instruments for shaving and cleaving the willow rods, knives and shears for cutting and trimming and devices for arranging the weave. The cleave, in skilled hands, will split a rod three ways while the two planes, the upright and shave, are used to reduce thickness or width. Split and shaved rods are used for binding. The shop knife is used for slyping rods (pointing one end) while shears and pick knife are the tools for trimming ends when the work is finished. Bodkins are greased from the grease horn and used to divide the weave so you can drive in other rods. You beat the weave down tight with the beating iron, using the ring end (the commander) to straighten the framework of square work.

walls, it seemed a delightful place to be. I asked Joe if he was not tempted to sit there sometimes and make his baskets. He told me no – the willow would dry out too quickly in the sunshine.

The essence of willow basket making is the flexibility of the withies. The willow is stored dry, however, and must be soaked well before it is used to restore its flexibility for the time when the basket is being worked. Most basket makers soak the willow for the next day the evening before. The willow bundles I saw soaking would be taken from the stone trough after an hour or so, depending on the sort of willow, and left to *mellow* overnight, that is to allow the surface water to penetrate to the pith of each withy, making it ready for use.

MORE ABOUT WILLOW

There are *brown withies*, *buff withies* and *white withies*. Brown withies simply have the bark left on them. They are used for large and rough baskets. Buff withies are boiled, in their jackets, for at least three hours (nearer five as a rule) and then skinned or stripped. The boiling causes the tannin and other dyes in the bark to stain the wood a pleasant tan colour. White withies are simply stripped without boiling. In order to make the stripping easier the bundles of withies for white withies are stood in muddy pools from the time they are cut, in winter, until they are transported in spring when they actually begin to sprout.

All this work had been done by the Shanahan firm, but now, alas, most of the material is imported. When people can make a fair living otherwise they are not going down the river in a boat to cut withies

it seems. A few are still cut by salmon fishermen in winter, but the bulk come from Somerset where farm workers and smallholders still make osier bed cultivation part of their livelihood.

THE YEAST BASKET

There is square basketwork and there is round basketwork. They are different mostly in the way you start the work and Joe was kind enough to show me the intricacies of both, while conveying great enthusiasm for his ancient craft. To demonstrate square basketwork he chose to make a yeast basket. Now this is a basket with a history that says much about the basket trade and its produce.

In days of old distillers used to produce as a by-product many tons of yeast, and this was sent out to bakers. The small bags of yeast were packed in baskets which were non-returnable. Shanahan's had once turned out as many as 1200 of these baskets a week, each man producing up to 40

KENT CRAFTSMAN
The Kentish basket maker, below, is approaching the border of a fine basket of brown and white withies, destined for use by some pampered dog. Basket makers work on a plank, sitting directly on its boards or on a low box or stool.

baskets every long working day.

"What used to happen to them after they had been delivered to the baker?" I asked.

"Into the fire with them! Under the oven."

It seemed to me to be a measure of the extreme cheapness of basketry, provided labor was cheap, that baskets could be made for such a transient use. True the basket was a rough creation put together, lid and all, in a quarter of an hour. But my belief is that that basket could have stood up to dozens of trips between distillery and baker before it would have come undone.

In 1957, the cardboard box came in and killed the industry because it was just a little cheaper than the yeast basket. The cost of human misery involved in the sacking of most of the hundred men working in the basketworks could not, of course, be taken into account. Nor could the fact that the cardboard boxes entailed the cutting down of forests, while baskets rely on the annual harvest from self-perpetuating willow beds.

Using the Clamp
The base is the start of any basket and to make a square base you need a *block*. This is two strips of wood with two bolts through them to form a clamp. In this Joe clamped 13 resilient withies so that they stood up vertically, and settled at his work station. He quickly wove two withies together along the bottom of this little fence. "We call that the *passover*," he said. He then started what he called *slewing*. This was ordinary plain weaving, but with five or six withies all together and parallel. It was obviously a very quick method of filling in space. He then finished off the little wall in front of him with two intertwined withies again, and this he called the *pass-off*.

High Speed Basketry
Now he took the piece of basketry he had woven out of the block and laid it on the slanting table before him. He dumped a large stone on it to keep it steady. The withies Joe had used projected way beyond the woven section of base, and now he *kinked* each withy where it projected and bent them up at right angles to make the *stakes*, or uprights of the basket body. Kinking is a matter of sticking a knife-blade in along the grain of the willow and giving it a slight twist. This opens the grain enough for the withy to be bent without breaking.

Basketry Techniques
The principles of basketry are similar to those of weaving. You need a row of parallel rods (stakes) through which you weave another rod at 90 degrees. You can use more than one weaving rod at once and you can weave in patterns if you like. To make a square of basketwork, you clamp the first set of stakes temporarily and when you reach the end of the row you can simply twist the weaving rod back on itself and continue the weave. For round basketry you must have an odd number of uprights so that the weaving rods weave alternatively in front and behind the same uprights every other circuit.

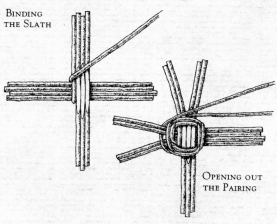

BINDING THE SLATH

OPENING OUT THE PAIRING

Tying the Slath
If you look in the middle of the bottom of a round basket, you will see the slath where the basket maker starts to work by laying three short rods over three others. He then binds the cross with a weaver and opens them out into a star shape, either weaving with two rods (pairing) or with one around an odd number of star points.

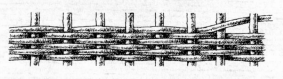

Three-rod Waling
You start three weavers and take each behind two, in front of one.

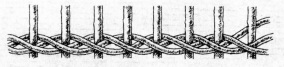

Randing
This is basic weaving, behind and in front, using one rod.

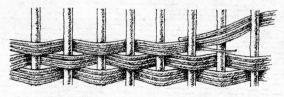

Slewing
Slewing is randing with three or more weavers. It is quick to do and looks good.

Five-rod Border
There are many decorative borders. This one involves five uprights at once.

Openwork
A basket maker will sometimes leave a section of a basket open, for decoration or for some practical purpose. The upright stakes have to be bound in tightly above it.

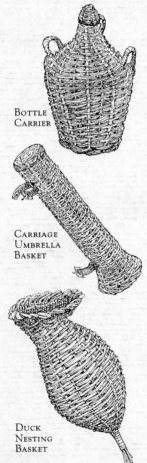

As each stake was bent up it was held there in a light loop. When all the stakes were in place he quickly slewed the two ends and the two sides of the basket. One side he continued slewing much further than the others, finishing off with a pass-off. The extension was bent down and became the lid. All loose ends were trimmed off with a pair of shears, like garden pruning shears but specially made.

Joe worked like lightning. It was hard to follow what he was doing.

"Anyone can make a basket, but if you want to make a living at it you've got to be fast!" he said.

THE TURF BASKET

The yeast basket was cast aside and at this point Joe held me to his assertion that I should make a basket. The basket I made, rather the basket that Joe made with a very little help from me, was a turf basket and it illustrates round basketwork nicely.

Turf is the name Irish people give to what we call peat, which is dug and dried for the fire (see p. 62). I have the basket still and it is a perfect general purpose basket. At the moment it is full of potatoes.

The *slath*, or beginning of the base of this basket, is made by cutting six short lengths of withy and laying them, three across three, at right angles. Now John Jones (my Gypsy friend, you will remember) had taught me to split one lot of these and stick the other lot through the slit. Joe abhorred this method and said he preferred the traditional way, which is just to lay one set on top of the other. He set his lap-board flat, put the crossed withies on top and steadied them with his foot. Stooping over, he bound them together with a very thin and whippy withy, which he twisted to make more flexible. Then, pulling the 13 rod points he had bound together into a star (the end of the binding withy forms one extra point of the star), he began to weave other withies in and out of them. The thirteenth point is vital as the number of withies that form the *warp* (to use a cloth weaving term) must be an odd number, for if this were not so, after one round of weaving the pattern would begin to repeat and all the weaving withies (the *weavers*) would be lying the same way and the basket would just not hold together.

As we got further from the middle of the base, the *warp* withies began to get too far apart, so extra withies were driven into the weave to augment them. The ends of these new withies were *slyped*, that is cut to a point with the knife. After about half of the bottom of the intended basket had been thus woven, we started slewing to fill out space more quickly before the edge of the circular base was completed by *pairing*, a sort of plait using two withies. Look at the underside of a circular basket and you will notice it is concave so that only the strong edge of the base contacts the ground. My turf basket is similarly dished.

THE SIDES AND BORDERING OFF

With round baskets the stakes for the side weaving have to be driven into the weave of the base. Twenty-nine strong rods are selected and slyped at their bottom ends. The slyped ends are driven hard into the edges of the circular base, then they are *kinked* and bent up sharply. This is called *upsetting*. Strong weaving holds the base of the stakes tight. Then a bit of slewing with four withies at once increased the pace. Next Joe showed me a new trick – a kind of plait he called *French weave*, which involved driving newly-slyped withies into the weave and plaiting them with alternate reverse turns of the basket.

When the top was near, Joe produced a complicated border, plaiting with five rods at once. The tops of the stakes were themselves woven into the border, their ends being bent down at right angles and driven into the weave below with a heavy iron tool, called the *hand iron*. Strong handles were made at each side from a simple hoop of withy pushed through the weave (a spike, known as a *bodkin*, was used to enlarge the holes for this). Slender withies were then selected, twisted hard to make them pliable, and wrapped round and round the hoop and woven into the basket below.

A WEALTH OF EXPERIENCE

After witnessing these displays of basketry I realised that Joe Shanahan could build any kind of basket there is or could be. I learned that he had even built balloon baskets. When he first started there were a hundred people employed full time in basketwork. They made a virtually endless variety of objects. A few of them were cane chairs, laundry baskets and heavy strong baskets for the railroads (you used to see baskets standing about on all railroad platforms). They made potato baskets, log baskets and shopping baskets, and plenty of industrial baskets in large quantities (mostly for protecting bottles and flasks), bread baskets, and even far-out things like wicker-work goal posts for polo fields (the ponies do not hurt themselves if they bang into them), calf muzzles (to stop calves from

sucking their mothers), bicycle baskets and even ducks' nests.

BASKETRY FOR THE SEA

I wanted some special basketry made for use on board my wooden boat *Dreoilin* (see p. 106). In the first place, I was going to go fishing in the estuary here where my home is and this body of water is famous for eels. You may not like the idea of eels, but I consider them one of the most delicious of seafoods, and smoked they are worth many times their weight in smoked salmon. I needed East Anglian eel *hives*.

The best hives are designed and made by the eel catchers themselves to suit the rivers they fish. A typical hive is up to five feet long and consists of two chambers connected by a funnel. The hive is flat bottomed to allow it to lie on the bed of the river where the eels swim. One end is wide open, the other narrow and enclosed. The hive is baited by placing a piece of dead fish in the chamber in the enclosed end, for the eel is a carnivore, and likes the dead flesh of fish as well as the occasional live newt, frog or small fish. Attracted by the smell, the eel swims in, and since it cannot find the small entrance, gets stuck in the hive. The English have a reputation for jellying eels but people of most other nations smoke them or simply fry or stew them.

I also wanted to set lobster and whelk pots. Of course, I know all about the advantages of lobster traps made of expanded metal, and wire mesh, and all the rest of it, but I am not a professional fisherman and derive more pleasure from using

FISHERMAN'S CREEL
The traditional fisherman's basket for tackle and catch is called a creel and is best made of fine wickerwork. It has a shoulder strap and is subtly shaped to hang snuggly by the user's hip, next to his free hand.

SHRIMPER'S CATCH
The harvesting basket, below, belongs to a shrimp fisherman from the north-west coast of England. The fish are an incidental bonus to the shrimp catch they rely on.

traditional methods, and so I wanted traditional pots. I thought that if I could watch a professional basket maker weave these items I would be able to copy him and make any extra that I needed myself. Joe was confident of producing any *exotica* I could mention and he made time to make me a whelk pot that day.

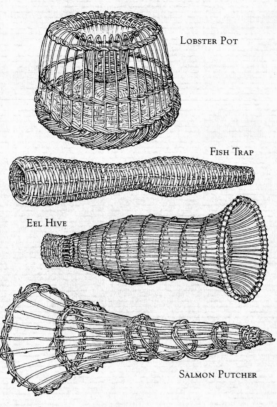

LOBSTER POT

FISH TRAP

EEL HIVE

SALMON PUTCHER

FISH TRAPS

Wicker fish traps come either in the form of pots that you bait to trap creatures that crawl across the sea-bed, such as lobsters, or funnels that allow swimming fish in but not out. Most famous of the funnel kind is the salmon putcher. Serried ranks of these devices have been built into the mud of the Severn estuary, near South Wales, for 500 years, waiting to trap the fish as the tide carries them to sea. Of course they need a little maintenance from time to time, as the picture below shows.

WHELK POTS

Now I have been to sea, many times, with the whelkers of Wells, in the east of England. I have a lovely little painting of a typical whelker (a very specialized open boat) in front of me as I write this. The east-coast fishermen use pots made of iron woven with tarred twine in between the iron bars. They shoot these pots 20 or 30 miles from land in shanks of 40 pots on a rope, each pot baited with fish. The whelks crawl in and, owing to the shape of the pots, cannot crawl out again. They are taken back, over the dangerous sand bar, and boiled in whelk sheds.

Joe made a shape exactly the same as the shape of the Wells pot. It took him about half an hour. The framework is established on a circular template with 17 small holes drilled in it. The funnel is made first, using a simple randing weave for a few inches. Then the stakes are bent over and the body of the pot is woven. The flat bottom is made separately and then woven into the pot. A lobster pot is made in the same way, with a broader base to accommodate the bigger lobster. I have the finished whelk pot hanging on a wall and I shall try it here down in Waterford harbour one day. If I am to have any catch at all I will need a few more pots to go with the one Joe made. Looking at it again, perhaps I was being optimistic to think I could copy them!

THE SOMERSET CHAIR

A GOOD BASKET MAKER CAN MAKE A CHAIR entirely out of wickerwork, and it will be strong and light, but it will not last forever; certainly not as long as the Windsor chair on page 65, for example. It is asking rather a lot of thin whippy withies, even when strongly woven, to stand up to the wear and stresses that a chair is put to. For a piece of furniture which has to be reasonably light but is destined to carry the weight of a large human being (who is quite likely to sway back and forth like a pendulum) has to be a piece of rigid engineering.

The Somerset chair – manages to combine basketwork with the more rigid construction necessary for a good chair. The solid elm seat which forms the foundation of a wooden country chair is expensive and difficult to obtain

and so using their native skills of basket working, the country chair makers of Somerset have evolved a chair in which basketwork forms the seat and back-rest, and hazel or heavier willow forms the framework and gives the chair its strength. Compared with the Windsor chair these chairs are very rustic, but no elaborate tools are required, and they are strong and light. What is so unique about the Somerset chair is that it is the only country chair made in the British Isles without using any hardwood. Even the most basic of rural chairs have at least the legs and back of wood, and the seat of rush or cane. It is a tribute to the basket workers of Somerset that they have developed a chair over the centuries that breaks all the rules of chair making, but doesn't break when sat on.

MAKING THE CHAIR
Once the basic framework of sturdy willow or hazel rods has been cut to length and tacked together, the basket worker starts to give the chair real strength by weaving the seat and back (left). Using a basic randing weave for the flat surfaces, the chair maker has to use a more complex weave to bend the willow rods over the sides and front of the seat to act as a cushion against the hard edges. He is tacking on the rounded batten that forms the mould for the roll of weave at the front of the seat, above.

THE COMPLETED CHAIR

RUSH & STRAW WORK

IF YOU PUSH STRAW OR RUSHES through a conical tube (into the larger end is recommended) it will emerge from the smaller end in the form of a rough, loose rope, but with no twist in it. If you tie straw or some other fiber or string around the rope at short intervals as it emerges from the cone, you will have a stable, although not very strong, untwisted rope. If you then coil this rope round and round in the shape you want, and tie each coil to the next at fairly frequent intervals, you can make a basket or other similar container. You might be wondering at this point how you can thrust your tie between two already tied coils of rope in order to tie a third one on. Well, traditionally, you have a goose's leg bone, cut off at an acute angle so that it makes a shape rather like the end of a giant hypodermic needle. You push this between the coils and feed the tie through the hollow center of the bone. The conical tube used for moulding the fiber rope in the first

place is, traditionally, a hollowed cow's horn. Objects like dog or cat baskets and other artifacts that do not take much stress and strain are made like this, as were old-fashioned straw beehives.

LIP WORK

Before the days of extruded plastic and aluminum, many domestic as well as farm objects were made of straw or rush, formed into coils as I have described and built up to make anything from a cradle to a chair. This process was called *lip work* and is probably a corruption of the Scandinavian *lob*, meaning coiled basketry. Rush work was popular and widespread throughout Europe and Scandinavia because the raw materials were readily available and the techniques employed needed no machinery, just a few simple tools. In Britain you can find examples of lip work anywhere from the Orkneys to Cornwall, and in Wales, where it was particularly popular, there are still some traditional craftsmen plying their trade, especially in Dyfed.

To make a straw object you need wheat and bramble. And winter wheat, which is the strongest variety, is considered the best to work with. After the wheat is thoroughly dry, the heads are removed and the stalks piled up. Bramble was commonly used as the binding material to keep the newly formed rope together. It is important that there is no sap between the bark and the core of the bramble, so winter, when there is no sap rising, is the the best time to go collecting. Before the bramble can be used, however, it has to be split in four using a sharp knife and the pith removed.

The base of a basket can be of three basic designs. In one, all the coils run from a single central point, making a shape a little like that of a snail. In another common design the coils form the shape of a cross and, finally, the coils can all radiate outwards somewhat like a rosette.

BEEHIVES

Straw beehives, or *skeps*, were usually made out of rye straw because it is longer and tougher, although wheat straw was sometimes used. These one-chamber beehives, however, went out of fashion for three main reasons. First, it was not possible for

CONSTRUCTION MATERIALS
All you need for making a wide variety of basketwork is wheat straw, formed into a loose rope by being pushed through a cow's horn, and brambles, tied at regular intervals and used to hold the straw together. Straw bee skeps are made from rye straw as this material is longer and tougher than the wheat straw variety.

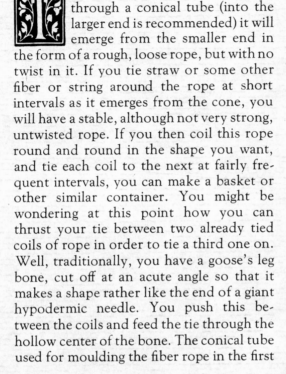

BEE SKEP

BASKET UNDER
CONSTRUCTION

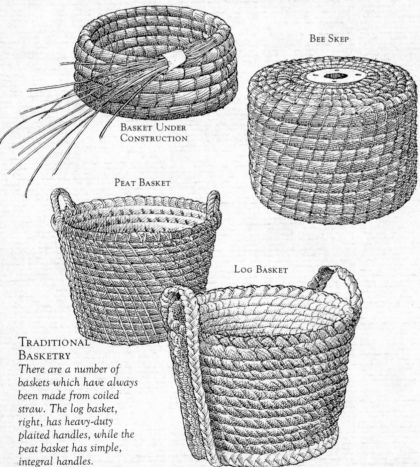

PEAT BASKET

LOG BASKET

TRADITIONAL BASKETRY
There are a number of baskets which have always been made from coiled straw. The log basket, right, has heavy-duty plaited handles, while the peat basket has simple, integral handles.

CUTTING RUSHES
There is some controversy about exactly when is the best time to cut rushes. It is generally accepted, though, that mid or late summer is probably preferable. You want maximum height without undue brittleness. The rush cutters use blades attached to long poles so that they can sever the rushes below water level. The rushes are then washed and dried – a process that can take from ten days to six weeks, depending on the weather.

your local friendly bee inspector to check your swarm for disease such as *foul brood* (he could not see the bees). Second, you cannot (or I should say could not) extract the honey without killing the bees. In the past, a little piece of sulphur was burned under the skep to achieve this. The third reason for the decline in popularity of the straw beehive is that you cannot put the comb in a centrifugal extractor and spin the honey out, free of the comb.

Fortunately, all these objections can now be overcome owing to a simple discovery, although unfortunately you cannot prevent the death of the larvae, or grubs, still in the cells – they have to go. The discovery is simply that you do not put a coiled straw bottom in the skep (in the past very few people probably ever did). When you want to extract the honey you carefully turn the skep upside down and place an empty, bottomless skep the right way up on top of it. The bees, which always tend to go upwards, crawl into the empty skep. You then remove the new skep, bees and all, and carry the old skep, full of honey and comb, away to some bee-proof place. I have never done this, but I have been assured that it works. And with a modern wooden, compartmental hive costing nearly $100, it is worth a try.

STRAW PLAITING

Straw plaiting was an important cottage-type industry in Britain even as late as the 1920s. Records indicate that this craft was introduced sometime in the sixteenth century. The popularity of straw plaiting is linked directly to that of the hat-making industry, which absorbed most of the plaiters' output. By the mid-nineteenth century the plaiting of straw was concentrated around the Dunstable and Luton area, and within this area there were plait markets every day of the week, with the exception of Sunday, of course.

Many simple but ingenious tools were introduced either to split or sort the wheat stalks. A series of sieves fitted into a wooden frame was sufficient to sort the straw into its different thicknesses. Bundles of stalks were placed, end on, over the sieves, starting first with the finest mesh sieve. As the stalks fell through, they were collected and bundled. Intricate work was not possible with complete, round stalks of plaited straw. Originally, the straw was split using a sharp knife, but by about 1820 a device containing up to 13 blades was being used. Each straw stalk was pushed into a hole at the center of the blades and emerged from the other side in as many strips as there were blades.

TEXTILES & HOMECRAFTS

For long periods my family and I have lived self-sufficiently. Such a life does not just depend on growing your own food. It includes, if at all possible, providing clothing, light and other such necessities as are needed in the daily life of a household. The making of textiles involves crafts that were once commonplace in most ordinary families – the history of words like spinster and distaff are witness to this – and many everyday items, such as soap, were home produced. I am not saying that we should all weave our own cloth, far from it. I am saying that it is wasteful of our limited resources to use oil to transport textiles, for example, half way round the globe when there is an excellent local tradition of cloth making to use and encourage.

SPINNING & WEAVING

T IS INTERESTING TO SPECULATE how such a difficult concept as turning raw, natural fibers into cloth by spinning and weaving was first discovered. Certainly people would quickly have discovered how to make *felt*. If you clobber wet wool fibers with a mallet, the minute scales which cover the individual fibers of the wool will knit together and you end up with felt. The Mongols make their *yurts*, or tents, of this material, and considering the climate they live in, if there was a more protective covering than felt they would surely be using it.

THE ORIGIN OF WEAVING

But how was weaving developed? My own belief is that weaving must have followed basket making. Early people hit upon the idea of weaving reeds or grasses together to make baskets to carry things in. It was only a short step from this for some modest cave lady to discover that if she twisted sheep's wool between her hands she could make coarse thread, and then if she lay some of these threads parallel on the ground, and wove another set of threads across them, basket fashion, she had a piece of cloth to make a garment out of. She was the first cloth weaver and she had invented the *warp* and the *weft* (or *woof*) too, for the first lot of parallel threads formed a warp, and the second lot at right angles to the first formed what is known as the weft.

SPINDLES

All early attempts at weaving must have been considerably hindered by the inadequacy of the thread or yarn with which the cloth was made. Yarn doesn't occur naturally on the sheep's back or on the cotton plant in long, ready-made lengths. It has to be twisted into lengths from the original fibers. The invention of the *drop spindle* to make the yarn, therefore, represents a very considerable advance in weaving technology.

The drop spindle is a simple device consisting of a small stick with a hook or notch at the top and a weight at the bottom. Many Neolithic archeological sites yield examples of such weights made of clay, two or three inches across with a hole in the middle through which the stick passes. To work a spindle like this is simple. Hook the notch on the top into the fluffy ball of raw wool or cotton, and give the stick a turn. The weighted end gives the spindle momentum, and as it spins the tangled threads are drawn out of the ball of fibers and twisted together to form a lengthening yarn. Pay out more

DROP SPINDLE

SPINNING WHEEL WITH SINGLE BAND AND FRICTION BRAKE

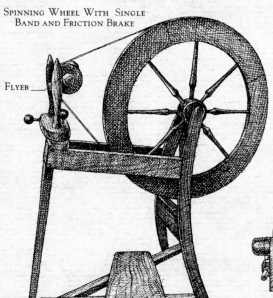

FLYER

SPINNING HEDGEHOG – ALTERNATIVE TO A SPINNING WHEEL

SPINNING MACHINES
Textile fibers are pulled through the flyer and its turning twists them into thread. The flyer also winds the thread on to the bobbin, which it surrounds, as the bobbin spins slower than the flyer, either because of a friction brake, as with the spinning wheel, far left, or because of a separate drive from the wheel, above.

loose fiber and the spindle will soon hit the floor below you, at which point you coil the thread round the spindle stem, and then start the process again. Soon you will have a spindle full of thread ready for weaving.

The Spinning Wheel

Drop spindles are laborious to work but need little concentration and are preferable to twisting yarn by hand. But at some stage or other, someone discovered that the drop spindle could be held horizontally in a frame and turned not by twisting with the fingers but by a wheel-driven belt. The spinning wheel had arrived, and with it a good supply of well-made, continuous yarn. Most wheels are operated by a crank connected to a foot treadle, which leaves the hands free to feed the loose tangled fibers on to the spindle. More complex spinners include a *flyer*, also driven by the wheel but at a different speed to that of the spindle, which ensures that the thread is always kept tensioned correctly.

Spinning wheels are great fun to work, but you need to work long and hard to produce enough yarn to weave with. One hand weaver working at full tilt needs 10 spinners to produce the necessary yarn.

The First Looms and Shuttles

Once you can spin, the next step is to weave what you have spun. All modern *looms* look fiendishly complex, but every working part is the product of many centuries' development, and once you have got to grips with what bit does what, and why, operating a loom becomes second nature.

The first loom was probably a simple square frame made by lashing four sticks together. The warp was wound round the frame, and the weft laboriously woven through it just with the fingers or using a simple shuttle, probably a stick with a notch in both ends around which the yarn was wound. To load any such shuttle involved the tedious business of first unwinding the yarn from the spindle. Thus came the development of the *boat shuttle*, which incorporates the already-loaded spindle inside it. A basic loom will only have one shuttle, but this means that a weft of only one color can be woven into the warp. For colorful cloth, you need lots of shuttles each loaded with a different color.

Tension and Longer Warps

When making cloth, it is very important that the weft is pulled together to produce a tight cloth. This is the task of the *reed*, originally a hand-held stick poked through the warp, but on a modern loom a frame with many vertical divisions, looking rather like a large comb, between which the warp passes. One sharp pull towards the weft every so often will ensure that the cloth remains tightly packed.

Boat Shuttles

Good, even weaving depends on the smooth passage of the shuttle through the warp. Boat shuttles are shaped like little canoes and they carry the weft yarn on a bobbin. With some shuttles the bobbin is the same spindle on which the spinning wheel winds the yarn, saving the time of winding bobbins separately.

The Heddle

The wonderfully simple device that separates alternate warp threads is called a heddle. Simple heddles are a series of alternate slots and holes. You can see below how threads that pass through the holes are lifted while those passing through the slots stay where they are.

DECORATED SCANDINAVIAN HEDGE

Fast Weaving

Mankind owes a great debt to the person who first thought of how much easier weaving would be if you could lift every other warp thread in turn and then simply pass the shuttle through the weft. The gap you pass the shuttle through is called the shed.

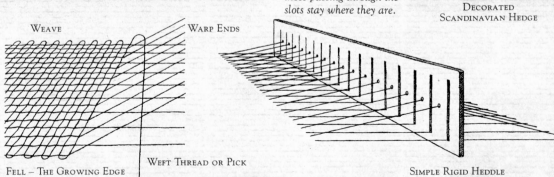

WEAVE   WARP ENDS

FELL – THE GROWING EDGE   WEFT THREAD OR PICK

SIMPLE RIGID HEDDLE

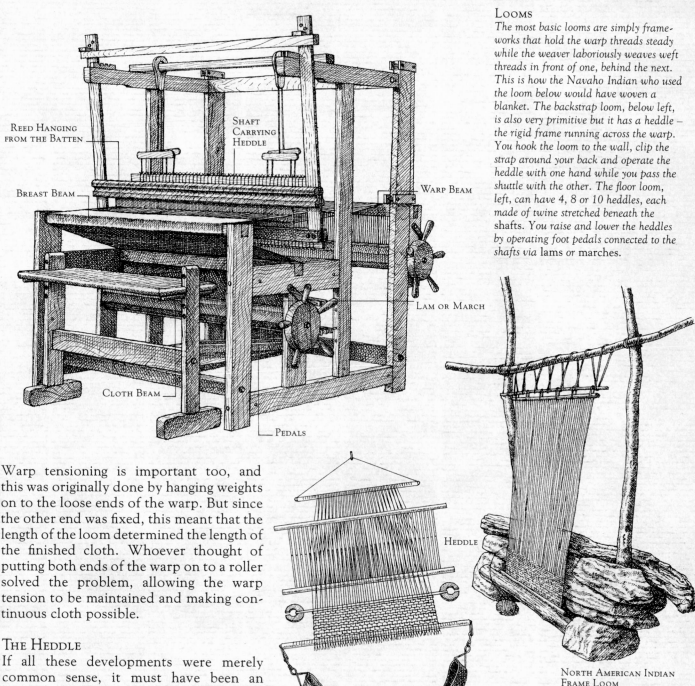

REED HANGING
FROM THE BATTEN

SHAFT
CARRYING
HEDDLE

BREAST BEAM

WARP BEAM

LAM OR MARCH

CLOTH BEAM

PEDALS

LOOMS
The most basic looms are simply frameworks that hold the warp threads steady while the weaver laboriously weaves weft threads in front of one, behind the next. This is how the Navaho Indian who used the loom below would have woven a blanket. The backstrap loom, below left, is also very primitive but it has a heddle – the rigid frame running across the warp. You hook the loom to the wall, clip the strap around your back and operate the heddle with one hand while you pass the shuttle with the other. The floor loom, left, can have 4, 8 or 10 heddles, each made of twine stretched beneath the shafts. You raise and lower the heddles by operating foot pedals connected to the shafts via lams or marches.

HEDDLE

NORTH AMERICAN INDIAN
FRAME LOOM

BACKSTRAP LOOM

Warp tensioning is important too, and this was originally done by hanging weights on to the loose ends of the warp. But since the other end was fixed, this meant that the length of the loom determined the length of the finished cloth. Whoever thought of putting both ends of the warp on to a roller solved the problem, allowing the warp tension to be maintained and making continuous cloth possible.

THE HEDDLE
If all these developments were merely common sense, it must have been an inventor of real genius who developed the *heddle*. If I had to choose the half-dozen most significant inventions of mankind, the heddle would be one of them. And like most inventions, it is stunningly simple.

Pushing the shuttle through every alternate thread of the warp to make the weft was a slow process when all the warps lay at the same level. But if they could be separated, allowing the shuttle to pass straight through in between them, rather than having to weave over and under them, then the shuttle could move with greater ease. Hence the invention of the heddle, which, like the reed, is a comb-like frame

with holes in the uprights through which are passed alternate warps. When the heddle is raised, up go those warps which pass through the holes, leaving the other warps which pass through the gaps between the uprights where they were. The space thus created, through which the shuttle can now be passed with ease, is known as the *shed*. From here it was only a short stage to developing a flying shuttle, which is caught

WARPING AND DRESSING

A WEAVER HAS TO PREPARE THE WARP THREADS so that they don't tangle and are easy to thread on to the loom; this is called *warping*. Most hand weavers use the technique called *chain warping*. You position two sets of three pegs apart by the length of the intended piece of cloth, plus about three feet extra *for the loom*, as weavers say. You do not cut every warp thread to length but instead wind the yarn around the pegs until you have the right number of threads. You leave cutting through the end loops until you have arranged the warp on the loom. The threads remain separate because you loop the ends in a figure-of-eight pattern around the three sets of pegs and then tie the group of threads before taking the warp off the pegs. It is at this stage that you gently pull the warp into a chain for safe-keeping until you come to thread it through the reed and heddles of your loom – known as *dressing* the loom. There are various ways of dressing the loom, but it is usual to work back from the warp beam to the cloth beam.

DRESSING ON SKYE
Weavers will tell you that they far prefer to work on big hand looms rather than small ones. One of the reasons it that it is easier to get inside a big loom in order to dress it – the threading of the warp yarns through reed and heddles. This weaver is dressing his loom on the Isle of Skye, Scotland. Notice the twin heddles in front of him.

WARPING FRAMES AND MILLS
To avoid running up and down the 30 or 40 yards of a long warp, warping frames and mills allow you to fold the warp on to a zig-zag of pegs, or wind it on to a framework, between the sets of three pegs where the figure-of-eight looping takes place. A warping mill is shown below, together with the business ends of a frame with its sets of three pegs. How you arrange pegs to take the warp between is up to you.

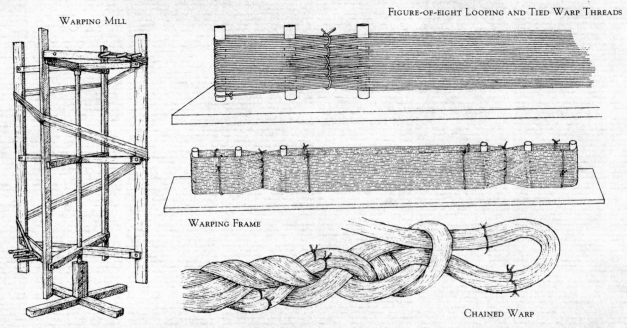

WARPING MILL

FIGURE-OF-EIGHT LOOPING AND TIED WARP THREADS

WARPING FRAME

CHAINED WARP

automatically before returning back through the shed at great speed. Equipped with a loom like this, any home weaver is really in business.

Not that operating a loom is an easy task. To co-ordinate the shuttle, heddle and reed requires great concentration, especially since many patterns of cloth require different colors on both warp and weft, using a number of heddles and shuttles.

Power looms are, of course, part of another world, making a pleasurable activity into an uncomfortable, noisy job people are forced to do for little money. The shuttle is flung around at 60 miles an hour, and the resulting noise is terrifying. Go into any pub in the weaving towns of the north country, and talk to a weaver. You will have to shout, for the noise in the factories has deafened them. And factory work has reduced them to mere extensions of their machines, for their tasks are merely to repair broken threads and refill shuttles.

But, thank God, there are still plenty of hand weavers left. The hand weavers of the Western Isles of Scotland, and of Donegal in Ireland, work flying shuttle looms completely manually, and generally run their small farms and go fishing as well. In India, Gandhi saved the hand weavers by mounting a campaign against machine-made cloth. And in the mountains in Crete, no self-respecting housewife would be without her loom (no flying shuttles there), and all her curtains, sheets and table cloths are made on it. I had only to see one of these looms to want one, and it will soon be installed safely in my house in Ireland. But I doubt if I will ever be able to produce work to the standard of those women on Crete.

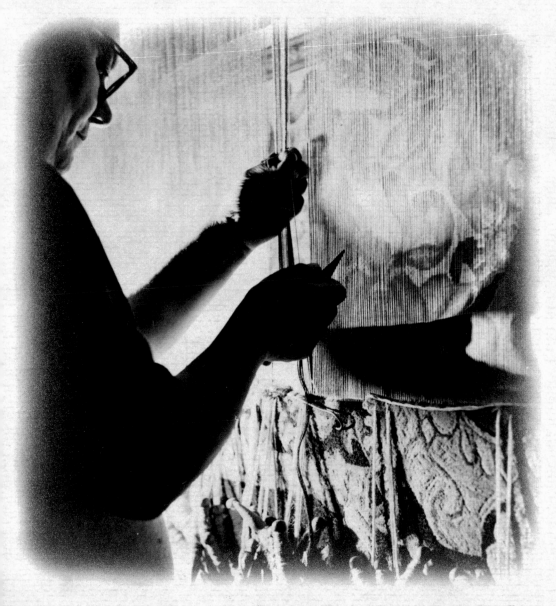

TAPESTRY WEAVING IN AUBUSSON
Tapestries are generally woven on upright looms so that you can see the design you are making clearly. Aubusson, in central France, has an ancient tradition of tapestry weaving and this is one of its practitioners, weaving against a guiding pattern that shows through the warp threads.

WOOL CRAFT

 AM THE HAPPY OWNER OF SEVERAL garments made from the wool of my own sheep, which had grazed on my own land. Now both land and sheep are gone but the cloth remains, a pleasant gray color produced without adding any other dye since some of my sheep were black.

I would like to be able to claim that I, or others on my farm, carded, spun and wove the wool too, but this was not the case. We had spinning wheels, we had looms, but, as I mentioned on page 168, if you are to spin and weave your own cloth you will spend 12 times as much time spinning as weaving. Now nothing is more soothing than to listen to the whirr of the flyers and the soft rumble of the spinning wheel itself as one sits by a warm fire. I have listened to this sound for many hours but, I have to admit, somebody else was turning the wheel. The pressure on our time nowadays sometimes makes spinning enough wool to weave with an impossible barrier, a luxury that cannot now be afforded.

Although my family did, over the course of the years, both spin and weave much wool (my daughter, Anne, spent three years at a college learning how to do it) on the whole, while my sheep provided my wool, it was spun and woven in a big mill.

CHOOSING THE WOOL

The hand spinner has to select the type of wool carefully. There are countless breeds of sheep, and each one has a distinctive type of wool. The so-called *Persian*, for example, found throughout Africa and Asia, has no wool at all, only straight hair like a dog that is quite useless for spinning. The best wool in the world, on the other hand, is *Merino* wool, which is from a sheep not hardy enough to keep in Britain, but it has to be said that it has rather a short *staple*, and is therefore difficult for hand spinners to use, though I have seen it spun. The staple, by the way, is the length of the individual fibers and is an important consideration when assessing the suitability of a wool for spinning and weaving.

In Britain there are three main classes of sheep: *Down Sheep*, *Mountain Sheep* and the long-wooled descendants of the *Leicester*. Down Sheep have a very short staple, the wool is fine, and non-lustrous. The Mountain breeds have medium length staple, and half-lustrous wool. The Leicester-founded breeds have very long staple (the Leicester itself produces a staple of up to 10 inches), very lustrous and silky, and very strong. Of the Leicester breeds, the *Lincoln* has superb wool, the staple as long as 18 inches and you can shear as much as 14 pounds, sometimes more, off one sheep.

There are two breeds considered intermediate between Mountain and Down: the

SUFFOLK-WELSH SHEEP
The sheep contentedly munching below are Suffolk-Welsh crosses on my farmland in Wales. One of their uses was to provide fleeces for spinning and weaving. Both the black and the white fleeces I sheared were combined in the process and the result was a good gray-colored cloth that needed no dye to color it.

A SPINNER'S VIEW OF SHEEP
If I lived in a mountain area and was a hand spinner I should choose the Cheviot as my breed of sheep. If I lived on lowland plains, I would choose between the South-down (despite its very short staple, or fiber length), the Oxford Down or the Romney Marsh, although the Shropshire gives a splendid wool, too.

LINCOLN

ROMNEY MARSH

KERRY

Kerry Hill and the *Ryeland*. The Kerry Hill has a soft, white, dense fleece, while the Ryeland has very fine, good quality wool with a staple length of three and a half to four and a half inches. I have kept Ryelands and while I admire their wool I don't think much of the sheep: I found them not very hardy. They probably do well enough in their own area though, which is the English-Welsh Marches.

Another sheep I must mention is the *Welsh Black*. This provides a rather coarse wool, but it is a rich brown-black color, makes an attractive cloth by itself and is fine mixed in with white wool – that is if you wish to keep the natural color of the wool and not dye it.

CONSIDERING CRIMP

As you work with wool you find all sorts of qualities about it. *Crimp* is important – it gives elasticity to the wool. It is the wavy pattern that each minute strand of a fleece has, and some breeds have far crimpier wool than others. It is desirable for knitting wools to be crimpy: the *Southdown*, which is a sweet little sheep (the smallest of our breeds) has very crimpy, fine wool, good for lightweight tweeds and hosiery. For heavier tweeds, the *Oxford Down* is good, being much longer in staple than the Southdown but coarser, and the *Cheviot* is famous for the best tweed wool in the world. The *Welsh Mountain* also makes tweed, although flannel is its main use – a much softer cloth than tweed. The long-wooled breeds are fine for carpets and hard-wearing, tough cloths. The *Romney Marsh*, which is a long-wooled breed, is fine for hand spinners: I know a lady at Chepstow whose husband keeps a flock and who spins the finest yarn from the wool. The *Shetland* is kept by some hand spinners: it has an inner layer and an outer layer to its fleece. The outer layer is fine for tweed, the inner for knitwear. A

new phenomenon which is hitting the spinning world is the *Friesian Milk Sheep*. This huge sheep, which is as tame as a dog, gives half a gallon of milk a day besides fine long wool. And I knew a lady in Suffolk who kept, and swore by (and sometimes at) Angora goats. Their hair spins into a yarn of delightful softness that knits or weaves into a soft and fluffy cloth which is much sought after.

PREPARING THE FLEECE

Now farmers sell wool either *washed* or *in-the-dirt*. To produce washed wool you simply throw your sheep in a pond or a

SHEARING IN CUMBRIA
Shearing with hand shears is something of a forgotten art in itself. It is very hard work but very satisfying when you become proficient. Good shearing is not a traumatic affair for the sheep and without the noise of electric shears and a frantic shearing shed the operation can be as relaxed as the Cumbrian scene above appears.

FRIESIAN

SOUTHDOWN

CHEVIOT

WELSH MOUNTAIN

WOOLEN-SPUN

WORSTED-SPUN

WAYS OF SPINNING
There are two distinct ways of allowing the twist of woolen yarn to form. If you let the fibers spiral together naturally you get a slightly shaggy yarn for soft warm cloth. Comb the fibers straight before spinning, you get a smooth yarn for finer cloth.

CARDING
Carding sorts and aligns the fibers of wool prior to spinning for woolen-spun yarn. The picture shows stripping off fibers from one carder to the other.

stream a few days before you shear them. The many villages in England called Wash-brook, or Sheep Wash, derive their names from this practice. You get more for washed wool but it has less weight, and the differential does not make up for the loss of weight and extra trouble, so practically no commercial farmers wash their sheep now. Hand spinners sometimes do though, for washed wool is easier and pleasanter to work with. Having got the fleece off the back of the sheep, either with hand or electric shears (it doesn't matter much which type you use), the spinner is now faced with spinning it.

ALTERNATIVE ROUTES TO YARN
If you go to a spinning factory, a mill where they turn fleece into yarn, you may be daunted by the complexity of the machinery needed to do it. The raw fleece is scoured clean in a large machine, dried, and then torn into pieces in what in a Greek mill I heard called *likos*, or wolf (and it had a very wolf-like biting action), before it goes into the *carding* machine. This consists of a large number of big drums all covered with fine wire brushes (called *cards*) which revolve at differential speeds so that the tiny wires tear the fibers of the fleece apart. The finely teased-out and fluffed up fibers are then put into the spiling machine which, very skillfully, collects and unites them in long continuous *spiles*. These can be various

thicknesses, but about as thick as a pencil is the average size for a spile.

The slowly moving spiles then travel straight to the spinning machine, which takes the place of the spinning wheel of old and which in modern mills has many spinning heads, not just one. This then spins the wool into yarn ready for weaving. If all this sounds very complicated, bear in mind that even in a very small mill, the whole series of machines can be 20 to 30 yards long and every inch of that length is used in the processing of the wool. All this may seem strange when you have seen your wife, as I have seen mine, take a fleece which has come straight off a sheep, lay it on the floor beside her and, leading a pinch of the wool from it to the spinning wheel, spin a perfect yarn straight off the fleece! But to do this needs considerable skill and it can be a very slow job.

HAND CARDING
The average hand spinner first *cards* the fleece. Hand carders are small tools with handles, covered on one side with that weird stuff called *card clothing*, a flexible fabric densely packed with tiny wire hooks. I don't know how to make it nor how it is made and all I can say is, that if I couldn't buy it I would have to use a *teasel*. The teasel, or *Dipsacus sativus* to give it its botanical name, is a thistle with a prickly head that grows almost everywhere in Europe, North Africa and North America. The teasel head, was the first carder, and is still used industrially today for *teasing* cloth, that is scratching it so as to *raise a nap* on it to make it fluffy. For this the thistle heads are set on a frame. In days of old spinsters set a few heads on a handle like a modern carder and carded the wool with that.

The carding of wool is a subtle process. A lump of raw wool is pulled apart by hand a little, and then placed between two hand carders. With the carders pulled in opposite directions, the wool is then combed or *scarified,* until the tiny wire hooks tease it apart. Then, with both the carders facing the same direction, the wool is collected on one carder only. Then one carder is turned around again, so that its hooks again oppose the hooks of the other, and with some more hard combing, the wool is scarified again. This process is repeated about five times until the wool is properly carded, that is when all the tiny fibers are separate from each other.

HARRIS TWEED
Tweed is a magnificent, slightly-rough woolen cloth which is still made on hand looms in the Western Isles of Scotland, particularly on Harris where traditional designs, such as Glen Urquhart (shown here) or Prince of Wales check, have ancient origins. The Harris island weaver is here using five shuttles to carry the weft back and forth.

When the combing is done, the wool is taken off by hand, and is rolled gently to form a *rolag*, which is the equivalent of the long, continuous, never-ending spile of the big mills. Your rolag, however, will only be the size of a long sausage, made of fluffy wool. Now it is easy to spin the wool, and subsequently knit or weave it into what is an incomparable material.

A FIBER FOR ALL SEASONS

I cannot finish without saying something about the qualities of wool, for I do not think it possible to sing the praises of woolen material too highly. Marvelously warm, extremely long lasting, water-shedding, weatherproof, with a pleasant feel about it, it is the perfect fiber for cold countries. No textile that man has invented comes anywhere near it for versatility. If you follow the process of preparing the wool fibers as I have outlined above, and then proceed to spin the wool you will end up with a springy yarn with the fibers spiraling around each other. It is termed *woolen-spun* and is light but bulky, and therefore warm. This is the sort of woolen fiber that is ideal for knitting.

But this method is not the one and only way of preparing and spinning wool. If you look at a piece of fine woolen cloth the individual fibers look very different from those knitted into a pullover. It will have been *worsted-spun*. Instead of carding the wool into a rolag, you pull locks of it through the teeth of a steel comb to sort out the long fibers (called *top*) from the short ones (*noil*) that occur in a fleece. You keep the long fibers parallel and twist them together a little to form a *roving* from which you spin. The yarn you end up with is very fine and smooth and is ideal to be woven into dense, flat cloth suitable for all the products of tailoring and dressmaking.

COLOR PATTERNS
Color patterns can be created by having different colored yarns in the warp, or by having more than one shuttle, each loaded with a colored yarn.

COTTON CRAFT

THE COTTON BOLL
The seeds of the cotton plant are contained in a seedhead called a boll, well protected by a white or creamy colored fiber. It is this fiber that is the raw material for cotton, the seeds producing an oil used in cooking and some cosmetics.

THE COTTON TWANGER
Cotton production is mostly mechanized but in India I have seen cotton twangers like this man, whose job it is to prepare the cotton for spinning by carding it, or fluffing it up with his bow.

SINCE PREHISTORIC TIMES, COTTON has been spun, woven and then dyed, and the ancient civilizations of India, China and Egypt produced fine quality cloth worked with ingenious and beautiful designs. The use of cotton slowly spread to Europe from India, and by the ninth century AD the Moors were growing cotton in Spain. But it is the New World that has been the biggest producer of cotton, first cultivated in the Jamestown colony in 1607. Vast numbers of slaves were employed on the plantations that turned the southern states of America into one big cotton field, laboriously harvesting the crop by hand. The raw cotton was then shipped off to England, where thousands of workers toiled in the mills of Lancashire and the mill owners made their fortunes in the production of cotton cloth.

The cotton plant belongs to the mallow family and is a shrubby plant that only grows in hot climates. The raw cotton *lint*, or fiber, surrounds the seeds in the *boll*, or seedhead. The seeds must first be removed, work which used to be done by the nimble fingers of the slave women. Nowadays this is done mechanically in a gin mill by a cotton-gin, which separates fiber from boll and then bails the raw cotton.

Cotton has a short *staple*, or fiber length, but is easily turned into thread. As the harvested cotton dries the fibers flatten and twist naturally, and must be *willowed*, whipped with willow rods to fluff out the cotton and clean it. Next it is *carded*, just like wool but easier to do because of its short staple, and then *combed*, its fibers laid parallel ready for spinning. When spinning cotton, you must keep your hands close together and treadle quickly, making sure that you do not hold back too much cotton from the bobbin or else it will kink. Once spun, it is strong enough for weaving.

When I was in India I came across workers whom I dubbed *cotton twangers*. These men sit, in darkened sheds, cross-legged on the floor and operate objects like bows, as in bows and arrows. In one hand the twanger holds the bow, in the other a wooden club with a sharp ridge cut round it. He keeps twanging the string with the wooden club and dips the vibrating string into the tangled mass of fibers. This fluffs it up for rolling into *rovings* – long, slightly twisted sausages of cotton for spinning.

LINEN CRAFT

INEN COMES FROM THE FLAX PLANT, and flax was probably the first vegetable fiber ever made use of by man. The Egyptians were growing and weaving flax four thousand years ago, and it is known that the Phoenicians were trading fine quality linen throughout the Mediterranean by 1250 BC. The Romans cultivated flax and introduced it to northern Europe, and it was being grown extensively in Ireland and Wales by the fifth century AD. In Ireland, as in ancient Egypt, the bodies of chiefs and kings were wrapped in linen for burial, and Irish linen is still considered to be the finest in the world. It is a superb fabric, infinitely superior to any of the man-made materials we have today. Consider the finest table cloths, sheets, napkins, shirts and other garments made of linen. Cloth from the flax plant, *Linum usitatissimum*, has qualities all of its own. And the plant has a second and a third use for man – it is *usitatissimum* indeed – for it provides linseed, the source of the best of all non-edible oils, and the residue of the crushed seeds makes linseed cake.

I have grown flax, experimentally, on my farm in Wales, and processed it through to linen thread ready for weaving. But few people grow flax any more. Two hundred years ago nearly every village in Europe was self-sufficient in linen, and the poorest peasant used freely what only rich people can afford today. Which causes one to question the whole idea of "progress". Progress from the widespread use of the very finest of materials to the use of third-rate synthetic rubbish seems to me to be progress in the wrong direction.

GROWING FLAX

Flax will grow in most soils, but it prefers a good loam and to make fine linen it should have fairly cool and damp weather throughout the summer months. If it be dry for harvesting, so much the better, but you can't have everything.

The little shiny black seeds which, when crushed, provide such magnificent oil, must be planted in a very fine tilth, in late March or early April in Wales, at a rate of about 90 pounds an acre. The seed can be drilled, or sown by hand by a skilled man, and then harrowed and rolled in.

The flax plant grows three or four feet high and produces beautiful pale blue

MARVEL OF FLAX
Linum usitatissimum, flax, is a most versatile plant. I have sailed in a trading barge under a linen mainsail which had been used for 40 years, winter and summer, night and day, with only a dressing of fish oil, linseed oil and cutch (a product of the Burmese betel tree) once every five years. On the other hand, linen can be made into the finest of handkerchiefs.

FRENCH HACKLING
This French flax worker is hackling the retted flax stems. Pulling the fibrous stems through a bed of nails separates out any non-fibrous material that may still remain among the line, or linen fibers, and also pulls out any short fibers. These go to make tow, used for caulking and stuffing.

flowers. A flax field in bloom is a delightful sight, and when the flowers die down the seed begins to form. If a crop is grown for linseed oil production only, this seed should be allowed to ripen completely, but if the flax fibers of the stem are the main object, the crop should be harvested as soon as the first of the seed begins to ripen in late July. Harvesting is done by hand. The plants are then tied together in *beets* (like wheat sheaves but smaller) and stooked up in order to dry.

RIPPLING AND RETTING
Once harvested, the next operation is *rippling*, which is the pulling of the seed heads through a fixed upright steel comb. This removes the seed bolls, which are then crushed for oil or fed to cattle.

The beets, minus their seed heads, now have to be *retted*. This means, encouraging

bacteria to attack and decompose the gum which holds the flax fibers together, and to rot the unwanted inner core of the stem. Retting can be done either by laying the beets out on the ground to let the dew and the sun work on them for from two to five weeks, turning them over from time to time, or by dunking the crop into a stagnant pond for from eight to 14 days. When the stems begin to crack and open, the retting is done. The warmer the weather the shorter the time the flax should spend in the pond, and it is important that the retting time should be correct for the quality of the finished linen depends largely on this factor. I am told that only experience can help the operator here. When I tried retting, I sunk the beets in the duck pond for a week and a half, and it worked perfectly well. But I may have just been lucky.

After retting, the stalks must be washed clean in water and then dried. This is sometimes done by opening the beets up and spreading the stalks out evenly on a cut grass field if the weather is fine, or by stooking the beets (standing them up in tiny stacks). In some places in England, where the weather is so unpredictable, the flax was laid up to dry on a platform under which a small fire was lit. This was risky, however, because it took just one stray spark and the crop was lost.

SCUTCHING AND HACKLING
Scutching is the process of removing the *line*, or true linen fibers, from the flax stems. On a small scale you use a *brake* – a very simple device consisting of two fixed parallel battens of wood with a hinged batten that falls between them. You drag a

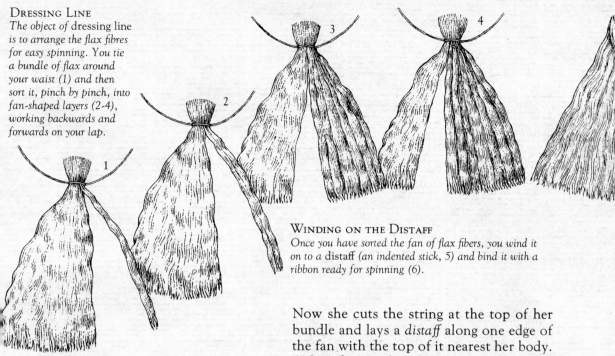

DRESSING LINE
The object of dressing line is to arrange the flax fibres for easy spinning. You tie a bundle of flax around your waist (1) and then sort it, pinch by pinch, into fan-shaped layers (2-4), working backwards and forwards on your lap.

DISTAFF

WINDING ON THE DISTAFF
Once you have sorted the fan of flax fibers, you wind it on to a distaff (an indented stick, 5) and bind it with a ribbon ready for spinning (6).

READY FOR SPINNING

handful of flax over the fixed battens while beating it with the hinged one. This breaks and crushes the woody pith in the fibers so that it can be removed.

Hackling is the next process. This consists of drawing the line through a large comb, once a bed of nails, to get rid of any fibers too short for spinning. The short fibers are known as *tow* and can be used for caulking decks, stuffing mattresses, making cord and hundreds of other uses.

DRESSING AND SPINNING
Before spinning, the line must be *dressed*. This can be a beautiful process if accomplished by a pretty woman wearing a long apron. Taking as much fiber as she can clasp into one hand, the dresser ties a piece of string around one end of this bundle, lays it on her lap and ties the two long ends of the string around her waist to secure it. She now lays the whole bundle on her left knee (assuming she is right handed), takes as much fiber as she can easily take between her finger and thumb and lays this on her right knee. She then takes a pinch more of the fibers and lays them next to the first pinch, but further to the left. She continues doing this until she has laid out a fan of fibers. Then she lays another fan of fibers on top of the first, working left to right, then another right to left, until the whole bundle is laid out in fan-shaped layers.

Now she cuts the string at the top of her bundle and lays a *distaff* along one edge of the fan with the top of it nearest her body. A distaff is simply a short stick with rippled edges. Winding the fan up on the stick, she keeps the top of the fan (which had the string around it) pretty tight, but the wide bottom of the fan looser. Then she sticks the distaff in the hole provided for it on her spinning wheel, takes a ribbon and ties this round the top and criss-crosses the two ends down to the bottom, tying the two ends in a bow.

Taking a bit of yarn that has already been spun, she winds this on to the bobbin of her wheel. The loose end of this is twisted into some of the loose ends of line at the bottom of her distaff and then she begins to spin, wetting her fingers in a bowl of water so as to moisten the flax to make it more supple. With her left finger and thumb she stops the spin from traveling up into the fiber on the distaff; with her right hand she draws the fibers out and clears any knots. Occasionally she turns the distaff as required and when necessary unties the bow in the ribbon and ties it again further up. In this way she spins the whole hank.

Once spun, the linen thread is ready to be woven on a loom like any other kind of thread. In days of old every farm which could grow it grew flax, every spinster spun it – and many a good wife too – and the distaff side of the family concerned itself for much of the year with its preparation. And, once a year, a traveling weaver would visit the farm, carrying his loom, and weave it all up for the family. And thus was real wealth created.

SILK CRAFT

I N 1900 A MILLION PEOPLE IN southern France were employed in the production or processing of native silk. By the 1960s this number had fallen to zero. Except for a few faithful souls who just kept a few silkworms and a few mulberry trees for fun or sentiment, the industry had died out. The great silk mills of Lyons were and are still operating, and so are those of Milan, another silk city, but they are operating on raw silk imported from China and elsewhere in the Far East.

THE FRENCH SILK INDUSTRY

The silkworm was introduced into France in the fifteenth century from Spain and Italy, and by the late seventeenth century

sericulture, the culture of the silkworm, flourished, supported by the government of Louis XIV. It was nearly wiped out by disease in 1853, but Louis Pasteur found a cure for the worms and the industry took off again and became the mainstay for many of the peasants living in the rural South of France. Alas, with the opening of the Suez Canal things took a turn for the worse, for the canal made it possible to import cheaper silk from the East. Now the production of native silk in France is almost but a memory.

Wherever you go in the Cévennes, in the South of France, look out for long buildings on the side of farmhouses, with very small windows and many chimneys. Look inside one and you will find the building empty, or merely being used for storage, and the walls blackened by ancient fires. You may still find the remains of the woven cane trays on which millions of silkworms once lived and munched their way through tons and tons of mulberry leaves. These buildings are called *magnaneries*, which is an Occitan word derived from the ancient *langue d'oc* word for silkworm, *magnans*. It was in these buildings that the silkworms were fed. Other, even larger, buildings, often special in that they have large pointed-arch windows, are the *filatures*. There is about one to a village. Into these the farmers brought their silk cocoons and sold them to the owner. He, or at least the young women he employed, performed the delicate task of winding the silk off the cocoons. The silk was then bought by traveling buyers who transported it to Lyons to sell to the big spinning and weaving mills there.

AN INDUSTRIAL RENAISSANCE

Although the French silk production industry all but died during this century, like many other so-called "Forgotten Crafts", it did not quite die, and is now experiencing marked re-birth.

In search of this I took myself to the village of Monoblet, where the young village schoolmaster is acting as midwife to this renaissance. Monsieur Wolgram Mollison has aroused enough interest in his locality to have raised the cash to build a small factory which takes silk from the cocoon stage to the finished, dyed, garment. He has delicate machines, invented by the

Japanese, which wind the silk off the cocoons, spinning machines, automatic looms and sewing machines. When I visited him, in 1983, the mill was still using some oriental silk, but it is hoped to phase this out as time goes on, for Monsieur Mollison has persuaded many landowners to let him plant mulberry trees on their disused land (of which there is an enormous amount) and he has already planted thousands. He is managing to persuade more and more peasant people, chiefly women, to start cocoon production again, though he admits that at the moment silk farming is something of a labor of love. Imported silk is still too cheap for it to be possible to compete against it economically, but he points out that wages in South Korea, where most imported silk comes from, are rising and the time will come when it will not pay them to produce it there and then transport it half way round the world. One day, he feels sure, the Cévennes silk producers will be in business again and, due to his efforts, off to a flying start. So, thanks largely to the enthusiasm of a small group of local people, inspired by the hard work and dedication of this one man, the skills of silk craft are being relearned and preserved for future generations.

LEAVES AND WORMS

To produce a decent amount of silk you need a prodigious quantity of leaves from the mulberry tree. *Morus alba*, the Chinese white mulberry, is hardy and most suitable, but M. *nigra*, the black mulberry, has a fruit which is nicer for *us* to eat than that of the white mulberry, and seems just fine for silkworms too. A young girl named Marie, whom I met on a farm near St. Hippolyte du Fort in the Cévennes, raises 10,000 worms, and they eat the leaves of 25 mulberry trees in a month – about three bushels of leaves a day. Marie has to pick the leaves fresh every day, which she does simply by holding each branch in a big sack and stripping the leaves off with her hand. To miss a day is fatal: it puts the worms off their routine and could kill them.

The worms occupy a corner of Marie's father's old *magnanerie*. From hatching eggs until starting to spin silk takes the worms about 27 days, and the larger they get the more they want to eat. Marie told me she has to be scrupulously careful about removing the droppings, which are abundant, and any leaves not eaten. When the worms are first hatched out she has to chop the leaves up small for them; after a few days this is not necessary. She uses racks of

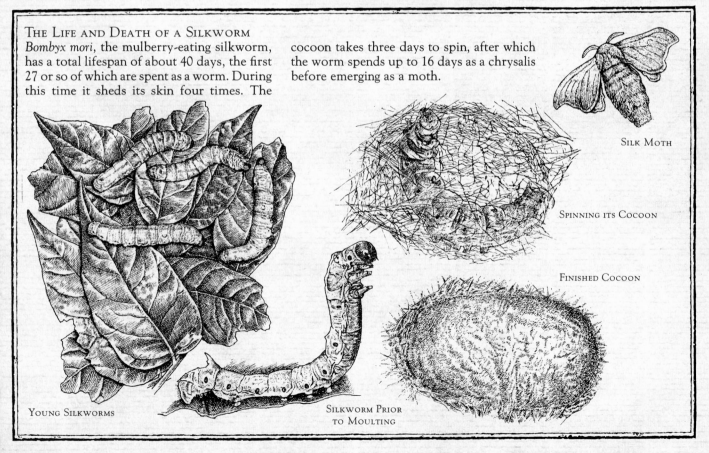

THE LIFE AND DEATH OF A SILKWORM
Bombyx mori, the mulberry-eating silkworm, has a total lifespan of about 40 days, the first 27 or so of which are spent as a worm. During this time it sheds its skin four times. The cocoon takes three days to spin, after which the worm spends up to 16 days as a chrysalis before emerging as a moth.

SILK MOTH

SPINNING ITS COCOON

FINISHED COCOON

YOUNG SILKWORMS

SILKWORM PRIOR
TO MOULTING

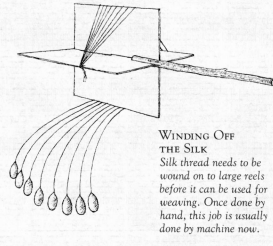

WINDING OFF
THE SILK
*Silk thread needs to be
wound on to large reels
before it can be used for
weaving. Once done by
hand, this job is usually
done by machine now.*

A HOME-MADE SPOOL
*Marie made her own
simple spool out of two
interlocking pieces of
cardboard, each about 10
inches square, and a twig
handle, around which she
can wind the threads of
silk off the cocoons.*

trays woven from osiers and, as the worms
get larger, she lays branches of heather and
bushy herbs on the worm-laden trays.
Feeling the urge to make their cocoons, the
worms climb up into the twigs of these
plants and spin their cocoons there.

When the worms have finished spinning,
after three days' solid work, they must be
killed, for if left alive they will secrete an
alkali which will eat its way through the
cocoon and ruin the silk. Marie kills them
by putting them in a paper bag and the bag
into an oven at 200°F for 20 minutes, but
she told me that if you lay them in hot sun
for a day it would do the same thing.

SPINNING THE SILK THREAD
After killing the worms, the silk must be
wound off fairly smartly because if it isn't
the worms will start to stink and taint the
silk. Marie showed me how she does this.

Although most of her cocoons go to the
new factory, she is producing thread herself
in a small way and does it with the simplest
possible method, using a homemade spool
made of two interlocking squares of cardboard with a twig handle.

Taking eight cocoons she flings them into
a bowl of water which is nearly – but not
quite – boiling. (The inside of the bowl is
black, making it easier to see the silk
threads.) Very soon the threads on each
cocoon begin to come loose and float in the
water. With a pair of tweezers she gathers
the eight loose ends up, twists them together, and fastens the end of the thread
thus formed to a notch in the "wheel".
Very carefully she then begins to turn the
spool and wind the silk thread. After the
silk is completely unwound from the
cocoon, a little wizened grub falls into the
water: quite unlike the three-inch-long fat
caterpillar that started to build the cocoon.

Marie told me she likes making silk, but
there is no way she can make a fortune at
it. It takes 500 silkworms or 80 kilos of
cocoons to create one kilo of raw silk. So
Marie's total production, from 10,000
worms and 25 mulberry trees, is 20 kilos a
year. Not a good return.

SILK AND STEEL
Silk production may seem a slightly frivo-
lous pursuit to be included in a book such as
this, but consider this: silk is by far the
strongest material we have, and thickness
for thickness, it is said to be stronger than
steel. It makes a superb fabric, warm when
it's cold and cool when it's hot. Why should
we Westerners deny ourselves such a
luxury, which we can produce quite well by
ourselves, even if it does require much
labor. It is a labor of love.

DYEING

HE INVENTION OF SYNTHETIC DYES in the last century made people accustomed to very bright, pure and garish colors but spoiled their taste for the more subtle hues derived from natural dyes. Yet using dyes derived from nature is a centuries-old craft.

A great many plants are a raw material for dyes but some, like beetroot, that one would think would be excellent, are no good at all: they merely stain the fiber and wash out later. Time and experience will soon teach you which provide *fast* dyes, that is dyes that hold their color, and an enthusiast can experiment endlessly to achieve a desired color or hue.

What is important in dyeing is the *mordant*, the chemical bridge that connects the dye to the fabric. Most natural dyes require a mordant, which used to be such products as vinegar, or ammonia supplied from the urine of horses. Nowadays chrome, tin, iron, cream of tartar and alum are used, a mixture of the last two being the commonest. The mordant can affect the final color of the dye, chrome making it brighter and purer, iron dimmer or *sadder*.

Mordanting a fiber is simple. Dissolve four ounces of alum and an ounce of cream of tartar in a little hot water and add it to four gallons of nearly boiling water, the softer the better. Dump your fiber, ready-washed, roughly a pound at a time, into the mordant and simmer for an hour. Then remove it and squeeze it dry. Don't twist or wring out wool as it will turn into felt. Now if it feels sticky, there is too much alum in the mordant – use more water next time. Sometimes it is best to mordant both before and after to ensure the dye holds.

To extract the coloring from the raw materials, you must crush, shred, pulverize, or generally beat them up, place them in cold water and leave overnight. Then simmer them for an hour or so before tipping the lot into the dyeing vat along with four gallons of soft water. If fleeces are being dyed, it is a good idea to put the dye material in a muslin bag, but this is unnecessary for skeins of wool. As for quantities, about two pounds of dye material should be ample, but it is very difficult to make the solution too strong, easy to make it too weak. When the dye is nearly boiling, in can go the fiber, all at once if you want it to be the same color. Leave it to simmer for up to an hour, though it is wise to keep checking that the color looks right, take it out when ready, rinse it in cold water and hang it up to dry.

DYEING WITH BRACKEN
Mrs MacDonald of Harris, Scotland, does all her dyeing in the open, using bracken to turn the wool a beautiful pale shade of green.

RAW MATERIALS
The natural world can provide every color dye. Dandelion produces magenta, sorrel dark brown, elder blue, broom and sloe tan, and birch a delicate green.

DANDELION   SORREL   ELDER   BROOM   BIRCH   SLOE

CANDLE MAKING

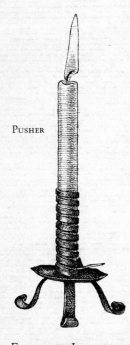

PUSHER

THE GOOD OLD-FASHIONED CANDLE is an important stage in the evolution from burning twig to fluorescent light. Many is the time, when I lived happily in the bush in central Africa, when I have followed an African on a pitch dark night, as we found our way along some winding path through the forest. The only light came from a blazing stick carried by my companion, which he swung round his head from time to time to keep it glowing.

For many centuries, northerners used rush-lights. The rush is carefully split so as not to damage the pith. The pith is then dipped in molten fat and allowed to harden. Rush-light holders can be seen in most country museums: they are fittings screwed into the wall which hold the rush-lights at the right angle in a sort of pincer. If you hold them upright they go out. They stink like, well, like burning mutton fat, they smoke badly, don't last long, and don't give out much light.

Candles, on the other hand, can be made so they don't smoke or smell. There are two elements to a candle: the fuel and the wick. The fuel can be made of various substances, some better than others.

FUELS

Tallow is melted-down animal fat. Tallow candles were the traditional lighting arrangements of poor country people. They smell as they burn, don't give a very good light, but are much better than rush-lights.

Beeswax was traditionally used for ecclesiastical candles. It is an excellent fuel for candles, smells delightful when it burns and gives a good light. Alas, because of our efficient method of obtaining honey we don't have very much beeswax. Originally, in order to extract honey all the comb had to be pulled out, and this of course contained the wax as well as the honey. Nowadays, we extract the honey centrifugally so as to leave the comb intact. First, though, the *cappings* of the combs have to be taken off so we still get some beeswax for candles.

But we come down with a bump to *paraffin wax*, which is what most of us have to use to make our secular candles. This

ENDURING LIGHT
Candles are a source of sympathetic light that it has been impossible to extinguish. The candle survives and has a use for special occasions. They provide the blacksmith with the job of making beautiful individual candlesticks. The spiral example above, has a pusher that you use to push the candle up the spiral as it burns short.

EVERYDAY TASK
When candlelight was the rule, dipping tallow candles had to be a regular activity and scenes, like this one in Wales, were commonplace.

POURED ECCLESIASTICAL
CANDLES

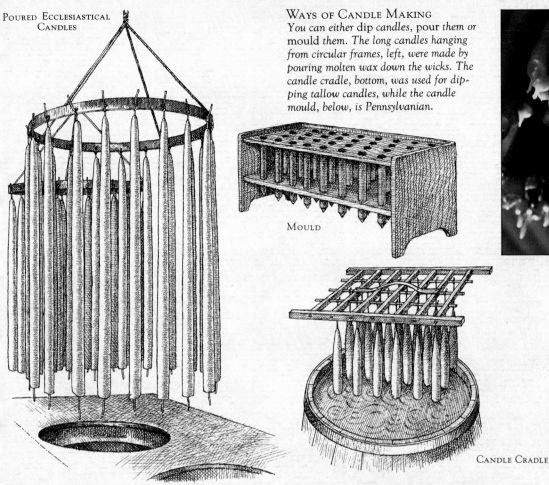

WAYS OF CANDLE MAKING
You can either dip *candles,* pour *them or* mould *them. The long candles hanging from circular frames, left, were made by pouring molten wax down the wicks. The candle cradle, bottom, was used for dipping tallow candles, while the candle mould, below, is Pennsylvanian.*

MOULD

THE FINISHED ARTICLE
Making a candle is easy; making a good one that has the right sort of wax-blend and diameter for the wick you use, so that it burns clear and gives that comfortable candlelight, takes experience and is a very worthwhile activity.

CANDLE CRADLE

substance is distilled we are told from coal. Depending on how it is distilled it has different melting temperatures, varying between 122° and 160° F. In cool climates 135° is suitable, while in the tropics the melting point should be higher or the candle will become too soft.

Stearine is often added to the paraffin to make it burn better. This is extracted from animal and vegetable fats. (A substance called *micro-crystalline wax* is often added to industrially produced candles to make them harder, but it is not necessary.)

WICKS

Traditionally, bleached cotton yarn was used for wicks: just thick cotton thread. This had the disadvantage of having to be trimmed constantly as it burned. Some genius then discovered that if you used flat, braided cotton the wick would curl downwards as it burned and thus be brought into the hottest part of the flame and consumed. As a result, it does not need trimming and the bewigged footmen of the eighteenth-century ballrooms lost their jobs. Braiding cotton is done by machine and it is highly

unlikely that anybody tried to do it by hand. The commercially produced stuff is very cheap to buy. You order it according to the number of strands it has. An ordinary candle, anything between, say, an inch and two inches in diameter, uses a 15-ply wick.

MANUFACTURE

Nearly every schoolchild knows how to make candles by buying moulds in a toy-shop, sticking a length of wick to the bottom of the mould with a piece of hot wax, melting the rest of the wax and pouring it in (holding the wick to keep it straight).

Dipping is a more pleasant technique. A small weight is tied to a wick, which is then dipped in a mixture of molten paraffin wax and stearine (in the ratio six to one). After dipping you allow the wax to solidify and repeat the process until the candle is as thick as required. Such a candle tends to be thicker at the bottom and is called a taper candle. If you want a cylindrical candle, invert the candle halfway through the dipping process. It is better to melt the wax in a water-jacketed container, so that the heat warms the water first.

SOAP MAKING

NE CAN LIVE VERY WELL WITHOUT soap. I have, and for long periods, without doing myself – or those close to me – any harm at all. Anybody who has been to India would have seen the *dhobi* or laundryman simply standing in a stream and bashing dirty clothes against any convenient rock. He is not trying to break the rock – he is knocking the dirt out of the clothes. He dips them in the water between each bash, and the actual shock of the water rushing through the fabric as it makes contact with the rock washes the dirt out. It generally knocks all the buttons off, too, which is why Indian garments tend not to have buttons.

THE RAW INGREDIENTS
But, if you must have soap it is very easy to make, and home-made soap can be quite as good as, or better than, the bought variety.

Long, long ago, I was forced to shoot a lion because it was eating domestic animals, and my employer's mother stripped all the fat off the carcass and made soap out of it. Ostriches, which, like male lions, also tend to chubbiness, are much sought after for this purpose as well (or they were – I don't think there are many of them left now). I am not suggesting that ostriches or lions should be bred specifically for making soap, or hunted either. I am simply trying to illustrate the undeniable fact that soap is simply fat, which surprisingly is classified chemically as an acid, neutralized by an alkali. The art of making it was no doubt discovered in rather a simple way. Everybody who has been camping knows that if you take some of the ashes from your camp fire and mix them into the fat in your frying pan, they clean the pan surprisingly easily. This is because you have made soap.

The strong alkali in the ashes neutralizes the fatty acids in the fat to form soap. This is soluble in water and can be washed away.

MAKING LYE
My employer's mother used caustic soda for neutralizing the fatty acid. The more traditional farmers' wives made their own alkali from ashes. Nothing could be easier. I have done it in Wales and it worked perfectly well. First, you drill a lot of holes in the bottom of a barrel and place a layer of gravel in the bottom and then some straw. This is to help with drainage. You then fill the barrel with hardwood ashes (softwood ashes are not as good). Next you must pour rainwater on top of the ashes. After a long time (and here you must exercise a deal of patience) liquid begins to dribble out of the holes in the bottom of the barrel. Collect this liquid and boil it down until it is concentrated enough for a fresh egg to float in it. This is then known as *lye*, and it is the traditional liquid employed to make soap. It is fairly powerful stuff – it will eat its way through an aluminum container.

LYE TESTING
To test the strength of lye made in this way, the experienced soap maker dissolves salt in water until no more will dissolve, to make a *saturated solution* of salt. He then takes a stick, attaches a small weight to one end of it and drops the stick in the salt solution. It bobs upright with the weight at the bottom, and a mark is made on the stick exactly at the water line.

Now this stick is an instrument for measuring the strength of lye, for it just so happens that you need the lye at exactly the same specific gravity as the saturated salt solution. You drop the weighted stick in the concentrated lye and it will probably float with its mark above the surface of the liquid. If so, you add rain water very carefully, stirring it as you do so, until the stick floats to its mark. This strength of lye is then correct for soap making.

HOW TO GET FAT
For the fat component of the soap, I think we can dismiss both lion and ostrich fat as being too unobtainable, and so we are left with more ordinary sources, and I would

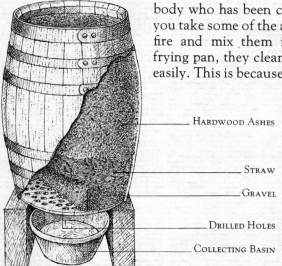

HARDWOOD ASHES

STRAW

GRAVEL

DRILLED HOLES

COLLECTING BASIN

HOME BREW
To make your own lye, first drill some holes in the bottom of a barrel and lay down some gravel as an aid to drainage. Place straw on top of the gravel and then hardwood ashes right to the top. Then pour rainwater into the barrel and wait patiently for it to filter out the bottom as lye.

put them in the following order of desirability: first, *tallow* (beef fat); second, sheep fat; and third, *lard* (pig fat). Vegetable oils can also be used, with olive oil being by far the best of its type. But who, unless they have their own grove, is going to use such wonderful stuff for making soap?

I have seen much good soap made of sheep fat. Most of the sheep kept in tropical Africa are what are known as *Persians*. This means that they have hair instead of wool and fat tails. These tails are the device of a desert animal to store energy in times of plentiful food for the lean times that are sure to follow. By the end of the wet season these tails are huge – great wide bags of fat. We used to kill about one sheep a week, and the surplus fat was always turned into excellent soap.

The fat must not be rancid, and if it is going to be stored for a long time, then it must first be *rendered*. To do this the fat is put into an equal quantity of water and boiled. When the mixture is cold, the solidified fat can be lifted off and it is then ready for soap making. For long-term storage, it is best to pour the fat mixture, while still hot, into an airtight container. Experienced soap makers have found that about one pint of lye for every two pounds of clean fat is about the right ratio.

The easiest method of making soap by hand involves buying caustic soda. Dissolve a pound of this in a gallon and a half of water, add seven pounds of fat and simmer gently for three hours, stirring gently at intervals. You can test if it has boiled sufficiently by pouring a few drops of it into boiling water – if it dissolves rapidly it is ready. Before it is cool, mix in one pound of salt. This will precipitate out and go to the bottom of the container, but it hardens the soap. Leave the brine behind as you pour the mixture into wooden moulds of the size you need. The wood should be wet and lined with damp cloth.

The Finishing Touches

After 24 hours in the mould, you can lift the soap out by the fabric lining and cut it into cakes by wrapping thin wire round it and pulling (like a cheese cutter). It is best to store the soap in the air but away from drafts and frost. After about a fortnight it will be ready for use but, like wine, soap matures, and after six months it will be better still. It will be at least the equal of anything you can purchase in a shop.

Before the soap mixture sets hard, you can mix in any perfumes you like. Any coloring is in order, too – provided it does not contain alcohol, which ruins the soap.

Soap Cakes
Pour the liquid soap into wet wooden moulds lined with damp cloth. Once set, lift the soap out by the cloth and cut into the right sized cakes using a thin wire cutter.

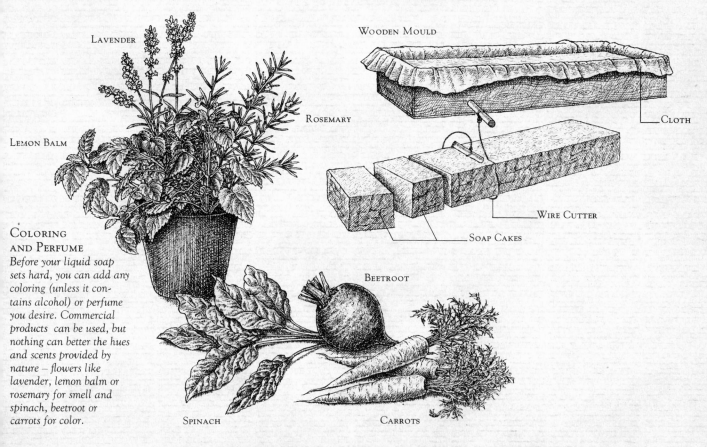

LAVENDER

WOODEN MOULD

LEMON BALM

ROSEMARY

CLOTH

Coloring and Perfume
Before your liquid soap sets hard, you can add any coloring (unless it contains alcohol) or perfume you desire. Commercial products can be used, but nothing can better the hues and scents provided by nature – flowers like lavender, lemon balm or rosemary for smell and spinach, beetroot or carrots for color.

WIRE CUTTER

SOAP CAKES

BEETROOT

SPINACH

CARROTS

INDEX

ACKNOWLEDGMENTS

Dorling Kindersley would like to thank Jonathan Hilton, Caroline Lucas, Moira J Mole, Steven Wooster, and Fred Ford and Mike Pilley of Radius, for their help in producing this book.

Many craftsmen have given the author and contributing artists the benefits of their considerable experience and expertise. In particular, thanks are due to William Brown, wheelwright and blacksmith, of Burwash, Sussex; Richard Carey, wheelwright, of Battle, Sussex; Mike Farmer, of G M Catterall, saddler, of Tonbridge, Kent; F Hawkins & Sons Ltd, carpenters, of Tunbridge Wells, Kent; H J Phillips, shipwright and boatbuilder, of Rye, Sussex; and Edgar and Trevor Stern, farriers and blacksmiths, of Maidstone, Kent.

Illustrations in this book are by:

David Ashby: 17, 19t, 24, 25l, 26, 27, 29, 44, 45, 49, 51, 56t, 57, 60, 61, 65, 86b, 90, 96, 97, 102, 104, 105, 108, 109r, 114, 115, 119, 121, 123, 126t, 130, 132, 135t, 137, 138t, 139, 142, 143r, 144m&b, 146r, 147, 149m&b, 150, 151r, 154, 159, 167, 168, 169, 170, 174, 175, 176, 178, 179, 181, 182, 183, 184, 185, 186, 187.

Brian Delf: 38, 39, 46, 47, 98, 99, 102, 103.

Peter Dennis: 18, 19b, 122, 125, 129, 135b, 143b, 144t, 145, 146t&l, 151b, 152, 153, 172, 173.

Robert Kettell: 2, 7, 8, 9, 10, 12, 13, 14, 15.

Peter Morter: 22, 23, 42-3, 74, 75, 109t&b, 110, 111, 113, 124, 126b, 127, 128, 136, 155, 160, 161, 162, 163, 164.

Peter Reddick: 16, 40, 52, 64, 166.

Les Smith: 20, 28, 37, 50, 54, 55, 58, 59, 63b, 72, 73, 86t, 95, 100, 101, 117, 138b, 140, 156, 157.

Eric Thomas: 25r, 32, 33, 34-5, 56b, 63t, 66-7, 69, 70-1, 76, 77, 78-9, 80, 81, 82, 83, 84, 85, 88, 89, 92, 93, 106-7, 120, 149r.

Typesetting by:

Vic Chambers and Tony Wallace
(Chambers Wallace Ltd)

Picture credits:

Bryan and Cherry Alexander: 41.

Bernard Barton: 6, 60.

BBC Hulton Picture Library: 75, 132, 173, 175.

British Tourist Authority: 48l, 62.

Michael Bussell Photo Library: 45.

Cliché Musée des Arts et Traditions Populaires, Paris: 145.

Andrew de Lory: 168, 185.

Farmers Weekly: 1, 27, 50, 73, 84, 94, 129, 158, 160, 162.

Kit Houghton Photography: 37, 77, 104, 127b, 156t, 159, 161, 174.

Jacqui Hurst: 38, 47t, 49, 87, 115, 148, 149, 150, 153, 154, 156b, 163.

Institute of Agricultural History and Museum of English Rural Life, University of Reading: 17, 21, 23, 25, 26, 29, 32, 33, 53, 55, 80, 83, 91, 93, 96, 98, 116, 118, 121, 131, 137, 138, 139, 140, 142, 165.

Jean Ribière: 11, 51, 133, 134, 171, 178, 180.

John Seymour: 43, 47b, 57, 65, 68, 108, 109, 111, 127t, 172, 176.

The Sutcliffe Gallery, Whitby: 112.

Topham: 167, 170, 182, 183.

Ulster Museum: 177.

Welsh Folk Museum, St Fagans: 97, 184.

Steven Wooster: 36, 48r.